ACI DEALING CERTIFICATE
questions and answers
(*September 2017 syllabus*)

for **Financial markets professionals**
and **ACI Dealing Certificate** candidates

Philip J.L. Parker

This book is published by
Multimedia TradeWind Limited

www.lywood-david.co.uk   www.multimediatradewind.co.uk

via **Lulu**

Second edition April 2019
ISBN 978-0-244-68316-0

Questions and answers in this book relating to the **ACI Dealing Certificate** September 2017 syllabus and examination format are correct at the time of going to press but these may be subject to change without notice. Information in this book has been produced in good faith. Many sources are used as reference in this book, wherever possible these are suitably accredited.

This book has been produced following the release of the September 2017 syllabus / examination format changes. It was at this date that the ACI Model Code was withdrawn from the syllabus after the publication of the BIS FX Global Code initially in May 2017. This Code is now itself the subject of a separate ACI examination - the **ACI FX Global Code Certificate**. The latest update of the BIS code (August 2018) may be downloaded here…

https://www.globalfxc.org/docs/fx_global.pdf

The **ACI Dealing Certificate** syllabus and examination format and **ACI Formulae** sheet (reproduced as *Appendix I* to this book) are published with the permission of **ACI - The Financial Markets Association**.

Candidates are advised to check the ACI website regularly (particularly before booking their examination) as there may be more up to date downloadable versions of ACI qualification syllabuses, examination formats, booking procedures and other associated documents.

ACI website: www.acifma.com

There is a comprehensive companion textbook "**Financial Markets and the ACI Dealing Certificate**" and **WinFOREX** interactive distance learning software (see also *Appendix III*) available from **Multimedia TradeWind Limited**.

Contents

Chapter 1

Introduction

ACI Dealing Certificate syllabus

Examination format

Examination administration

Introduction

ACI - The Financial markets Association and the wholesale markets

Global wholesale financial markets are dynamic and fast changing and these conditions demand highly qualified people with wide-ranging market skills and knowledge. ACI's Education Programme provides globally acknowledged, portable, professional qualifications that enhance career prospects, improve job performance and set benchmarks within the industry. ACI communicates regularly with a wide range of national Regulators on the education and training of market participants. ACI also works closely with regulatory bodies in a number of countries to ensure that market standards, ACI examinations and regulatory requirements all find common ground.

ACI provides a suite of specialised examinations targeting Foreign Exchange, Fixed Income, Money Markets, Derivatives, Repos, Asset & Liability management, Risk management and Conduct for front, middle and back-office staff. The **ACI Dealing Certificate** offers candidates both technical and practical dealing experience in financial markets elements as well as ethical behaviour principles expected from someone working within a front office role with the ACI Operation Certificate offering procedural and operational topics and behavioural principles expected from someone working within the Middle and back Office environments. All ACI exams are in English and electronically delivered.

ACI Dealing Certificate syllabus

The **ACI Dealing Certificate** is a foundation programme that allows candidates to acquire a working knowledge of the structure and operation of the major foreign exchange and money markets as well as their core products (cash, forwards and derivatives), and the basic skills required for competent participation, including the ability to apply the fundamental mathematics used in these markets.

The programme is designed for the following groups:

• Recent entrants and junior dealers (0-18 month's experience) in the dealing room
• Middle office and operations personnel
• Compliance and risk officers

The **ACI Dealing Certificate** is a precursor to the ACI Diploma.

In addition to the topics outlined below, candidates will be expected to be up-to-date with the latest events and changes in the markets.

Topic 1: Basic Interest Rate Calculations

Overall Objective: To understand the principles of the time value of money. To be able to calculate short-term interest rates and yields, including forward-forward rates, and to use these interest rates and yields to calculate payments and evaluate alternative short-term funding and investment opportunities. Candidates should know what information is plotted in a yield curve, the terminology describing the overall shape of and basic movements in a curve, and the classic theories which seek to explain changes in the shape of a curve. They should also know how to plot a forward curve and understand the relationship between a yield curve and forward curves.

At the end of this section, candidates will be able to:

• calculate present value and future value using the arithmetic techniques of discounting and compounding for both a money market instrument terminated at maturity and one that is rolled over at maturity
• calculate simple interest rates using different day count and annual basis conventions
• identify the day count and annual basis conventions for the euro, sterling, Swiss franc, US dollar and Japanese yen
• fix same-day, next-day, spot and forward value dates, and maturities under the modified following business day convention and end/end rule
• fix the conventional frequency and timing of payments by cash money market instruments, including those with an original term to maturity of more than one year
• calculate broken dates and rates through linear (straight line) interpolation
• define EURIBOR, LIBOR and EONIA
• convert interest rates and yields between the money market basis and bond basis in currencies for which there is a difference
• convert interest rates and yields between annual and semi-annual compounding frequencies
• calculate a forward-forward rate from two mismatched cash rates
• calculate a cash rate from a series of forward-forward rates for consecutive periods
• calculate the value of a discount-paying money market instrument from its discount rate (straight discount) and convert a discount rate directly into a true yield
• plot a yield curve, describe its shape and the basic changes in its shape using market terminology, and outline how the Pure Expectations Theory, Liquidity Preference Theory and Market Segmentation Hypothesis explain the shape of the curve

Topic 2: Cash Money markets

Overall Objective: To understand the function of the money market, the differences and similarities between the major types of cash money market instrument and how they satisfy the requirements of different types of borrower and lender. To know how each type of instrument is quoted, the quotation, value date, maturity and payment conventions that apply and how to perform standard calculations using quoted prices. Given the greater inherent complexity of repo, a good working knowledge is required of its nature and mechanics.

At the end of this section, candidates will be able to:

• define the money market
• describe the main features of the basic types of cash money market instrument - i.e. interbank deposits, bank bills or bankers' acceptances, treasury or central bank bills, commercial paper, certificates of deposit and repos - in terms of whether or not they are securitised, transferable or secured; in which form they pay return (i.e. discount, interest or yield); how they are quoted; their method of issuance; minimum and maximum terms; and the typical borrowers/issuers and lenders/investors that use each type

• use generally-accepted terminology to describe the cashflows of each type of instrument

• understand basic dealing terminology

• distinguish between and define what is meant by domestic, foreign and euro- (offshore) money markets, and describe the principal advantages of euromarket money instruments

• describe the differences and similarities of classic repos and sell/buy-backs in terms of their legal, economic and operational characteristics

• define initial margin and margin maintenance

• list and outline the main types of custody arrangements in repo

• calculate the value of each type of instrument using quoted prices, including the secondary market value of transferable instruments

• calculate the present and future cashflows of a repo given the value of the collateral and an agreed initial margin

• define general collateral (GC) and specials

• describe what happens in a repo when income is paid on collateral during the term of the repo, in an event of default and in the event of a failure by one party to deliver collateral

Topic 3: Foreign exchange

Overall Objective: To understand and be able to apply spot exchange rate quotations. To understand basic spot FX dealing terminology and the role of specialist types of intermediary. To recognise the principal risks in spot and forward FX transactions. To calculate and apply forward FX rates, and understand how forward rates are quoted. To understand the relationship between forward rates and interest rates. To understand time options. To be able to describe the mechanics of outright forwards, FX swaps and forward-forward FX swaps, explain the use of outright forwards in taking currency risk and explain the use of FX swaps in rolling spot positions, hedging outright forwards, creating synthetic foreign currency assets and liabilities, and in covered interest arbitrage. To display a good working knowledge and understanding of the rationale for NDFs. To be able to recognise and use quotes for precious metals and demonstrate a basic understanding of the structure and operation of the international market in precious metals.

At the end of this section, candidates will be able to:

• identify the base currency and the quoted currency in standard exchange rate notation

• select which currency should be the base currency in any currency pair

• recognise the ISO codes for the currencies of the countries affiliated to ACI - The Financial Markets Association

• distinguish between the "big figures" and the "points/pips"

• apply a bid/offer spot exchange rate as price-maker and price-taker to convert either a base or quoted currency amount

• select the best of several spot rates for the buyer or seller of an amount of base or quoted currency

• understand basic spot FX dealing terminology

- calculate cross-rates from pairs of exchange rates where the common currency is the base currency in both rates, where the common currency is the base currency in only one rate and where the common currency is the base currency in neither rate
- calculate and explain the reciprocal rate of an exchange rate
- define the function of market-making and explain the incentives to make markets and the particular risks of market-making
- outline what a voice-broker does and distinguish voice-brokers from principals
- outline what an automatic trading system (ATS) or electronic broker does in spot FX
- calculate a forward FX rate from a spot FX rate and interest rates
- calculate an outright forward FX rate from a spot rate and the forward points, and vice versa
- explain the relationship between the outright forward rate, the forward points, the spot rate and interest rates, including the concept of interest rate parity, and the possibility and concept of covered interest arbitrage
- fix forward value dates for standard periods and list those periods
- describe the structure and mechanics of an FX outright, and outline how an outright forward can be hedged with a spot transaction and deposits
- describe the structure and mechanics of an FX swap, and outline how it can be used in place of deposits to hedge an FX outright and the advantages
- use generally-accepted terminology to specify an FX swap
- outline the applications of FX swaps in creating synthetic foreign currency asset and liabilities, and in covered interest arbitrage
- describe forward-forward FX swaps,
- outline the application of tom/next and overnight FX swaps in rolling over spot positions and hedging value-tomorrow and value- today outright rates, and calculate
a value-tomorrow rate from a spot rate and tom/next points, and a value-today rate from a spot rate, tom/next points and overnight points
- calculate broken-dated forward FX rates through linear interpolation
- calculate forward cross-rates
- define an NDF and explain its rationale
- describe the structure and the features of NDFs as well as their pricing and valuation
- define a time option and explain its reasoning
- list the commodities called precious metals (gold, silver, platinum and palladium) and give their ISO codes
- describe the conventional method of quoting gold in the international market in US dollars per ounce
- apply a bid/offer spot price as price-maker and price-taker to calculate the value of a given weight of precious metals
- distinguish between precious metals trading for physical delivery and book entry
- distinguish between the spot, forward and derivative markets in precious metals
- outline the mechanics and role of the London gold price fixing
- explain the role of gold lending/borrowing and define the gold offered forward rate or lease rate

Topic 4: Forward-forwards, FRAs and Money market Futures & Swaps

Overall Objective: To understand the mechanics of and how to use money market interest rate derivatives to hedge interest rate risk.

At the end of this section, candidates will be able to:

• describe the mechanics and explain the terminology of a forward-forward loan or deposit, and the interest rate risk created by such instruments
• explain how FRAs, money market futures and money market swaps are derivatives of forward-forward positions, and outline the advantages of derivatives
• describe the mechanics and terminology of FRAs, use quoted prices, select the correct contract, decide whether to buy and sell, identify the settlement rate and calculate the settlement amount
• explain how FRAs can be used to hedge interest rate risk
• describe the mechanics and terminology of money market futures, use quoted prices, select the correct contract, decide whether to buy and sell, identify the settlement rate and calculate variation margin payments
• explain how money market futures can be used to hedge interest rate risk
• give the contract specifications of the Eurodollar, 3-month Euribor, short sterling, euro-Swiss franc and Japanese Euroyen futures
• outline the principal differences between OTC instruments like FRAs and exchange-traded instruments like futures, and describe how a futures exchange and clearing house works
• describe the mechanics and terminology of money market interest rate swaps, including overnight indexed swaps (OIS), use quoted prices, select the correct contract, decide whether to buy and sell, identify the settlement rate and calculate settlement amounts
• explain how swaps can be used to hedge interest rate risk
• explain how money market futures can be used to hedge and price FRAs and money market swaps
• identify the overnight indexes (OI) for euro, sterling, Swiss francs and US dollars

Topic 5: Options

Overall Objective: To understand the fundamentals of options. To recognise the principal classes and types, and understand the terminology, how they are quoted in the market, how their value changes with the price of the underlying asset and the other principal factors determining the premium, how the risk on an option is measured and how they are delta hedged. To recognise basic option strategies and understand their purpose.

At the end of this section, candidates will be able to:

• define an option, and compare and contrast options with other instruments
• define strike price, market price, the underlying, premium and expiry
• calculate the cash value of a premium quote
• describe how OTC and exchange-traded options are quoted, and when a premium is conventionally paid
• define call and put options
• explain the terminology for specifying a currency option
• describe the pay-out profiles of long and short positions in call and put options
• describe the exercise rights attached to European, American, Bermudan and Asian (average rate) styles of option

• define the intrinsic and time values of an option, and identify the main determinants of an option premium
• explain what is meant by in the money, out of the money or at the money
• define the delta, gamma, theta, rho and vega
• interpret a delta number
• outline what is meant by delta hedging
• outline how to construct long and short straddles and strangles, and explain their purpose
• outline how options can be used to synthesise a position in the underlying asset
• define an interest rate guarantee
• describe the function of cap and floor options, and how they are used to produce long and short collars

Topic 6: Principles of Asset and Liability management

Overall Objective: To understand the fundamentals of Asset & Liability Management as a practice of managing and hedging risks that arise due to mismatches between the asset side and the liability side of the balance sheets of a bank. To explain how main risk factors like funding and liquidity risk, market risk (FX, Interest Rate, Equity, Commodity, etc.), credit risk, leverage risk, business risk and operational risk are interrelated and how they affect the balance sheet of a financial institution. To describe common risk management and hedging techniques which help control these effects and to understand how these techniques are used to set up a state-of-the-art ALM approach.

At the end of this section, candidates will be able to:

• define the meaning and the general concepts of ALM
• describe the impact of main risk factors on the asset and the liability side of the balance sheet: Impact of Interest Rate Risk, Currency Risk , Liquidity Risk and Credit Risk
• understand the importance of an efficient and reliable organizational infrastructure delivering the necessary data with accuracy and frequency in order to manage ALM Risks
• describe the organisational and infrastructure set up of ALM in a bank: - ALM information systems (Management Information System, Information availability and accuracy) - ALM organisation (Structure and responsibilities, ALM Committee, Role of Controlling, Level of top management involvement) - ALM process (Risk parameters, Risk identification, Risk measurement, Risk management, Risk tolerance levels)
• understand the use of Gap management: interest and duration mismatches
• explain Asset and liability management techniques: Cash Flow Management, Duration Management, Gap Limits
• describe the use of different types of interest rate and FX derivatives for implementing hedging techniques against ALM risks
• describe the use of Credit Risk Transfer Instruments for Balance Sheet Management: Credit Derivatives and Asset Securitizations
• explain the impact of Basel III (Liquidity Coverage Ratio, Net Stable Funding Ratio, Leverage Ratio) on the structure of a bank's balance sheet

• explain the concept of funds transfer pricing as a means to ensure that funding and liquidity costs & benefits are transparently allocated to respective businesses and products
• describe the interaction between bank capital and leverage and the role of economic and regulatory capital
• describe the formulation of Liquidity Stress Test Scenarios and the use in ALM

Topic 7: Principles of Risk

Overall Objective: To understand why risk is inherent in banks business models and why effective risk management is a key driver for banks success. Candidates will be able to describe major risk groups: credit, market, liquidity, operational, legal, regulatory, and reputation risk. They will understand the significance of risk groups for different banking businesses and units. Candidates will also get an overview about methods and procedures needed to manage these risk types and extend their understanding to different risk/return profiles of shareholders, regulators and debt providers.

At the end of this section, candidates will be able to:

• Understand the following aspects of Market Risk: o Types of market risk (Interest Rate, Equity, Currency, Commodity) - Market Risk in the Trading Book : How it arises and accounting impact -The use of Risk Measures: key concepts of Value at Risk (holding periods, confidence levels, VaR calculation, Limitations of VaR, Expected Shortfall) - the use of quantitative techniques (Risk Factors and Loss Distributions, Variance-Covariance Method, Historical Simulation , Monte Carlo) - Limit structures in the dealing room - Capital treatment of market risk under Basel III
• Understand the following aspects of Credit Risk: - Categories of credit risk: lending, issuer, settlement, counterparty credit risk - Managing credit risk: Limits and safeguards, Credit approval authorities and transaction approval process, Aggregating exposure limits by customers, sectors and correlations -Credit mitigation techniques: collateral; termination clauses, re-set clauses, cash settlement, netting agreements - Documentation: covenants, ISDA / CSA and other collateral - Fundamentals of credit risk capital measurement: probability of default (PD), exposure at default (EAD), loss given default (LGD) and correlation - Capital treatment of credit risk under Basel III (Standardised approach, Foundation and advanced internal ratings based approaches, Regulatory capital treatment for derivatives)
• Understand the following aspects of Operational Risk: - Sources of operational risk; systems, people, processes and external events - Reasons for banks to control operational risk: legal and regulatory requirements - Best practice management procedures
• Understand the following aspects of Legal, Regulatory and Reputation Risk: - Sources of reputation risk and relationship to other risk groups
• Understand the following aspects of Liquidity Risk: - Objectives and importance of a funding strategy - Lessons learned from crises in liquidity risk management; Off-balance sheet contingencies, complexity, collateral valuation, intra-day liquidity risks and cross-border liquidity, Measuring and managing stress scenarios, Early warning indicators of liquidity risk - Liquidity coverage ratio and Net stable funding ratio

Text reproduced from ACI website with permission <u>www.acifma.com</u>

Examination Procedure

Format: The examination lasts 2 hours and consists of 70 multiple-choice questions.

Calculators: Some questions will require the use of a calculator. A basic one will be provided on the computer screen. You may also use your own hand-held calculator, provided it is neither text programmable nor capable of displaying graphics with a size more than 2 lines. ACI have published a list of approved calculators on their website.

Topic Basket		Number of questions	Minimum of correct answers	Minimum score level
1	Basic Interest Rate Calculations	6	3	50%
2	Cash Money Market	6	3	50%
3	Cash Money Market Calculations	6	3	50%
4	Foreign Exchange	12	6	50%
5	Foreign Exchange Calculations	6	3	50%
6	Forward-forward, FRAs and Money Market Futures & Swaps	12	6	50%
7	Options	6	3	50%
8	Asset & Liability Management	8	4	50%
9	Principles of Risk	8	4	50%
Totals		70	42	60%

Results: The **overall pass level** is **60%** (42 correct answers) and there is a **minimum score criterion** of **50%** for each Topic Basket which must also be achieved for a pass.

Examination administration

ACI Dealing Certificate examination registration

Registration and booking for ACI Certificates and Diploma can be made through the ACI Global Education Centre via the ACI website www.acifma.com.

ACI oversees an extensive and ever-growing test centre network with centres available to candidates in over 50 countries. If your country is not listed or you cannot find a convenient test centre you should contact ACI direct.

Calculators

Candidates are allowed to take a non-programmable calculator into the exam as long as it is not text capable and does not display graphics greater than 2 lines.

> **HINT** It is recommended that during your revision sessions you use the calculator you will take with you into the examination. Familiarity with the calculator to be used will save a considerable amount of time in the examination itself.

The standard MS Windows on-screen calculator is also available during the examination proper on the test screen together with access to the ACI formulae sheet.

Erasable boards (for rough workings) are also available at the test centre on request.

Dictionary

If you are taking the examination in a language other than your native tongue a standard language dictionary may be taken into the examination – **NOT** a business terms dictionary.

Formula Sheet

You can obtain a copy of the Formula Sheet through the following sources:

- Your National Association, or ACI education officer
- Your trainer will be able to supply you with a copy
- Examination test centres will supply you with a copy
- **Appendix I of this text** *(though this has been annotated to assist candidates)*
- You can download a copy from the ACI website: www.acifma.com.

> **HINT** This final alternative is recommended to avoid any problems of non-availability at the test centre on the day.

Certificates

Successful candidates will receive an email with confirmation of their result immediately after the exam with an electronic copy of their Certificate attached to the email. A formal paper version of the Certificate can only be produced under specific request made by candidates to ACI Head Office at a cost of EUR 50.00 per certificate.

Appeal

A candidate has the right to appeal the result of his or her exam to ACI's Board of Education, within four weeks of sitting the exam.

Appeals may be made by candidates who experience unexpected physical, organisational or technical difficulties at the test centre, or who believe that reasonable doubts exist about an exam question. In the latter case, the candidate must offer a detailed submission about the specific question and topic basket.

The request for an appeal is submitted on ACI's website www.acifma.com exclusively by the candidate who failed the exam and will only be accepted if the candidate makes a detailed statement with supporting reasons for his or her appeal.

Once a decision on his or her appeal is made the candidate cannot submit an appeal for the same examination again.

Text reproduced from ACI website with permission www.acifma.com

Chapter 2

Approaching the
ACI Dealing Certificate
examination

Key points when revising for the
ACI Dealing Certificate
examination

Approaching the ACI Dealing Certificate examination

Preparation

During your study and revision, you will probably not have had the time or the opportunity to have been able to read and revise everything on the subject matter of the examination. Rather than worry about what you haven't done or read concentrate on what you <u>have</u> done. When you finally sit the examination that is the point when you demonstrate to the examiner what you know and will be judged on that performance on the day.

Last minute revision may give rise to doubts in your mind. You should not allow these to detract from your understanding of the syllabus topics Where you have been on a specific training course towards the examinations or you are relying on personal study you should refer back to what you have learnt and use your preparation for the examination to pull things together.

> **HINT** Don't worry about what you haven't done. No one can understand everything. Concentrate on making the best use of what you have covered.

"Honing" examination techniques

Most trainers agree that the single most useful revision activity of all is attempting old examination questions. When the ACI examinations were paper delivered old examination papers were available from ACI Education. With the introduction of electronic examination delivery these are no longer available. This book looks to provide a selection of **ACI Dealing Certificate** questions set out in separate 'mock' examinations (70 questions correctly weighted by topic) but, unlike the examination proper, the topic heading is included with each question meaning that these questions can be attempted as individual 'mock' examinations or, if preferred, can be used for topic by topic revision.

'Mock' (trial) examination

It is certainly well worth the discipline of attempting one (or more) full mock examinations as listed in this book. You can complete one or more of them without reference to any textbook or other outside assistance, i.e. under examination conditions and, most importantly, *against the clock*.

Using this book

The aim of this book is to provide ACI candidates with practical experience of multiple choice questions covering all topics of the **ACI Dealing Certificate** examination syllabus. It can be used as stand-alone distance learning material or better as an accompaniment for other textbooks - such as **Financial Markets and the ACI Dealing Certificate** (September 2017) also published by Multimedia TradeWind Limited. This latter mentioned textbook also provides **Hints** in approaching the multiple-choice format questions and selecting the correct answers in the examination.

The style of questions and marking methodologies of the **ACI Dealing Certificate** examination are as set out in this textbook and also available in Multimedia TradeWind Limited's distance learning product **WinFOREX** with its unique approach to interactive questions / answers. The PC based **WinFOREX** product replicates the electronic delivery format of the examinations themselves making them invaluable study aids with the principal objective to ensure that at the end of the day **YOU** are confident in your personal approach to the examination. Please see *Appendix III* of this book for further details and screenshots of the **WinFOREX** product.

Mock examination - Multiple choice questions

In the ACI examination each multiple-choice question consists of the question including any calculation data required followed by four (4) alternative answers of which only one (1) is correct.

In Chapter 4 of this text the topic title of all questions is quoted in each mock examination whereas this is not the case in the examination proper.

As in the examination proper all questions are worth 1 mark each. There is no penalty for an incorrect answer.

HINT It is recommended that candidates use a separate sheet of paper to note down the answers to questions so that the contents of the q&a book can be used on more than one occasion – either topic by topic or when attempting a full mock (trial) examination.

Mock examination - Answers and explanations

Similarly, in Chapter 5 of this text the topic title of all correct answers is quoted and accompanied by a brief explanation / reason for its selection as 'Correct'.

Key points when revising for the ACI Dealing Certificate examination

- Study any previous examination questions and sample questions available
- Carefully select the topics of the syllabus you intend to revise
- Draw up a timetable for revising
- Seek out the core elements of the syllabus topics you have chosen to revise
- Condense the contents of your chosen topics into brief bullet points / notes
- Practise examination techniques
- Read the Model Code

Final revision

Approach your final revision in a planned way. Use your time efficiently dividing it between reading and examination theory / calculation practice. Obviously you will want to concentrate on those syllabus topics in which you feel least confident. Bear in mind the incidence of examination questions in these topics in the examination proper. For example it would be very frustrating to spend hours revising just one topic of the "catch all" question baskets (e.g. **ACI Dealing Certificate Topic 4 Forward-forwards, FRAs and Money markets and Swaps**) only to find that through the random selection process no questions from your revised topic were included in the examination.

However, the reverse can also be the case so a sensible background knowledge level per topic is recommended.

The ACI Dealing Certificate examination

Multiple choice questions (and answers)

Many people find the multiple-choice format the most off-putting style of examination. There are several reasons for this. One is that an answer must be right or wrong - there are no near misses or marks for "showing all workings" in calculation questions. Another is that the examination delivery and answering processes may differ dramatically from the candidate's experience and use of the subject matter of the syllabus. A final and most significant one is that the nature of the examination permits a large number of questions to be set meaning that questions must be answered quickly and accurately given the examination time constraints. Calculation questions by their very nature will probably take more time than theory questions.

Examination questions are written to test your knowledge or a particular product or subject. Always read and re-read the question and in the case of multiple choice questions read and re-read each choice of answer carefully. The multiple-choice format of the examination means that the answer on each occasion is literally "staring you in the face". If it happens to be in one of your weaker topic areas and you cannot immediately identify the correct answer it may end up being down to a process of elimination and logic to select the correct answer.

ACI Dealing Certificate examination

Theory and Calculation multiple choice questions

The textual multiple-choice questions (with the usual four alternative answers) are randomly selected and displayed in the examination proper in topic order but without the topic heading being identified. There are **70** multiple choice questions worth *1 mark* each with the PASS mark set at **50%** per question basket. There are four theory question baskets (**Topics 2, 3, 6** and **7**) three separate Calculation question baskets (**Topics 1, 2** and **3**) and two (**Topics 4** and **5**) which include both theory and calculation questions. Additionally, to pass you must achieve an overall 60% pass mark (42 correct answers).

> **HINT** This means that to achieve an overall 60% pass mark in the **ACI Dealing Certificate** you must score better than 50% in more than one of the topic question baskets.

Examination techniques

Order of attempting questions

Once the exam proper has started, take each question in turn, answer those you are immediately confident about and then spend time on questions which are more involved (needing careful reading and/or more than one calculation) or those you are unsure about.

Of those questions requiring further attention, many of these can be answered by a logical method of elimination of obviously wrong answers.

"Who wants to be a millionaire?" style quiz

The examination multiple choice format has been used in general knowledge quiz shows such as the TV quiz show "Who wants to be a millionaire?". Reading the question and the available choice of answers is equally important in both environments.

Where all else fails the examination differs from the quiz in one major way. The lifelines available in the TV quiz - "Ask the audience", "50:50" and "Phone a friend" are unfortunately **not** able to be used by the candidate. However, an approach along similar lines to the "50:50" option can sometimes be invoked to good effect in the examination itself.

Process of elimination

We are talking here about a process of elimination. Of the four possible answers there is probably one which may be immediately discarded (a "red herring"). If you are lucky there may be *two* such answers giving you an immediate "50:50" option.

Just as with the TV quiz there may then be left a choice between two "obvious" answers which in your mind may be "to close to call". Unlike other examination formats multiple choice questions are often designed to lead you towards an answer including a silly error. If a question involves a calculation, no matter how simple, it is often worth using the calculator to re-check the result.

Bearing in mind your time management plan, if after say 2 minutes concentrating on one calculation question you still cannot identify the correct answer you should move on. Don't take this as a suggestion to rush through the examination in a "mad panic" but it is far better to cut your losses and move on after an expensive use of time on a question which continues to puzzle you.

> **HINT** Remember under the current **ACI Dealing Certificate** marking regime there is no penalty for an unanswered question or for a wrong answer in any examination.

Key points for the examination itself

- Remember your time management plan for the examination and stick to it
- Scan through the examination identifying questions you have prepared for
- Begin selecting answers as soon as you are confident to do so – it helps "unfreeze" you.
- As you tackle a question:
    - Examine the wording carefully
    - Beware of "Negatives" in the question
    - In "list style" multiple choice questions be extra careful in reading the available answers
    - If the correct answer is still not evident 'pass' on it move on
    - Make sure your time management permits all such passed over questions to be returned to

---

Time management

You have a total of 2 hours (120 minutes) to complete the 70 questions of the **ACI Dealing Certificate** examination.

120 minutes remaining

Review – You should probably allow yourself some time at the end of the examination for an overall review of your answers.

Don't forget the system permits you to go back to any question whether answered or not and change your choice of answer. Let us assume you allow 15 minutes at the end for this purpose

105 minutes remaining

Theory multiple choice questions

As these theory-style questions are easier to read and probably mostly easier to select the correct answer, you may find that you can answer many without too much effort. The way some questions are worded will mean you can almost instantly identify the correct answer whilst the random selection process of the system will mean that others may require more careful study before a final choice is made.

Remember, if there are any which seem more complex than others you can pass on these to return to them later.

Calculation multiple choice questions

Don't forget there are *at least* 14 calculation multiple choice questions which may necessitate use of a calculator and/or the ACI formulae sheet.

The more key strokes required for a calculation the longer the time per question.

Overall there should be a balance between easier and more difficult questions in the random selection process. Also, bear in mind that sometimes even correct answers to calculation questions can sometimes be reached by a simple process of elimination.

Allowing 105 minutes for the 70 questions means an average of 90 seconds (1½ minutes) per question. Many will take you less but the more complex questions, needing reading and re-reading and/or complex calculations may take considerably more time.

15 minutes remaining

Time to re-check questions where doubt remains in your mind (using the functionality of the electronic examination delivery) or perhaps to double check more complicated calculations. Don't forget when all is said and done, and you find you cannot identify a correct answer to one or more questions it is always worth taking a guess (there is a 1 in 4 chance of being correct).

HINT with 70 questions in 120 minutes, most candidates do **not** experience any time pressures in the **ACI Dealing Certificate**. Provided you are well prepared you should find that the time allowed is sufficient to answer all questions and review answers.

Once you are happy with your examination you must **Quit** the examination.

If after the examination, you are able to recall issues of concern to you during the examination, please make ACI aware of any such problems you have encountered with a particular question or its answers (grammar, ambiguity etc.) or the examination overall.

Chapter 3

Specific points in respect of
dealing and financial instruments
to bear in mind on reading ACI
Dealing Certificate examination
questions (not exhaustive)

Specific points in respect of dealing and financial instruments to bear in mind on reading ACI Dealing Certificate examination questions

The following is a list (not exhaustive) of areas where participants can make silly but expensive mistakes when reading the multiple-choice questions or answer choices in the **ACI Dealing Certificate** examination.

Money market Theory and Calculations

Loans and deposits - Do not confuse loans and deposits.

A **Loan** in banking terminology is an advance to a customer (counterparty), an **asset**, a debit balance on a loan account in the bank's books or balance sheet, the lender charges and eventually receives the interest due. This transaction is sometimes described as a "Deposit Placed", placing or **Money OUT** on effective date. Such loans are subject to **Credit limits** (clean advances).

To create a loan, you lend cash. Having lent cash, you are **Short** (Cash). As market maker you lend on your Offer (the higher interest rate in a two-way quote). As a market user the opposite applies, you have to lend to the market maker's Bid (the lower interest rate in a two-way quote).

A **Deposit** in banking terminology is an acceptance from a customer (counterparty), a **liability**, a credit in a Deposit account in the bank's books or balance sheet, the borrower (bank as deposit taker) eventually pays the interest due. This transaction is sometimes described as a "Deposit accepted" or **Money IN** on effective date. Deposits accepted do not reduce utilization of **Credit limits** (there is **NO** automatic right of set-off).

To take a deposit, you borrow cash. Having borrowed cash, you are **Long** (Cash). As market maker you borrow cash on you Bid (the lower interest rate). As a market user the opposite applies, you have to take from the Offer (the higher interest rate).

In all questions, ask yourself "Am I market maker or market user?"

Remember there is a big difference between the English <*You quote*> and <*You **are** quoted*>. If the question is worded "*You quote*" you are the **market maker**. If the question is worded "*You **are** quoted*" you are the market user. If rates quoted are "Market rates" or quoted by a broker, you must always assume that you are the market user. i.e. that is the cost to you to cover.

Loan/Deposit quotations

Some questions will be worded in London terms (Offer–Bid) and some in international or continental terms (i.e. Bid-Offer). An examination may include a mix of quotation methods.

Remember loans/deposits and many derivatives are often quoted in **Basis points**. A basis point = 0.01 percent. i.e. the second decimal place.

Interest calculations

Interest on US Dollars in the international Eurocurrency money markets is calculated on an **Actual / 360** annual basis. Most currencies follow this annual basis approach although some have differing day bases for international and domestic markets.

The exceptions to this rule are Sterling and typically currencies which are ex- British Empire, Commonwealth or Sterling area. These exceptions must be learnt. GBP interest calculations annual basis = **Actual / 365** for ALL money market cash and financial instruments (except Financial Futures).

Government bonds (when considering the **ACI Dealing Certificate** this probably refers to questions on Repos) in the major markets of London, the EU, New York and Tokyo are quoted on an **Actual /Actual** annual basis though coupon (dividend) payment frequencies may differ between centres. e.g. a semiannual coupon for London, New York and Tokyo government bonds whilst EU governments pay an annual coupon. The repo interest rate however is **always** calculated on the appropriate money market basis for the currency i.e. **Actual/360** in most cases (Sterling Actual/365) regardless of on what day count the bond itself is based.

Money market cash market transactions pay interest on a simple interest basis. Loans and deposits with maturities in excess of 12 months pay interest annually on their anniversary and then again at final maturity.

When switching from a Bond basis (**30/360** or **Actual/Actual** annual basis) interest rate to an equivalent Money market (**Actual/360** annual basis) interest rate the Money market will always be numerically **LOWER**. The Money market rate pays five days more interest in a full year therefore the equivalent must be a lower number. The Calculation involved is 'multiply by 360 and divide by 365'.

When switching from a Money market basis (**Actual/360**) interest rate to an equivalent Bond basis market (**30/360** or **Actual/Actual**) interest rate the Bond basis will always be numerically **HIGHER**. The Bond basis rate pays five days less interest in a full year therefore the equivalent must be a higher number. The Calculation involved is 'multiply by 365 and divide by 360'.

The more frequently interest is paid the higher the return. i.e. semiannual 5 p.c. gives a better return than annual 5 p.c.

If the question states "use straight line interpolation" it is a simple average price along a straight (upwards or downwards sloping) yield curve or graph line.

Discount rates will always give a higher yield than the "Pure" discount rate quoted. (i.e. 5 p.c. discount for 90 days = yield of 5.0633 p.c.

Compound interest rates

ACI do not provide the formulae for any form of compounding of interest. The most complex question you will see is the rolling-over (renewal) of a deposit *plus* interest for a number of consecutive periods at different rates of interest.

Interest rate derivatives Theory and Calculations

Forward rate agreements (FRAs)

On FRA Fixing date, FRA rates are compared with the appropriate LIBOR Cash rate following common practice for the currency involved. e.g. **GBP** Fixing date = Settlement date as GBP is a same day value currency. For **USD** and other **Eurocurrencies** Fixing = Settlement *minus* two working days, i.e. currencies are rated from value Spot.

The FRA Settlement formula does not identify the difference payment direction. Remember as you input the FRA rate first followed by the LIBOR if the result is "*Negative*" (i.e. LIBOR higher than FRA) the **Buyer is reimbursed** with the difference. If the result is "*Positive*" (i.e. LIBOR lower than FRA) the **Seller is reimbursed** with the difference.

FRA Settlement (the payment of the "difference" between the parties following the fixing procedure) takes place on "Settlement date" – the start of the hedge period originally dealt.

CARE! The exam questions have been known to refer to Settlement date when the FRA rate is compared with LIBOR. This really means 'Fixing' date.

OIS questions

OIS settlement is dictated by the currency involved. **GBP** and **CHF** are settled on **Maturity date. EUR** denominated OIS are settled on **Maturity date *plus* 1** and **USD** denominated **OIS** are settled on **Maturity date *plus* 2.**

Spot FX quotations

Spot is always quoted Low-High and typically referred to as **Bid–Offer** for the Base Currency < **B O B**> Bid-Offer for Base).

Spot FX / Forward FX calculated rates

When calculating cross FX rates, dealers tend to round down or truncate the Bid side and round up the Offer side of any such quote. Only ever effect rounding at the end of a sequence of calculations. Keep rates to as many decimal places as you can during any such sequence.

Forward FX quotations

Forward quotes are swap points High-Low is referred to in continental terms as **Bid – Offer** for the Base currency (currency movement on the FORWARD date). <**B O B**> Bid-Offer for Base.

Base currency Discount

Forward points quoted **High - Low** means that you should **SUBTRACT** those points from the Spot rate to achieve the Outright forward rate.

The Base currency *at a forward Discount* will have a **higher interest rate** than the variable currency (countercurrency). e.g. USD at a Discount against the Japanese Yen = USD interest rate is higher than JPY.

Note: In **London terms** dealers may refer to **High - Low** as a forward Premium because traditionally London dealers refer to the countercurrency (quoted currency) i.e. in GBP/USD dealings in London a dealer may refer to a forward Premium (meaning a USD Premium) whereas the dealer in Paris will refer to a forward Discount (meaning a GBP Discount). It is the description only which differs, the arithmetic is unchanged.

Base currency Premium

Forward points quoted **Low-High** means that you should **ADD** the points to the Spot rate to achieve the Outright forward rate.

The Base currency *at a forward Premium* will have a **lower interest rate** than the variable currency (countercurrency). e.g. USD at a Premium against Singapore Dollars = USD interest rate is lower than SGD.

Note: In **London terms** dealers may refer to **Low-High** as a forward Discount because traditionally London dealers refer to the countercurrency (quoted currency) i.e. in GBP/USD dealings in London a dealer may refer to a forward Discount (meaning a USD Discount) whereas the dealer in Paris will refer to a forward Premium (meaning a GBP Premium). **Once again, it is the description only which differs, the arithmetic is unchanged.**

Dealing periods for both Money market and Foreign exchange

In both FX and money markets **Overnight** refers to a swap price or money market price for the period Today against Tomorrow. **Tom/Next** (US markets = *rollover*) refers to Tomorrow against the Next day (Spot date). **Spot/Next** refers to Spot date against the day after Spot. **Spot a week** (Week fixed) Spot date for 7 days fixed.

Short date transactions tend to refer to market deals dealt for periods up to 1 month.

Days and dates for both Money market and Foreign exchange

Money market fixed date quotations and **Forward FX** swap points (two-way spreads) are quoted from 1 month. A typical run-through from a broker or on a Reuters screen display would be 1, 2, 3, 6 and 12 months prices. Sometimes there are only four periods (1 to 6 months) in less liquid markets. If there are six periods quoted then a 9 months has been added (1, 2, 3, 6, 9, and 12).

Make sure you are familiar with "end/end" principles for forward value dates towards the end of a month.

Most questions will indicate the actual number of days in any period (for inclusion in formulae in the calculation multiple choice question section) or state the assumption you are to follow e.g. 'assume 30 day months'. (1 month = 30, 3 months = 90, six months = 180). Always make sure you calculate the correct number of days if 'calendar months' are used in any question.

Market maker / Market user

In all questions, ask yourself "Am I **market maker** or **market user**?"

Remember there is a big difference between the English <You quote> and <You **are** quoted>. If the question is worded "*You quote*" you are the **market maker**. If the question is worded "*You **are** quoted*" you are the market user. If rates quoted are "Market rates" or quoted by a broker, you must always assume that you are the market user. i.e. that is the cost to you to cover.

Calculations

Where there is a choice of formulae and you are initially uncertain that you have used the correct one, if you have time, you can usually check your choice via a different formula or by looking at the cash flows generated by the sequence of transactions suggested by the question under consideration.

Before starting any lengthy calculations always convert all fractions into decimals and use them to the full number of decimal places. This will avoid silly errors like using or identifying as a correct answer 5.14 (decimal) instead of 5.25 (5 1/4) decimal equivalent of pure fraction. Also do **NOT** round or truncate figures in the middle of a sequence of calculations. Only round as instructed in the exam question or at the very end of a sequence of calculations and then only if you are asked to do so in the examination question or this requirement is obvious from the calculation multiple choice answers available.

HINT Administration-wise the examination questions are infrequently updated so any questions relating to "current" issues or rates could be many months out of date.

We hope you will find the practice examinations in this book useful in your studies and revision towards the **ACI Dealing Certificate** examination.

There is a comprehensive companion textbook "**Financial Markets and the ACI Dealing Certificate**" and **WinFOREX** interactive distance learning software (see also *Appendix III*) available from **Multimedia TradeWind Limited**.

Further information on these and other of the company's ACI training and distance learning products can be found on the **Multimedia TradeWind Limited** website www.lywood-david.co.uk or www.multimediatradewind.co.uk where all software products and financial textbooks can be purchased on-line.

Chapter 4

Mock examinations Nos. 1 – 6
correctly weighted topic by topic
(420 questions in total)

ACI Dealing Certificate - MOCK EXAMINATION No.1

(Please note that in the examination proper topic titles are not advised.)

QUESTION 1: TOPIC: Basic Interest Rate Calculations

ACCORDING TO SOME TEXTBOOKS ON INVESTMENT WHAT IS THE SHAPE OF A 'NORMAL' YIELD CURVE?

A: gently upwards sloping

B: steeply upwards sloping

C: negative

D: flat

QUESTION 2: TOPIC: Basic Interest Rate Calculations

A RATE OF 3.50 P.C. IS QUOTED ON AN ANNUAL BASIS, WHAT IS THE EQUIVALENT SEMI-ANNUAL RATE?

A: 3.548 p.c.

B: 3.470 p.c.

C: 3.452 p.c.

D: 3.530 p.c.

QUESTION 3: TOPIC: Basic Interest Rate Calculations

CONVERT AN ANNUAL EUR BOND COUPON OF 4.00 P.C. TO A SEMI-ANNUAL COMPOUNDING FREQUENCY.

A: 3.945 p.c.

B: 4.055 p.c.

C: 3.960 p.c.

D: 4.040 p.c.

QUESTION 4: TOPIC: Basic Interest Rate Calculations

WHICH OF THE FOLLOWING GIVES YOU THE BEST RETURN?

A: an annual bond market rate of 4.00 p.c.

B: a semi-annual bond market rate of 4.00 p.c.

C: a semi-annual money market rate of 4.00 p.c.

D: an annual money market rate of 4.00 p.c.

QUESTION 5: TOPIC: Basic Interest Rate Calculations

CALCULATE THE 6 MONTHS GBP INTEREST RATE FROM THE 2 MONTHS (61 DAYS) GBP INTEREST RATE OF 4.50 P.C. AND THE 2s V. 6s FORWARD-FORWARD (122 DAYS) GBP INTEREST RATE OF 5.0247 P.C.

A: 5.00 p.c.

B: 4.7624 p.c.

C: 4.875 p.c.

D: 4.75 p.c.

QUESTION 6: TOPIC: Basic Interest Rate Calculations

WHAT DO YOU CALL A YIELD CURVE WHERE SHORTER RATES ARE HIGHER THAN LONGER RATES?

A: Inverted

B: Positive

C: Flat

D: Parabolic

QUESTION 7: TOPIC: Money market Theory

WHEN A GILT COUPON PAYMENT IS RECEIVED BY THE REVERSE REPOER DURING THE LIFE OF A CLASSIC REPO THESE ARE...

A: not paid

B: paid to the owner of the bonds as an addition to the repurchase price at maturity

C: paid to the owner of the bonds as an allowance against the repurchase price at maturity

D: paid to the owner of the bonds as a manufactured dividend

QUESTION 8: TOPIC: Cash Money markets Theory

WHICH OF THE FOLLOWING IS A TYPE OF CUSTODY ARRANGEMENTS IN REPOS?

A: tri-party agreement

B: all of these

C: Euroclear/Clearstream service level agreements

D: HIC agreement

QUESTION 9: TOPIC: Cash Money markets Theory

WHAT IS THE VALUE OF A BASIS POINT?

A: 1/32nd p.c.

B: 0.0001 p.c.

C: 1/10th of 1 p.c.

D: 0.01 p.c.

QUESTION 10: TOPIC: Cash Money markets Theory

IN AN INTEREST ARBITRAGE OPERATION TO RAISE THE VARIABLE CURRENCY FOR 3 MONTHS AS A MARKET USER YOU MUST...

A: sell and buy the base currency on the market maker's 3 mos OFFER FX swap and borrow the base currency

B: sell and buy the base currency on the market maker's BID FX swap and borrow the base currency

C: sell and buy the base currency on the market maker 's OFFER FX swap and lend the base currency

D: buy and sell the base currency on the market maker's 3 mos OFFER FX swap and borrow the base currency

QUESTION 11: TOPIC: Cash Money markets Theory

WHAT ARE THE PRIMARY REASONS FOR TAKING AN INITIAL MARGIN IN A CLASSIC REPO?

A: Collateral illiquidity and legal risk

B: Counterparty risk and legal risk

C: Collateral illiquidity and counterparty risk

D: Counterparty risk and operational risk

QUESTION 12: TOPIC: Cash Money markets Theory

A LONDON CERTIFICATE OF DEPOSIT IS ISSUED AT AN INTEREST RATE OF 3.00 P.C., AND SOME TIME THEREAFTER YOU BUY IT IN THE SECONDARY MARKET AT A YIELD OF 2.75 P.C. WHICH OF THE FOLLOWING WOULD YOU EXPECT TO PAY?

A: Less than the face value

B: More than the face value

C: The face value

D: Impossible to say

QUESTION 13: TOPIC: Cash Money markets Calculations

YOU HAVE PAID USD 4,950,000.00 FOR 90 DAY US T-BILLS (FACE VALUE USD 5,000,000). WHAT DISCOUNT RATE IS BEING APPLIED?

A: 4.00 p.c.

B: 4.0404 p.c.

C: 3.9596 p.c.

D: 4.0268 p.c.

QUESTION 14: TOPIC: Cash Money markets Calculations

WHAT WOULD YOU PAY FOR USD 1,000,000 60 DAY US T-BILLS QUOTED AT A DISCOUNT RATE OF 4.85 P.C.?

A: USD 991,916.67

B: USD 997,972.60

C: USD 992,027.40

D: USD 1,000,000.00

QUESTION 15: TOPIC: Cash Money markets Calculations

YOU HAVE BOUGHT 3 MONTH UK T-BILLS FACE VALUE GBP 20 MILLION AT A TRUE YIELD OF 4 P.C. IF, ON THE SAME DAY, YOU SELL THEM AT 3.875 P.C. DO YOU...

A: make a profit of GBP 6,250.00.?

B: make a loss of 12.5 basis points?

C: make no profit or loss?

D: make a profit of 0.125 p.c.?

QUESTION 16: TOPIC: Cash Money markets Calculations

YOU INVESTED USD 5 MILLION IN A NEWLY ISSUED 3 MONTH CD AT 5.50 P.C. TWO MONTHS AGO (30 DAY MONTHS). YOU DECIDE TO SELL THE CD INTO THE SECONDARY MARKET TODAY. THE YIELD FOR THE REMAINING ONE MONTH PERIOD HAS FALLEN TO 5.10 P.C. WHAT PROCEEDS WILL YOU RECEIVE FOR THIS CD IN THE SECONDARY MARKET?

A: USD 5,063,750.00

B: USD 5,047,298.98

C: USD 5,068,750.00

D: USD 5,046,653.75

QUESTION 17: TOPIC: Cash Money markets Calculations

YOU INVESTED GBP 5 MILLION BY BUYING AT ISSUE A 3 MONTH CD FROM MERKEL INTERNATIONAL BANK LONDON AT 4.75 P.C. TWO MONTHS AGO (30 DAY MONTHS). TODAY YOU DECIDE TO SELL THE CD IN THE SECONDARY MARKET. THE YIELD FOR THE REMAINING ONE MONTH PERIOD HAS FALLEN TO 4.50 P.C. IGNORING FUNDING COSTS, DO YOU MAKE A PROFIT OR A LOSS ON THE CD AND HOW MUCH?

A: GBP 39,920.84 Profit

B: GBP 39,920.84 Loss

C: GBP 58,561.64 Profit

D: GBP 58,561.64 Loss

QUESTION 18: TOPIC: Cash Money markets Calculations

A 95 DAY USD BANKERS ACCEPTANCE IS QUOTED AT A DISCOUNT RATE OF 6.85 P.C. WHAT IS THE TRUE YIELD?

A: 6.85 p.c.

B: 7.00 p.c.

C: 6.95 p.c.

D: 6.98 p.c.

QUESTION 19: TOPIC: Foreign exchange Theory

WHAT IS THE OFFICIAL VALUE DATE FOR SETTLEMENT OF SPOT GOLD OR SILVER TRANSACTIONS VERSUS THE US DOLLAR?

A: deal date + 1

B: two business days after deal date

C: value same day

D: gold/silver settlement on deal date + 1, US Dollars two business days after deal date

QUESTION 20: TOPIC: Foreign exchange Theory

YOUR VOICE BROKER QUOTES YOU 3 MONTHS GBP/USD 25–20. YOU HAVE AN INTEREST TO SELL AND BUY GBP/USD IN AN AMOUNT OF GBP 3 MILLION AT 23 POINTS WHICH OF THE FOLLOWING IS THE CORRECT WAY OF ADVISING HIM OF THIS ORDER?

A: I offer 3 million at 23 points my favour in the three months

B: I offer 3 million at 23 points against me in the three months

C: I pay 23 points my favour for 3 million in the three months

D: I pay 23 points against me for 3 million in the three months

QUESTION 21: TOPIC: Foreign exchange Theory

THE EXTENSION OF A CONTRACT AT OFF-MARKET RATES MAY HAVE WHICH OF THE FOLLOWING IMPLICATIONS?

A: All of these

B: Deferring a loss to a future date

C: Credit risk

D: Deferring a profit to a future date

QUESTION 22: TOPIC: Foreign exchange Theory

IF THE USD/ZAR SPOT EXCHANGE DEALER SAYS HE IS CURRENTLY "FIVE LONG". WHAT IS HIS ACTUAL POSITION?

A: Overborrowed ZAR 5 million overnight

B: Overbought USD 5 million against ZAR

C: None of these

D: Overbought ZAR 5 million against USD

QUESTION 23: TOPIC: Foreign exchange Theory

WHAT IS THE ROLE OF A VOICE BROKER IN THE FOREIGN EXCHANGE MARKET?

A: to match interbank buyers with sellers in the spot and forward FX markets

B: to match lenders with borrowers in the spot and forward FX markets

C: to guarantee completion of all transactions in the FX spot and forward FX markets

D: to quote its own spot and forward FX bids and offers

QUESTION 24: TOPIC: Foreign exchange Theory

IF YOU ARE TOLD THAT THE FORWARD POINTS FOR 1 MONTH USD/ZAR ARE QUOTED AT A USD DISCOUNT (INTERNATIONAL TERMINOLOGY), HOW WOULD YOU EXPECT THEM TO BE DISPLAYED ON A DEALER'S RATES SCREEN?

A: 'High-Low'

B: 'Low-High'

C: insufficient information to decide

D: Around PAR

QUESTION 25: TOPIC: Foreign exchange Theory

THE GBP/USD 3-MONTH SWAP IS QUOTED TO YOU AS 104-102. IF YOU TAKE A NEW POSITION BY DEALING AT 104, THIS WOULD PROBABLY BE BECAUSE YOU EXPECT...

A: GBP to strengthen against USD

B: the interest differential between GBP and USD to widen

C: GBP to weaken against USD

D: the interest differential between GBP and USD to narrow

QUESTION 26: TOPIC: Foreign exchange Theory

WHICH ASSOCIATION REGULATES PRECIOUS METALS TRADING IN LONDON?

A: LBMA

B: Bank of England

C: FSA

D: ICMA

QUESTION 27: TOPIC: Foreign exchange Theory

YOU QUOTE A CALLING BANK A 3 MONTHS GBP/USD FX SWAP OF 35-38. HE ASKS TO DO 10 MILLION AT 35. WHAT HAVE YOU DONE?

A: you have sold and bought GBP 10 million Spot against 3 mths at 35 pts against you

B: you have bought and sold GBP 10 million Spot against 3 mths at 35 pts your favour

C: you have bought and sold GBP 10 million Spot against 3 mths at 35 pts against you

D: you have sold and bought GBP 10 million Spot against 3 mths at 35 pts your favour

QUESTION 28: TOPIC: Foreign exchange Theory

YOU NEED TO BUY SPOT GBP AGAINST EUR AND YOU ARE QUOTED THE FOLLOWING RATES. WHICH RATE IS THE BEST FOR YOU?

A: 1.11 08/13

B: 0.89 92/99

C: 1.11 15/20

D: 0.89 96/90

QUESTION 29: TOPIC: Foreign exchange Theory

WHICH OF THE FOLLOWING PRICES DO YOU NEED TO CALCULATE WHERE CAN YOU BUY GBP AGAINST USD FROM A CLIENT VALUE TODAY? EUR/USD SPOT: 1.5520-23, O/N: 1.65-1.75, T/N: 1.30-1.40.

A: Spot Bid for GBP, O/N Bid for GBP

B: Spot Bid for GBP, O/N Offer of GBP and T/N Offer of GBP

C: Spot Bid for GBP and O/N Offer of GBP

D: Spot Bid for GBP, O/N Bid for GBP and T/N Bid for GBP

QUESTION 30: TOPIC: Foreign exchange Theory

DURING THE DAY, THE EUR/USD 6-MONTH FORWARD POINTS MOVE FROM 2-5 TO 6-1. IF THE SPOT EUR/USD RATE AND EUR INTEREST RATES HAVE NOT CHANGED, THIS INDICATES THAT...

A: USD interest rates have risen

B: USD interest rates have remained the same but the market expects rates to fall in 6 months time

C: USD interest rates have fallen

D: USD interest rates have remained the same but the market expects rates to rise in 6 months time

QUESTION 31: TOPIC: Foreign exchange Calculations

YOU ARE QUOTED SPOT EUR/CHF: 1.1005, 6 MONTHS (180 DAY) EUR: 3.45 P.C., 6 MONTHS (180 DAY) CHF: 1.25 P.C. CALCULATE THE EUR/CHF 6 MONTH SWAP POINTS?

A: +203

B: -203

C: -119

D: +119

QUESTION 32: TOPIC: Foreign exchange Calculations

YOU ARE QUOTED THE FOLLOWING RATES: SPOT GBP/USD: 1.6250/55. O/N SWAP: 1.50/1.45. T/N SWAP: 1.35/1.25. S/N SWAP: 1.60/1.55. WHERE CAN YOU SELL GBP AGAINST USD FOR VALUE TOMORROW?

A: 1.625375

B: 1.625635

C: 1.625125

D: 1.624875

QUESTION 33: TOPIC: Foreign exchange Calculations

YOUR FORWARD DEALER HAS JUST QUOTED POLLY PECK LIMITED A 3 MONTHS OUTRIGHT USD/JPY OF 89.75 (BANK SELLS OUTRIGHT USD). IF THE 3 MONTHS USD/JPY SWAP IS CURRENTLY QUOTED 20-15 WHAT IS THE SPOT RATE ON WHICH THE OUTRIGHT WAS BASED?

A: 89.90

B: 90.00

C: 89.60

D: 89.95

QUESTION 34: TOPIC: Foreign exchange Calculations

CALCULATE THE PROFIT OR LOSS ON THE FOLLOWING POSITION: LONG JPY 500,000,000 AGAINST USD AT 109.00, REVALUED AT 109.35.

A: profit JPY 14,682,260

B: profit USD 14,682.25

C: loss JPY 14,682,260

D: loss USD 14,682.25

QUESTION 35: TOPIC: Foreign exchange Calculations

IF SPOT EUR/GBP IS 0.88 75-80 AND THREE MONTHS FORWARD OUTRIGHT EUR/GBP IS 0.86 60-70, WHAT ARE THE 3 MONTHS SWAP POINTS?

A: 21-21.5

B: 21.5-21

C: 210-215

D: 215-210

QUESTION 36: TOPIC: Foreign exchange Calculations

IF SPOT GBP/USD IS QUOTED TO YOU AS 1.6020/25 AND 1 MONTH FORWARD IS QUOTED TO YOU AS 20/25, AT WHAT RATE CAN YOU BUY USD 1 MONTH OUTRIGHT?

A: 1.6040

B: 1.5995

C: 1.6000

D: 1.6050

QUESTION 37: TOPIC: Fwd/fwds, FRAs Money market Futures and Swaps

IT IS JUNE 1X, IF THE SEPTEMBER 1X SHORT STERLING FUTURES PRICE ON NYSE EURONEXT.LIFFE CLOSES LOWER WHAT DOES THIS MEAN IN TERMS OF GBP INTEREST RATES?

A: 3s v.6s GBP interest rates have fallen during the day

B: 3s v.6s GBP interest rates have risen during the day

C: 3 month LIBOR has fallen today

D: 3 month LIBOR has risen today

QUESTION 38: TOPIC: Fwd/fwds, FRAs Money market Futures and Swaps

WHICH OF THE FOLLOWING IS AN ADVANTAGE OF FINANCIAL FUTURES OVER THE CASH MARKET FORWARD-FORWARD ALTERNATIVE?

A: standard contracts

B: all of these

C: liquid market

D: zero credit risk

QUESTION 39: TOPIC: Fwd/fwds, FRAs Money market Futures and Swaps

IF THE OFFER OF SPOT AGAINST 3 MONTHS EUR IS QUOTED 3.00 P.C. AND THE BID FOR SPOT AGAINST 6 MONTHS EUR IS QUOTED 3.25 P.C. (ASSUME 30 DAY MONTHS), WHAT FRA RATE WOULD YOU QUOTE TO A CORPORATE CUSTOMER WHO WANTS TO PROTECT AGAINST FALLING EUR INTEREST RATES IN THE 3s V. 6s. PERIOD?

A: 3.00 p.c.

B: 3.12 p.c.

C: 3.54 p.c.

D: 3.47 p.c.

QUESTION 40: TOPIC: Fwd/fwds, FRAs Money market Futures and Swaps

THE FLOATING RATE OF AN ISDA BASED 5 YEAR USD INTEREST RATE SWAP IS ALWAYS...

A: LIBOR Actual/360

B: LIBOR Actual/Actual

C: Prime rate Actual/360

D: US T-Note Actual/Actual

QUESTION 41: TOPIC: Fwd/fwds, FRAs, Money market Futures and Swaps (FRAs)

YOU TOOK A POSITION ON FUTURE INTEREST RATES BY BUYING A 1 X 4 (89-DAY) EUR 150 MILLION FRA AT 3.15 P.C. TODAY BBA EUR LIBOR FOR THE FRA CONTRACT PERIOD IS FIXED AT 3.27 P.C., WAS YOUR VIEW ON THE EUR INTEREST RATES CORRECT, WHAT IS THE FRA SETTLEMENT AMOUNT AND DO YOU PAY OR RECEIVE?

A: Yes, you receive EUR 44,143.14

B: No, you pay EUR 44,500.00

C: No, you pay EUR 44,143.14.

D: Yes, you receive EUR 44,500.00

QUESTION 42: TOPIC: Fwd/fwds, FRAs Money market Futures and Swaps

WHICH OF THE FOLLOWING IS A REASON TO USE AN OIS TO HEDGE INTEREST RATE RISK?

A: to switch the risk from 3 months fixed to overnight

B: to receive interest in one compound amount at maturity

C: to avoid paying interest for three months

D: to cover a 3 months interest rate risk by dealing Tom/next

QUESTION 43: TOPIC: Fwd/fwds, FRAs Money market Futures and Swaps

WHAT IS THE VALUE OF 1 TICK ON THE SHORT STERLING FUTURES CONTRACT ON NYSE EURONEXT.LIFFE?

A: GBP 25.00

B: GBP 10.00

C: GBP 12.50

D: GBP 6.25

QUESTION 44: TOPIC: Fwd/fwds, FRAs Money market Futures and Swaps

IT IS MID-JUNE AND AFTER CLOSE OF BUSINESS ON THE FUTURES EXCHANGE. IF YOU SOLD 10 DECEMBER ED CONTRACTS ON NYSE EURONEXT.LIFFE TODAY AT 95.575 AND TODAY'S SETTLEMENT PRICE WAS 95.50 WHAT VARIATION MARGIN IS PAYABLE AND TO WHOM?

A: USD 937.50 to the buyer

B: USD 1,875.00 to the seller

C: USD 1,875.00 to the buyer

D: USD 937.50 to the seller

QUESTION 45: TOPIC: Fwd/fwds, FRAs Money market Futures and Swaps

WHICH OF THE FOLLOWING IS TRUE?

A: The CME EURODOLLAR futures contract has a minimum price interval of one-quarter basis point value (0.0025) for the nearest contract

B: The 3-month EURIBOR futures contract has a minimum price interval of half a basis point value (0.0050) for the nearest contract

C: The EUROYEN TIBOR futures contract has a basis point value of JPY 25,000 and a face value of JPY 1,000,000,000

D: The 3-month Sterling (SHORT STERLING) futures contract has a basis point value of GBP 25.00 and a face value of GBP 1,000,000 .00

QUESTION 46: TOPIC: Fwd/fwds, FRAs Money market Futures and Swaps

IF AN INTEREST RATE SWAP INCLUDES SYNCHRONISATION AND NETTING, THE INTEREST PAYMENTS ARE...

A: agreed to be compared with the appropriate fixed rate on each rating date and re-set accordingly

B: agreed to be compounded throughout the life of the swap and paid on final maturity

C: agreed to be netted and paid on each re-rating date

D: agreed not to be exchanged on each re-rating date

QUESTION 47: TOPIC: Fwd/fwds, FRAs Money market Futures and Swaps

WHICH OF THE FOLLOWING CAN BE DESCRIBED AS AN OIS (OVERNIGHT INDEX SWAP)?

A: pay USD LIBOR, receive GBP LIBOR

B: receive USD LIBOR, pay USD 3 year fixed

C: receive USD 1 week fixed, pay USD 1 year fixed

D: pay SONIA receive GBP 1 week fixed

QUESTION 48: TOPIC: Fwd/fwds, FRAs Money market Futures and Swaps

A USD 10,000,000 3 MONTH FRA (92 DAYS) THAT YOU BOUGHT AT 5.50 P.C. IS NOW DUE FOR SETTLEMENT. THE SETTLEMENT RATE (LIBOR) IS FIXED TODAY AT 5.5625. WHAT IS THE SETTLEMENT AMOUNT AND IN WHOSE FAVOUR IS IT?

A: You receive USD 1,574.84

B: You pay USD 1,574.84

C: You receive USD 1,547.48

D: You pay USD 1,334.75

QUESTION 49: TOPIC: Options

WHEN DOES AN AT THE MONEY OPTION PREMIUM EXHIBIT GREATEST THETA, ALL OTHER THINGS BEING EQUAL?

A: None of these

B: When the option is most in-the-money

C: When the time to expiry of the option is longest

D: Just before expiry

QUESTION 50: TOPIC: Options

WHICH OF THE FOLLOWING BEST DESCRIBES AN INTEREST RATE COLLAR?

A: a speculative trading strategy

B: a combination of buying a Cap and selling a Floor at different strike prices

C: a combination of buying a Call and selling a call at the same strike price

D: a combination of buying a Cap and buying a Floor at different strike prices

QUESTION 51: TOPIC: Options

WHEN CAN AN OPTION NOT HAVE INTRINSIC VALUE?

A: when it is out-of-the money

B: when it is in-the-money

C: when it has expired

D: when volatility is low

QUESTION 52: TOPIC: Options

WHICH OPTIONS MODEL IS MOST OFTEN USED FOR PRICING OTC CURRENCY OPTIONS?

A: Elliot Wave

B: Random Walk

C: Bollinger Bands

D: Black and Scholes

QUESTION 53: TOPIC: Options

WHAT IS THE NAME FOR AN OPTION WHICH GIVES THE HOLDER THE RIGHT BUT NOT THE OBLIGATION TO EXERCISE THE OPTION ON ANY ONE OF A NUMBER OF DATES SPREAD OVER THE LIFE OF THE OPTION?

A: Asian

B: American

C: European

D: Bermudan

QUESTION 54: TOPIC: Options

WHICH OF THE FOLLOWING MIGHT USE AN INTEREST RATE FLOOR IN HIS HEDGING STRATEGY?

A: an options trader to speculate on interest rates rising

B: a fund manager worried about falling interest rates

C: a bank dealer to guarantee his funding cost for fixed rate mortgages

D: a corporate treasurer worried about rising interest rates

QUESTION 55: TOPIC: Principles of ALM

ALL OTHER THINGS BEING EQUAL, IF A BANK BORROWS SHORT AND LENDS LONG WHAT IS THE EFFECT ON THE LIQUIDITY RISK OF THE BANK?

A: changes only when interest rates levels are low

B: positive

C: negative

D: changes only when interest rates levels are high

QUESTION 56: TOPIC: Principles of ALM

WHICH OF THE FOLLOWING STATEMENTS IS CORRECT?

A: the Macaulay duration of a coupon paying bond is always lower than its maturity

B: the higher the coupon of a bond the higher the Macaulay duration

C: the more frequent the coupon of a bond the higher the Macaulay duration

D: the duration of a zero coupon bond is zero

QUESTION 57: TOPIC: Principles of ALM

WHICH OF THE FOLLOWING IS THE DEFINITION OF SECURITISATION?

A: Securitisation is the financial practice of pooling various types of contractual debt in the form of bonds to investors

B: Securitisation is the pooling of liabilities by a mortgage bank

C: Securitisation is ensuring that borrowers have collateral against loans accepted

D: Securitisation is how CCPs manage risk on securities settlements

QUESTION 58: TOPIC: Principles of ALM

WHAT IS A CREDIT DEFAULT SWAP (CDS)?

A: a financial instrument issued by a company with an 'in default' credit rating

B: a funded credit derivative

C: an agreement whereby the seller will compensate the buyer in the event of a specified loan default or other credit event

D: an agreement whereby the buyer will compensate the seller in the event of a specified loan default or other credit event

QUESTION 59: TOPIC: Principles of ALM

WHICH OF THE FOLLOWING IS NOT THE RESPONSIBILITY OF ALCO?

A: gap management

B: compliance

C: interest rate risk management

D: balance sheet management

QUESTION 60: TOPIC: Principles of ALM

WHAT IS INTEREST RATE IMMUNIZATION IN THE CONTEXT OF BANK GAP MANAGEMENT?

A: the strategy of holding more interest rate sensitive assets than interest rate sensitive liabilities

B: the strategy of holding fewer interest rate sensitive assets than interest rate sensitive liabilities

C: reducing the size of the balance sheet

D: structuring a bank's portfolio so that its net interest revenue and/or the market value of its portfolio will not be adversely affected by changes in interest rates

QUESTION 61: TOPIC: Principles of ALM

ALCO REPORTAGE FOR THE 12 MONTH TIME BUCKET IDENTIFIES THAT THE BANK HAS GBP 600 MILLION IN LIABILITIES THAT WILL BE MATURING AND GBP 800 MILLION IN ASSETS THAT WILL BE MATURING. THE REPORTED GAP FOR THIS PERIOD IS THEREFORE...

A: A funding gap of GBP 200 million

B: A negative gap of GBP 600 million

C: A positive gap of GBP 200 million

D: A negative gap of GBP 0.2 billion

QUESTION 62: TOPIC: Principles of ALM

IF YOU BUY A 3 YEAR BOND AND ENTER INTO A USD PAYER'S SWAP AGAINST 3 MONTHS LIBOR HOW WOULD THESE TRANSACTIONS BE RETURNED IN THE BANK'S GAP REPORTAGE?

A: Asset at 3 years, asset and liability at 3 months

B: Asset and liability at 3 months, liability at 3 months

C: Asset and liability at 3 months, asset at 3 years

D: Asset and liability at 3 years, asset at 3 months

QUESTION 63: TOPIC: Principles of Risk

WHO SETS ECONOMIC CAPITAL LEVELS FOR A BANK?

A: the bank itself

B: the regulators

C: the external auditors

D: The Basle Committee on Banking Supervision

QUESTION 64: TOPIC: Principles of Risk

YOU HAVE JUST SOLD A SECONDARY MARKET USD 5 MILLION CD ORIGINALLY ISSUED BY MEGA BANK TO MAJOR BANK VALUE SPOT - HOW WOULD YOU DESCRIBE THE CREDIT RISK IN YOUR BOOKS IN THE NAME OF MAJOR BANK?

A: Legal risk

B: Delivery Risk

C: Market risk

D: Market replacement risk

QUESTION 65: TOPIC: Principles of Risk

WHAT IS THE LOSS-GIVEN DEFAULT (LGD) RATIO FOR SENIOR CLAIMS ON CORPORATES, SOVEREIGNS AND BANKS NOT SECURED BY RECOGNISED COLLATERAL?

A: 100%

B: 45%

C: 25%

D: 50%

QUESTION 66: TOPIC: Principles of Risk

THE PAYMENTS SYSTEM YOUR BANK IS USING FOR SETTLEMENT OF A MARKET TRANSACTION FAILS. WHAT TYPE OF RISK IS THIS?

A: Legal

B: Market

C: Credit

D: Operational

QUESTION 67: TOPIC: Principles of Risk

FOR WHAT IS STRESS TESTING INTENDED?

A: to evaluate VaR models in arrears

B: to estimate potential economic losses in abnormal markets

C: to evaluate VaR models by using historical simulation

D: to estimate potential economic losses in normal markets within a given time horizon

QUESTION 68: TOPIC: Principles of Risk

WHICH OF THE FOLLOWING COULD BE CONSIDERED TRUE OF VAR-TYPE LIMITS?

A: VaR limits are only used for operational limit control

B: VaR limits based on statistical measurements are only used for credit limit control

C: VaR limits attempt to indicate the level of market risk before its economic consequences are realised

D: VaR limits identify current mark to market risks in absolute terms

QUESTION 69: TOPIC: Principles of Risk

WHICH OF THE FOLLOWING STATEMENTS CONCERNING A VAR-BASED APPROACH TO MEASURING MARKET RISK IS TRUE?

A: It is only useful for assessing economic capital, not regulatory capital

B: It is not applicable to option portfolios

C: It guarantees a maximum loss

D: It permits aggregation of market risks across asset classes

QUESTION 70: TOPIC: Principles of Risk

YOU ARE SHORT ON USD/JPY. HOW CAN THE FED "SQUEEZE" YOU?

A: Lower interest rates

B: Raise interest rates

C: None of these

D: Lower reserve obligations

End of Mock examination No. 1

ACI Dealing Certificate - MOCK EXAMINATION No. 2

(Please note that in the examination proper topic titles are not advised.)

QUESTION 1: TOPIC: Basic Interest Rate Calculations

IF YOU RECEIVE INTEREST OF GBP 132,278.77 ON AN INVESTMENT OF GBP 5,500,000.00 FOR 181 DAYS WHAT INTEREST RATE ARE YOU RECEIVING?

A: 4.75 p.c.

B: 4.95 p.c.

C: 4.85 p.c.

D: 5.00 p.c.

QUESTION 2: TOPIC: Basic Interest Rate Calculations

A FINANCIAL INSTRUMENT HAS AN ANNUAL BOND YIELD OF 4.20 P.C. WHAT IS THE EQUIVALENT ANNUAL MONEY MARKET YIELD?

A: 4.186 p.c.

B: 4.142 p.c.

C: 4.175 p.c.

D: 4.213 p.c.

QUESTION 3: TOPIC: Basic Interest Rate Calculations

UNDER NORMAL CIRCUMSTANCES WHEN IS INTEREST PAID ON AN 18 MONTH STERLING INTERBANK DEPOSIT?

A: after one year and at maturity

B: every 6 months

C: all at maturity

D: quarterly

QUESTION 4: TOPIC: Basic Interest Rate Calculations

AT THE END OF TEN YEARS WHAT IS THE FUTURE VALUE OF AN AMOUNT OF USD 10,000,000.00 INVESTED AT 2.70 P.C. PER ANNUM?

A: USD 10,555,989.00

B: USD 13,052,822.61

C: USD 12,709,661.74

D: USD 12,389,022.37

QUESTION 5: TOPIC: Basic Interest Rate Calculations

WHICH OF THE FOLLOWING IS THE BENCHMARK INTEREST RATE AVERAGE FOR OVERNIGHT EUR FUNDS TRADED IN THE EUROZONE?

A: EONIA

B: EURONIA

C: EURIBOR

D: Eurepo

QUESTION 6: TOPIC: Basic Interest Rate Calculations

A 3-MONTH (90-DAY) DEPOSIT OF GBP 10 MILLION IS MADE AT 4.00 P.C. AT MATURITY, IT IS ROLLED OVER THREE TIMES AT 4.10 P.C. FOR 91 DAYS, 4.25 P.C. FOR 92 DAYS AND 4.35 P.C. FOR 92 DAYS. WHAT IS THE EQUIVALENT ANNUAL RATE (3 DECIMAL PLACES) PAID ON THIS DEPOSIT?

A: 4.217 p.c.

B: 4.350 p.c.

C: 4.176 p.c.

D: 4.242 p.c.

QUESTION 7: TOPIC: Cash Money markets Theory

WHICH ONE OF THE FOLLOWING IS TRADED ON A DISCOUNT BASIS?

A: Short Sterling Financial Futures contracts

B: London CDs denominated in USD

C: CHF Interbank deposits

D: US Treasury Bills

QUESTION 8: TOPIC: Cash Money markets Theory

WHICH OF THE FOLLOWING STATEMENTS BEST DESCRIBES THE MAIN FEATURE OF THE EURO COMMERCIAL PAPER MARKET IN THE UK AND EUROPE?

A: ECP is traded as a discount-paying instrument quoted as a yield

B: ECP is issued at face value as an interest bearing instrument

C: ECP is traded as a discount-paying instrument quoted as a rate of discount

D: ECP is issued at face value at a price like a bond

QUESTION 9: TOPIC: Cash Money markets Theory

WHICH OF THE FOLLOWING STATEMENTS BEST DESCRIBES THE MAIN FEATURES OF THE STERLING CD MARKET IN LONDON?

A: Sterling CDs pay a return at maturity calculated as a yield using the simple interest formula

B: Sterling CDs may only be issued by top rated commercial companies in the UK

C: Sterling CDs must always be issued in security printed paper form

D: Sterling CDs may only be issued for periods in excess of 5 years in the UK

QUESTION 10: TOPIC: Cash Money market Theory

WHEN CALCULATING THE DIRTY PRICE OF A GILT REPO WHAT IS THE MARKET CONVENTION FOR THE DAY COUNT FRACTION USED ON THE UK GILTS INVOLVED?

A: Actual/360

B: 30/360

C: Actual/Actual

D: 30/365

QUESTION 11: TOPIC: Cash Money market Theory

WHICH COUNTERPARTY IN A CLASSIC REPO CAN MAKE A MARGIN CALL?

A: the repoer only

B: the party charging the initial margin

C: neither party

D: the reverse repoer only

QUESTION 12: TOPIC: Cash Money markets Theory

WHICH OF THE FOLLOWING IS NOT NORMALLY NEGOTIABLE?

A: Certificate of Deposit

B: Bankers acceptance

C: Treasury bill

D: Money market deposit

QUESTION 13: TOPIC: Cash Money markets Calculations

WORLD TRADE CENTRE INVESTMENTS INC. ISSUES 1 MONTH (30 DAYS) US DOMESTIC CP IN NEW YORK IN THE AMOUNT OF USD 25,000,000.00 AT 2.00 P.C. WHAT IS THE CP WORTH AT MATURITY?

A: USD 25,000,000.00

B: USD 25,041,095.89

C: USD 24,958,333.33

D: USD 25,041,666.67

QUESTION 14: TOPIC: Cash Money markets Calculations

IF YOU PAY EUR 15,097,159.94 FOR A SECONDARY MARKET CD ISSUED BY TRUMP NATIONAL BANK LONDON ORIGINALLY ISSUED IN THE AMOUNT OF EUR 15,000,000 AT A RATE OF 2.00 P.C. FOR 180 DAYS AND THEN YOU SELL THE CD WITH 40 DAYS REMAINING TO MATURITY AT A YIELD OF 1.20 P.C. IGNORING ANY FUNDING COST WHAT IS THE GROSS PROFIT ON THIS CD FOR THE HOLDING PERIOD?

A: EUR 34,487.36

B: EUR 32,666.96

C: EUR 29,437.80

D: EUR 33,527.78

QUESTION 15: TOPIC: Cash Money markets Calculations

IF A GBP THREE MONTHS (90 DAYS) DISCOUNT RATE IS QUOTED 4 1/8 P.C. WHAT IS THE EQUIVALENT TRUE YIELD PER ANNUM?

A: 4.21 p.c.

B: 4.07 p.c.

C: 4.13 p.c.

D: 4.17 p.c.

QUESTION 16: TOPIC: Cash Money market Calculations

IN A 5.25 P.C. 1 MONTH REPO OF GBP 10 MILLION UK GILTS 5.5% TREASURY 201Y TRADED AS A SPECIAL WITH A DIRTY PRICE OF 95.813256 (WHICH UNDER THE GMRA IS ROUNDED) WHAT IS THE INITIAL CONSIDERATION PAID?

A: GBP 9,500,000.00

B: GBP 10,081,369.86

C: GBP 9,581,000.00

D: GBP 10,000,000.00

QUESTION 17: TOPIC: Cash Money markets Calculations

TODAY YOU BUY A EUR CD YIELDING 3.875 P.C. FOR 90 DAYS. THE CD HAS A FACE VALUE OF EUR 10 MILLION AND WAS ORIGINALLY ISSUED AT A RATE OF 4 P.C. FOR 180 DAYS. WHAT IS THE MATURITY VALUE?

A: EUR 10,100,749.69

B: EUR 10,200,000.00

C: EUR 10,099,009.40

D: EUR 10,102,135.56

QUESTION 18: TOPIC: Cash Money markets Calculations

WHAT IS THE SECONDARY MARKET VALUE OF A GBP 200 MILLION 4 P.C. CD ORIGINALLY ISSUED BY MILLIBAND INTERNATIONAL BANK PLC FOR 3 MONTHS (91 DAYS) THAT IS TRADING AT 3.65 P.C. AFTER 60 DAYS?

A: GBP 201,370,272.70

B: GBP 200,789,781.86

C: GBP 200,800,684.72

D: GBP 201,389,244.64

QUESTION 19: Foreign exchange Theory

HOW WOULD YOU DESCRIBE THE RELATIONSHIP OF STERLING TO THE JAPANESE YEN?

A: it is freely floating

B: it is managed on a 'crawling peg' basis

C: it is managed by Gordon Brown by means of his five tests

D: it is managed on an unsterilised intervention basis

QUESTION 20: Foreign exchange Theory

WHICH OF THE FOLLOWING SCENARIOS MIGHT GIVE YOU THE OPPORTUNITY TO CREATE A COVERED INTEREST ARBITRAGE PROFITABLE POSITION?

A: a differential between interest rates and forward FX swap points in a currency pair

B: a devaluation of the EUR against the USD

C: parallel drops in the EUR and USD yield curves

D: a revaluation of the EUR against the USD

QUESTION 21: Foreign exchange Theory

AS FAR AS FINENESS AND WEIGHT ARE CONCERNED, WHAT ARE THE LONDON BULLION MARKET ASSOCIATION (LBMA) REQUIREMENTS FOR A "GOOD DELIVERY BAR"?

A: minimum 999.9/1000 pure gold; weight between 350 and 430 fine ounces

B: minimum 995/1000 pure gold; weight of 400 fine ounces

C: at least 995/1000 pure gold; weight between 350 and 430 fine ounces

D: at least 995/1000 pure gold; weight of 400 fine ounces

QUESTION 22: Foreign exchange Theory

IGNORING ANY RISK ON UNCOVERED INTEREST FLOWS, WHICH OF THE FOLLOWING IS AN EXAMPLE OF A COVERED INTEREST ARBITRAGE TRANSACTION?

A: Lend 3 months EUR, buy and sell EUR against USD in a FX swap spot against 3 months, Borrow USD for 3 months

B: Lend 3 months EUR, sell and buy EUR against USD in a FX swap spot against 3 months, Borrow USD for 3 months

C: Lend 3 months EUR, buy and sell EUR against USD in a FX swap spot against 3 months, Lend USD for 3 months

D: Borrow 3 months EUR, sell and buy EUR against USD in a FX swap spot against 3 months, Borrow USD for 3 months

QUESTION 23: Foreign exchange Theory

WHICH OF THE FOLLOWING WOULD YOU CONSIDER THE STANDARD PERIODS FOR FORWARD EUR/USD SWAP QUOTATIONS IN THE INTERBANK MARKET?

A: all of 1, 2, 3, 6 and 12 months

B: 1, 2, 3, 6 months only

C: 1, 3, 6, 12 and 24 months

D: none of these

QUESTION 24: Foreign exchange Theory

YOU ARE A BUYER OF USD 1,000,000. WHICH OF THE FOLLOWING SPOT GBP/USD QUOTES MADE BY FOUR DIFFERENT MARKET MAKING BANKS BEST SUITS YOU?

A: 1.54 01-06

B: 1.53 98-03

C: 1.53 99-04

D: 1.54 00-05

QUESTION 25: Foreign exchange Theory

IF USD INTEREST RATES ARE QUOTED AT 2.00 P.C. IN 3 MONTHS AND THE SAME PERIOD GBP INTEREST RATES ARE QUOTED AT 4.00 P.C. HOW WOULD YOU EXPECT THE FORWARD CABLE SWAP POINTS TO BE QUOTED?

A: High-Low

B: insufficient information to decide

C: Low-High

D: around PAR

QUESTION 26: Foreign exchange Theory

A CUSTOMER ASKS A PRICE IN GBP/SEK 3 MONTHS AND YOU QUOTE 370/350. THE CUSTOMER DEALS AT 350. WHAT HAVE YOU DONE?

A: you have sold GBP 3 months forward outright against SEK

B: you have bought GBP spot against SEK and sold SEK 3 months forward against GBP

C: you have bought GBP spot against SEK and sold GBP 3 months forward against SEK

D: you have bought SEK spot against GBP and sold SEK 3 months forward against GBP

QUESTION 27: Foreign exchange Theory

IF YOU MAKE A QUOTE OF 1.5720/25 IN SPOT CABLE AND THE CALLER "GIVES YOU 2", WHAT DEAL HAS BEEN DONE?

A: They sold you GBP 2,000,000 at 1.5720

B: They sold you GBP 2,000,000 at 1.5725

C: They sold you USD 2,000,000 at 1.5720

D: They sold you USD 2,000,000 at 1.5725

QUESTION 28: Foreign exchange Theory

WHAT IS THE INCENTIVE FOR MARKET-MAKING IN THE FOREIGN EXCHANGE MARKET?

A: Bid/offer spread

B: Flow information

C: Relationships

D: All of these

QUESTION 29: Foreign exchange Theory

IF A 6 MONTH EUR/GBP SWAP IS QUOTED 197-203, WHICH OF THE FOLLOWING STATEMENTS WOULD YOU CONSIDER TO BE MOST ACCURATE?

A: 6 months EUR rates are lower than 6 months GBP rates

B: 6 months EUR rates are higher than 6 months GBP rates

C: GBP yield curve is positive whilst the EUR curve is negative

D: Spot EUR/GBP will be higher by approximately 2 big figures in 6 months time

QUESTION 30: Foreign exchange Theory

IF A 6 MONTH EUR/USD SWAP IS QUOTED 72/68, WHICH OF THE FOLLOWING STATEMENTS WOULD YOU CONSIDER TO BE MOST ACCURATE?

A: 6 months EUR rates are higher than 6 months USD rates

B: 6 months EUR rates are lower than 6 months USD rates

C: EUR yield curve is positive whilst the USD curve is negative

D: Spot EUR/USD will be lower by approximately 70 points in 6 months time

QUESTION 31: TOPIC: Foreign exchange Calculations

IF SPOT EUR/USD IS QUOTED TO YOU AS 1.24 06/09. HOW MANY EUR WOULD YOU PAY IN EXCHANGE FOR YOUR PURCHASE OF USD 6,000,000 DEALING ON THAT PRICE?

A: EUR 7,445,400.00

B: EUR 4,835,200.26

C: EUR 4,836,369.50

D: EUR 7,443,600.00

QUESTION 32: TOPIC: Foreign exchange Calculations

YOUR EMERGING MARKETS CLIENT SIBERIAN IRON ORE COMPANY HAS AN OUTSTANDING USD/INR N-D-F WITH YOU - HIS PURCHASE OF INR 55 MILLION AT 54.60. TODAY IS FIXING DATE AND THE COMPARATOR RATE IS FIXED AT 55.00 AND THE N-D-F IS SETTLED. THE CLIENT NOW CALLS ANOTHER BANK AND IS QUOTED 54.90-95. HE DEALS ON THIS PRICE. A) WHAT IS THE SETTLEMENT AMOUNT ON THE N-D-F AND B) WHAT IS THE ALL-IN EXCHANGE RATE ACHIEVED BY THE CLIENT?

A: a) client pays Bank USD 7,326.00, b) 54.10

B: a) Bank pays client USD 7,326.00, b) 54.10

C: a) Bank pays client USD 7,326.00, b) 54.50

D: a) client pays Bank USD 7,326.00, b) 54.60

QUESTION 33: TOPIC: Foreign exchange Calculations

GIVEN THE FOLLOWING FX AND MONEY MARKET RATES MID-MARKET DATA CALCULATE A 3 MONTHS OUTRIGHT RATE FOR GBP/USD. SPOT GBP/USD: 1.55 00, 3 MONTHS GBP/USD SWAP: 29 POINTS GBP DISCOUNT.

A: 1.5529

B: 1.5471

C: 1.5500

D: 1.5469

QUESTION 34: TOPIC: Foreign exchange Calculations

A CUSTOMER ASKS TO BUY JPY AGAINST USD OUTRIGHT VALUE TOMORROW. SPOT USD/JPY IS: 89.00-05 AND THE SHORT DATE USD/JPY SWAPS ARE QUOTED OVERNIGHT: 2-1.5 AND TOM/NEXT: 2.25-1 75. CALCULATE THE OUTRIGHT PRICE REQUIRED.

A: 89.0250

B: 89.0225

C: 89.0150

D: 89.0175

QUESTION 35: TOPIC: Foreign exchange Calculations

CURRENT MID-MARKET RATES, SPOT GBP/JPY: 132.00, 1 MONTHS GBP INT: 1.125 P.C., 1 MONTHS JPY INT: 0.25 P.C. WHAT IS THE 1 MONTH FORWARD OUTRIGHT GBP/JPY MID RATE? ASSUME A 30 DAY MONTH.

A: 132.09

B: 132.12

C: 131.93

D: 131.90

QUESTION 36: TOPIC: Foreign exchange Calculations

CURRENT MID-MARKET RATES, SPOT EUR/USD: 1.3750, SPOT USD/JPY: 88.00, 1 MONTHS EUR INT: 2.875 P.C., 1 MONTHS JPY INT: 0.50 P.C. WHAT ARE THE SPOT AND 1 MONTH FORWARD OUTRIGHT EUR/JPY MID RATES? ASSUME A 30 DAY MONTH.

A: 121.00 and 120.76

B: 120.76 and 121.00

C: 121.00 and 121.24

D: 121.00 and 120.65

QUESTION 37: TOPIC: Fwd/fwds, FRAs, Money market Futures and Swaps

WHICH OF THE FOLLOWING IS THE CORRECT ISDA BRIDGE (FRABBA) RULE REGARDING PAYMENT DIRECTION ON SETTLEMENT OF A USD FRA?

A: If Settlement rate lower than FRA contractual rate - Seller pays Buyer

B: If Settlement rate higher than FRA contractual rate - Buyer pays Seller

C: None of these

D: If Settlement rate higher than FRA contractual rate - Seller pays Buyer

QUESTION 38: TOPIC: Fwd/fwds, FRAs Money market Futures and Swaps

YOU ARE PAYING 1,00% PER ANNUM PAID SEMI-ANNUALLY AND RECEIVING 6-MONTH LIBOR ON A USD 10,000,000.00 INTEREST RATE SWAP WITH EXACTLY TWO YEARS TO MATURITY. 6-MONTH LIBOR FOR THE NEXT PAYMENT DATE IS FIXED TODAY AT 0.95%. HOW WOULD YOU HEDGE THE SWAP USING FRAS?

A: sell a 5 year payer's swaption

B: buy a strip of 0x6, 6x12, 12x18 and 18x24 futures

C: sell a strip of 6x12, 12x18 and 18x24 FRAs

D: sell a strip of 0x6, 6x12, 12x18 and 18x24 FRAs

QUESTION 39: TOPIC: Fwd/fwds, FRAs Money market Futures and Swaps
ON WHICH OF THE FOLLOWING EXCHANGES CAN YOU TRADE THE 3 MONTH EURODOLLAR CONTRACT?

A: NYSE Euronext.liffe and EUREX

B: MATIF and FINEX

C: IMM and NYSE Euronext.liffe

D: MATIF and SGX

QUESTION 40: TOPIC: Fwd/fwds, FRAs Money market Futures and Swaps

IN 3 MONTHS TIME YOUR GBP DEPOSIT BOOK WILL BE OVER BORROWED FOR 4 MONTHS. YOU EXPECT INTEREST RATES TO FALL. USING THE FRA MARKET WHAT WOULD BE THE MOST APPROPRIATE HEDGE?

A: Sell 3x7

B: Buy 3x7

C: Sell 4x6

D: Buy 4x7

QUESTION 41: TOPIC: Fwd/fwds, FRAs Money market Futures and Swaps

IN THE CONTEXT OF FINANCIAL FUTURES WHAT IS MEANT BY OPEN INTEREST?

A: on any day the total number of futures contracts that have not yet expired, or fulfilled by delivery

B: on any day the total number of futures contracts that are delivered

C: on any day the total number of futures contracts traded

D: on any day the total number of futures contracts purchased

QUESTION 42: TOPIC: Fwd/fwds, FRAs Money market Futures and Swaps

YOU ARE TOLD THAT 3s V. 6s USD FRAS ARE QUOTED AT 4.5466 P.C. AND SPOT AGAINST 3 MONTHS USD ARE QUOTED AT 4.70 P.C. (BOTH MID RATES). WHAT IS THE MID RATE FOR SPOT AGAINST 6 MONTHS? (ASSUME 30 DAY MONTHS)

A: 4.65 p.c.

B: 4.88 p.c.

C: 4.55 p.c.

D: 5.00 p.c.

QUESTION 43: TOPIC: Fwd/fwds, FRAs Money market Futures and Swaps

IF AN INTEREST RATE SWAP INCLUDES SYNCHRONISATION AND NETTING, THE INTEREST PAYMENTS ARE...

A: agreed not to be exchanged on each re-rating date

B: agreed to be compounded throughout the life of the swap and paid on final maturity

C: agreed to be compared with the appropriate fixed rate on each rating date and re-set accordingly

D: agreed to be netted and paid on each re-rating date

QUESTION 44: TOPIC: Fwd/fwds, FRAs Money market Futures and Swaps

IT IS MARCH 201X. WHICH OF THE FOLLOWING SETS OF TRANSACTIONS WOULD SET UP A PROFITABLE ARBITRAGE POSITION?

A: buy June ED futures at 98.00, sell 3X6 USD FRA at 2.07 p.c.

B: buy June ED futures at 98.00, buy 3X6 USD FRA at 2.07 p.c.

C: sell June ED futures at 98.00, sell 3X6 USD FRA at 2.07 p.c.

D: sell June ED futures at 98.00, buy 3X6 USD FRA at 2.07 p.c.

QUESTION 45: TOPIC: Fwd/fwds, FRAs Money market Futures and Swaps

A 1s V. 4s USD FRA DEALT ON THURSDAY 15TH FEBRUARY 201X WILL HEDGE A PERIOD OF THREE MONTHS FROM...

A: Tuesday 19th June 201X

B: Thursday 15th March 201X

C: Monday 19th February 201X

D: Monday 19th March 201X

QUESTION 46: TOPIC: Fwd/fwds, FRAs Money market Futures and Swaps

WHICH OF THE FOLLOWING ARE THE PRINCIPAL DIFFERENCES BETWEEN OTC INSTRUMENTS LIKE IRS AND FRAS AND EXCHANGE TRADED INSTRUMENTS LIKE FUTURES?

A: all of these

B: IRS and FRAs can be tailor-made to suit individual requirements, futures are only available for 4 delivery months in the year

C: there is no up-front cost in IRS or FRAs, futures involve margining

D: with IRS and FRAs there is a credit risk on the counterparty, futures do not generate any credit risk

QUESTION 47: TOPIC: Fwd/fwds, FRAs Money market Futures and Swaps

WHICH OF THE FOLLOWING CONTAIN TWO EXAMPLES OF CONTRACTS FOR DIFFERENCE?

A: FX Swap and Eurocurrency Deposit

B: Spot FX deal and Non Deliverable Forward (NDF)

C: FX Swap and Interest Rate Swap

D: Forward Rate Agreement (FRA) and Non Deliverable Forward (NDF)

QUESTION 48: TOPIC: Fwd/fwds, FRAs Money market Futures and Swaps

IT IS OCTOBER 201X, I BUY 100 MARCH 201Y ED CONTRACTS ON NYSE EURONEXT.LIFFE AT 98.71. THE MARKET MOVES FOUR TICKS MY FAVOUR. WHAT VARIATION MARGIN WILL I RECEIVE ON THIS POSITION?

A: USD 4,000.00

B: USD 2,500.00

C: USD 5,000.00

D: USD 500.00

QUESTION 49: TOPIC: Options

AS THE WRITER OF A PUT OPTION YOUR RISK PROFILE IS BEST DESCRIBED AS...

A: unlimited downside risk, limited profit potential

B: limited downside risk, unlimited profit potential

C: limited downside risk, limited profit potential

D: unlimited downside risk, unlimited profit potential

QUESTION 50: TOPIC: Options

THE PREMIUM FOR A USD/CHF OPTION IS 2 CENTIMES I.E. 0.02 SWISS FRANCS. THE UNDERLYING VALUE OF THE OPTION IS USD 3 MILLION. HOW MUCH IS THE PREMIUM?

A: CHF 600,000

B: CHF 300,000

C: USD 60,000

D: CHF 60,000

QUESTION 51: TOPIC: Options

WHAT IS THE AIM OF DELTA HEDGING?

A: to reduce the market risk by taking a 100% equal and opposite exchange traded options position

B: to reduce the market risk by dealing in the cash market up to the gamma ratio of the position

C: to reduce the market risk by taking a 100% equal and opposite cash position

D: to reduce the market risk by an offsetting cash position

QUESTION 52: TOPIC: Options

HOW IS THE PREMIUM NORMALLY PAID FOR EXCHANGE-TRADED OPTIONS?

A: Only on the expiry date

B: As part of the daily variation margin

C: On the trade date

D: On the underlying market value date

QUESTION 53: TOPIC: Options

WHAT IS THE STRIKE PRICE OF AN OTC CURRENCY OPTION?

A: the premium payable on deal date

B: the price at which the option may be exercised

C: the exchange rate at expiry

D: the current spot rate

QUESTION 54: TOPIC: Options

"AN ESTIMATE OF HOW MUCH THE THEORETICAL VALUE OF AN OPTION CHANGES WHEN VOLATILITY CHANGES BY 1.00%." TO WHICH OF THE GREEKS DOES THIS DEFINITION APPLY?

A: gamma

B: rho

C: lambda

D: vega

QUESTION 55: TOPIC: Principles of ALM

WHAT IS A 'DURATION GAP'?

A: the average maturity of liabilities on a balance sheet

B: the difference between the duration of the longest-held and shortest-held liabilities on the balance sheet

C: the average maturity of the portfolio on the asset side of a balance sheet

D: the difference between the duration of assets and liabilities

QUESTION 56: TOPIC: Principles of ALM

WHICH STATEMENT ABOUT MODERN MATCHED-MATURITY TRANSFER PRICING IN BANKS IS CORRECT?

A: Modern matched-maturity systems differentiate transfer prices by the maturity of the commitment and also apply a marginal funding cost perspective.

B: It is now a widely accepted standard that banks should use a single representative transfer price across the entire maturity spectrum.

C: Modern matched-maturity pricing systems include an additional liquidity surcharge that is specifically applied to more liquid short maturities.

D: Matched-maturity transfer prices should represent a weighted average cost of capital that incorporates the cost of equity into the cost of borrowed funds.

QUESTION 57: TOPIC: Principles of ALM

SUPERVISORS WOULD GENERALLY CONSIDER INTEREST RATE RISK EXPOSURE IN THE BANKING BOOK EXCESSIVE BEGINNING AT WHAT LEVEL OF LOSSES GIVEN A +1-200 BPS MARKET RATE MOVEMENT?

A: >2% of 6 months forward earnings

B: <10% of regulatory capital

C: <5% of 12 months forward earnings

D: >20% of regulatory capital

QUESTION 58: TOPIC: Principles of ALM

A CUSTOMER SELLS A 3-MONTH EURO SWISS FRANC (EUROSWISS) FUTURES CONTRACT. WHICH OF THE FOLLOWING RISKS COULD HE BE TRYING TO HEDGE?

A: A decrease in forward USD/CHF

B: Rising CHF interest rates

C: An increase in forward USD/CHF

D: Falling CHF interest rates

QUESTION 59: TOPIC: Principles of ALM

WHICH OF THE FOLLOWING STATEMENTS IS TRUE?

A: hedging a long US Government bond position with a USD receiver's swap involves basis risk

B: hedging a long US Government bond position with a USD payer's swap involves basis risk

C: hedging a long US Government bond position with a USD payer's swap involves interest rate risk

D: hedging a long US Government bond position with a USD payer's swap becomes a liability swap

QUESTION 60: TOPIC: Principles of ALM

UNDER BASEL RULES, WHAT IS THE MEANING OF EEPE?

A: Effective Expected Payment Exposure

B: Effective Expected Potential Exposure

C: Effective Expected Price Earning

D: Effective Expected Positive Exposure

QUESTION 61: TOPIC: Principles of ALM

WHAT IS THE PRINCIPAL RISK IDENTIFIED BY GAP MANAGEMENT REPORTAGE?

A: interest rate risk

B: Currency risk

C: Credit risk

D: Operational risk

QUESTION 62: TOPIC: Principles of ALM

HOW DO CENTRAL BANKS IN MANY FINANCIAL CENTRES SEEK TO CONTROL A LOCAL BANK'S LIQUIDITY POSITION?

A: by issuing T-bills into the local market

B: by prohibiting banks to lend local currency externally

C: by imposing minimum reserve requirements

D: by authorising foreign banks to operate in the local market

QUESTION 63: TOPIC: Principles of Risk

WHAT BEST DEFINES MARKET RISK?

A: The risk involved between two different markets

B: The risk your position might be wrong

C: The risk you might choose the wrong currency pair to trade for a certain movement

D: The risk your position might change in value because of a move in the rate/price

QUESTION 64: TOPIC: Principles of Risk

HOW IS THE HOLDING PERIOD IN VAR CALCULATIONS DEFINED?

A: the time the portfolio or position is not altered or sold

B: the time that a trader normally holds his position

C: the time between the opening of a position and the moment that the position is first monitored by the risk manager

D: the time between the moment that the risk manager monitors a limit break and the moment that a trader is ordered to close his position

QUESTION 65: TOPIC: Principles of Risk

UNDER BASEL RULES IN ASSESSING MARKET RISK IN THE TRADING BOOK WHICH OF THE FOLLOWING COUNTS AS TIER ONE CAPITAL?

A: Equity

B: Goodwill

C: Undisclosed Reserves

D: Provision for bad debt

QUESTION 66: TOPIC: Principles of Risk

WHICH OF THE FOLLOWING LEGAL DOCUMENTATION IS A MEANS TO MITIGATE MARKET REPLACEMENT RISK BY BI-LATERAL AGREEMENT?

A: ICC 500

B: ICMA

C: ISMA

D: IFXCO

QUESTION 67: TOPIC: Principles of Risk

UNDER BASEL III RULES THE MEANING OF RSF IS...

A: Riskless Stable Funding

B: Riskless Supervised Funding

C: Required Stable Funding

D: Reviewed Supervisory Factor

QUESTION 68: TOPIC: Principles of Risk

WHAT IS THE PURPOSE OF RISK CAPITAL?

A: to absorb credit losses

B: to survive a liquidity crisis

C: to pay for expected losses

D: to pay for unexpected losses

QUESTION 69: TOPIC: Principles of Risk

WHICH ONE OF THE FOLLOWING STATEMENTS ABOUT MARK-TO-MODEL VALUATION IS CORRECT?

A: Mark-to-model valuation refers to prices determined by financial models, rather than actual market prices.

B: Mark-to-model valuation is used for complex financial instruments; it is always accurate and in line with potential tradable prices.

C: Asset managers are not allowed to use mark-to-model valuation.

D: Mark-to-model valuation is used for exchange-traded positions to ensure correct pricing.

QUESTION 70: TOPIC: Principles of Risk

WHAT TYPE OF RISK IS FRAUD GENERALLY CONSIDERED TO BE?

A: Legal

B: None of these

C: Operational

D: Market

End of Mock examination No. 2

ACI Dealing Certificate - MOCK EXAMINATION No. 3

(Please note that in the examination proper topic titles are not advised.)

QUESTION 1: TOPIC: Basic Interest Rate Calculations

CALCULATE THE 6 MONTHS EUR INTEREST RATE FROM THE 3 MONTHS (91 DAYS) EUR INTEREST RATE OF 2.90 P.C. AND THE 3s V. 6s FORWARD-FORWARD (92 DAYS) EUR INTEREST RATE OF 3.7187 P.C.

A: 3.0625 p.c.

B: 4.6446 p.c.

C: 3.3094 p.c.

D: 3.325 p.c.

QUESTION 2: TOPIC: Basic Interest Rate Calculations

WHO IS RESPONSIBLE FOR CALCULATING AND ANNOUNCING THE DAILY SONIA INDEX AVERAGE?

A: WMBA

B: ACI London

C: Bank of England

D: UK Treasury

QUESTION 3: TOPIC: Basic Interest Rate Calculations

IF YOU RECEIVED USD 10,000,000 AT THE END OF FIVE YEARS AFTER HAVING INVESTED A SUM OF MONEY AT 3.00 P.C. PER ANNUM, WHAT WAS YOUR ORIGINAL INVESTMENT?

A: USD 8,500,000.00

B: USD 9,151,416.59

C: USD 8,626,087.84

D: USD 9,327,873.23

QUESTION 4: TOPIC: Basic Interest Rate Calculations

CALCULATE THE 180 DAY USD INTEREST RATE FROM THE 3 MONTHS (90 DAYS) USD INTEREST RATE OF 1.50 P.C. AND THE 3s v 6s FORWARD-FORWARD (90 DAYS) USD INTEREST RATE OF 1.15 P.C.

A: 1.327 p.c.

B: 1.375 p.c.

C: 1.3624 p.c.

D: 1.625 p.c.

QUESTION 5: TOPIC: Basic Interest Rate Calculations

WHAT IS THE RATE OF 2.30 P.C. EQUIVALENT TO ROUNDED UP TO THE NEAREST 1/16 P.C.?

A: 2 3/16 p.c.

B: 2 1/4 p.c.

C: 2 7/16 p.c.

D: 2 5/16 p.c.

QUESTION 6: TOPIC: Basic Interest Rate Calculations

IF SHORT TERM INTEREST RATES ARE LOWER THAN LONG TERM INTEREST RATES, WHAT BEST DESCRIBES THE SHAPE OF THE YIELD CURVE?

A: Negative

B: Positive

C: Inverted

D: Flat

QUESTION 7: TOPIC: Cash Money markets Theory

WHAT IS A "TERM REPO"?

A: a Repo which may be terminated daily

B: an overnight Repo trade

C: a Repo using DBV (delivery by value) collateral

D: a Repo trade (of a maturity over one day) with a fixed end or maturity date

QUESTION 8: TOPIC: Cash Money markets Theory

WHICH OF THE FOLLOWING IS THE MAJOR DIFFERENCE BETWEEN US DOMESTIC COMMERCIAL PAPER AND ECP (EURO COMMERCIAL PAPER) DENOMINATED IN USD ISSUED IN LONDON?

A: US Domestic CP is quoted as a true yield and ECP is quoted on a discount rate basis

B: US Domestic CP is issued for 1 day up to 1 year and ECP is quoted only up to 270 days

C: US Domestic CP is always Investment grade and ECP is unrated

D: US Domestic CP is quoted on a discount rate and ECP is quoted on a true yield basis

QUESTION 9: TOPIC: Cash Money markets Theory

IN RESPECT OF THE PURCHASE OF A GBP CERTIFICATE OF DEPOSIT AT ISSUE (TO BE HELD TO MATURITY) WHICH OF THE FOLLOWING ARE DESCRIPTIONS OF THE CASH FLOWS INVOLVED IN THIS TRANSACTION IN THE MARKET?

A: discounted proceeds OUT on value date, principal plus interest for full issue period IN on maturity date

B: secondary market proceeds OUT on value date, principal plus interest for full issue period IN on maturity date

C: principal invested OUT on value date, principal plus interest IN on maturity date

D: discounted proceeds OUT on value date, face value IN on maturity date

QUESTION 10: TOPIC: Cash Money markets Theory

WHICH OF THE FOLLOWING RATES REPRESENTS THE BEST YIELD OVER A FULL YEAR?

A: Annual money market rate of 2.50 p.c.

B: Annual bond yield of 2.50 p.c.

C: Semi-annual bond yield of 2.50 p.c.

D: Semi-annual money market yield of 2.50 p.c.

QUESTION 11: TOPIC: Cash Money markets Theory

WHICH OF THE FOLLOWING IS SOMETIMES CALLED TWO-NAME PAPER?

A: BA or bank bill

B: Treasury bill

C: ECP

D: CD

QUESTION 12: TOPIC: Cash Money markets Theory

IF YOU DEAL A SINGLE CURRENCY REPO IN WHICH THE COLLATERAL IS A JGB, THEN YOU HAVE DEALT IN COLLATERAL ORIGINALLY ISSUED BY...

A: the UK Government

B: the Spanish Government

C: a commercial company

D: the Japanese Government

QUESTION 13: TOPIC: Cash Money markets Calculations

YOUR CORPORATE CUSTOMER WOOLWORTHS PLC ISSUES GBP 15,000,000 30 DAY UK COMMERCIAL PAPER AT LIBOR PLUS 75 BP. LIBOR TODAY IS FIXED AT 4.00 P.C. WHAT AMOUNT WILL THEY RECEIVE TODAY?

A: GBP 14,941,666.10

B: GBP 14,941,438.36

C: GBP 14,940,859.10

D: GBP 15,000,000.00

QUESTION 14: TOPIC: Cash Money markets Calculations

LEHMAN BROTHERS NEW YORK QUOTES YOU 2.50-2.60 P.C. FOR 3 MONTHS SECONDARY MARKET USD CDS. HOW MUCH WOULD YOU PAY FOR A USD 10,000,000.00 CD IF IT WAS ORIGINALLY ISSUED WITH A COUPON RATE OF 2.25 P.C. FOR 180 DAYS?

A: USD 10,049,689.44

B: USD 10,068,365.44

C: USD 10,000,000.00

D: USD 10,049,012.93

QUESTION 15: TOPIC: Cash Money markets Calculations

WHAT ARE THE SECONDARY MARKET PROCEEDS OF A CD WITH A FACE VALUE OF EUR 5 MILLION ISSUED AT A RATE OF 3.00 PERCENT FOR 182 DAYS AND IS STILL TRADING AT 3.00 PERCENT BUT NOW WITH 7 DAYS REMAINING TO MATURITY?

A: EUR 5,000,000.00

B: EUR 4,997,085.03

C: EUR 5,072,874.16

D: EUR 5,071,086.45

QUESTION 16: TOPIC: Cash Money markets Calculations

WHICH ONE OF THE FOLLOWING STATEMENTS IS TRUE IN RESPECT OF INTEREST RATE CALCULATIONS?

A: A 90 day CD for USD 5 million at an issue rate of 3 p.c. is worth USD 5,000,000.00 at maturity

B: A 90 day CD for USD 5 million at an issue rate of 3 p.c. is worth USD 4,962,500.00 in the secondary market

C: A 90 day CD for USD 5 million at an issue rate of 3 p.c. is worth USD 5,037,500.00 at maturity

D: A 90 day CD for USD 5 million at an issue rate of 3 p.c. is worth USD 5,037,500.00 in the secondary market

QUESTION 17: TOPIC: Cash Money markets Calculations

WHAT MATURITY CONSIDERATION DOES A DEALER PAY ON A 3 DAY REPO AGAINST GERMAN GOVERNMENT BUNDS AT 2.00 P.C. WITH A DIRTY PRICE OF EUR 10,008,219.18 AND THE COUNTERPARTY BANK CHARGING AN INITIAL MARGIN OF 1.25%?

A: EUR 9,886,624.88

B: EUR 1,647.44

C: EUR 9,886,308.36

D: EUR 9,884,660.92

QUESTION 18: TOPIC: Cash Money markets Calculations

YOU BUY USD DOMESTIC COMMERCIAL PAPER ISSUED BY CLINTON WHITEWATER INVESTMENTS INC. USD 25,000,000 14 DAYS AT 4.00 P.C. WHAT AMOUNT DO YOU PAY FOR THIS CP?

A: USD 24,961,111.11

B: USD 24,961,171.51

C: USD 25,000,000.00

D: USD 24,916,943.52

QUESTION 19: TOPIC: Foreign exchange Theory

THE DISCOUNT OR PREMIUM ON FORWARD FOREIGN EXCHANGE POINTS IN THE 3 MONTHS PERIOD IS CALCULATED FROM.

A: the shape of the yield curve of interest rates in the currency for one to twelve months

B: the current volatility in the FX markets

C: the expected appreciation or depreciation of the base currency against the quoted currency

D: the differential between the interest rates in the two currencies for that period

QUESTION 20: TOPIC: Foreign exchange Theory

FORWARD FOREIGN EXCHANGE PRICES ARE QUOTED IN THE INTERBANK MARKET...

A: as an upfront premium payable by the buyer

B: as FX swap points

C: as an interest rate differential

D: as a two way outright price

QUESTION 21: TOPIC: Foreign exchange Theory

WHAT IS BEING DESCRIBED HERE? A SYSTEM REQUIRING PARTICIPANTS TO ENTER INTO A RESTRICTED ACCESS DATABASE THEIR CREDIT LIMITS PERMITTING THEM TO DEAL EITHER AS MARKET MAKERS INPUTTING THEIR BID, OFFER OR TWO WAY DEALING PRICES OR MARKET USERS.

A: netting arrangements in the spot and forward FX markets

B: a settlements system for FX transactions

C: an electronic deal matching system for Spot FX markets

D: a guaranteed completion of all transactions in the FX spot and forward FX markets

QUESTION 22: TOPIC: Foreign exchange Theory

WHAT IS THE GOLD/SILVER RATIO?

A: The price of Gold divided by the price of Silver

B: The forward price of gold divided by the spot price of silver

C: The number of ounces of silver that can be bought with one ounce of gold

D: The number of ounces of gold silver that can be bought with one ounce of silver

QUESTION 23: TOPIC: Foreign exchange Theory

FORWARD FOREIGN EXCHANGE SWAP POINTS ARE CALCULATED FROM...

A: the interest rates in the two currencies

B: the level of interest rates in the base currency

C: the level of interest rates in the quoted currency

D: the market's expectation for the spot rate in the period quoted

QUESTION 24: TOPIC: Foreign exchange Theory

IF YOU SET UP A POSITION IN 1 MONTH GBP/USD FORWARD SWAP AT 30 POINTS YOUR FAVOUR WHEN GBP SWAPS ARE QUOTED TO YOU AT A DISCOUNT WHAT IS YOUR VIEW ON GBP INTEREST RATES (ASSUMING SPOT GBP/USD AND USD INTEREST RATES REMAIN THE SAME)?

A: GBP interest rates will remain stable

B: impossible to tell

C: GBP interest rates will rise

D: GBP interest rates will fall

QUESTION 25: TOPIC: Foreign exchange Theory

A CUSTOMER ASKS A PRICE IN GBP/SEK 3 MONTHS AND YOU QUOTE 370/350. THE CUSTOMER DEALS AT 350. WHAT HAVE YOU DONE?

A: you have bought SEK spot against GBP and sold SEK 3 months forward against GBP

B: you have bought GBP spot against SEK and sold SEK 3 months forward against GBP

C: you have sold GBP 3 months forward outright against SEK

D: you have bought GBP spot against SEK and sold GBP 3 months forward against SEK

QUESTION 26: TOPIC: Foreign exchange Theory

WHICH OF THE FOLLOWING LISTS OF COUNTRIES ARE ALL CURRENTLY MEMBERS OF THE EU EURO ZONE?

A: Sweden, Ireland, Italy and France

B: Luxembourg, Belgium, Finland and Norway

C: Austria, Spain, Germany and Ireland

D: Finland, Denmark, Germany and Netherlands

QUESTION 27: TOPIC: Foreign exchange Theory

A 1 MONTH EUR/USD SWAP IS QUOTED 5-8. IF US INTEREST RATES FALL AND EUR INTEREST RATES REMAIN STABLE WHAT EFFECT WOULD YOU EXPECT ON THE FORWARD RATE?

A: USD discount would increase

B: EUR premium would increase

C: EUR premium would reduce

D: insufficient information to decide

QUESTION 28: TOPIC: Foreign exchange Theory

IF 6-MONTH EUR/AUD IS QUOTED AT 29-32, WHICH OF THE FOLLOWING STATEMENTS IS CORRECT?

A: AUD interest rates are higher than EUR interest rates in the 6 months

B: EUR interest rates are higher than AUD interest rates in the 6 months

C: There is a positive EUR yield curve

D: There is a positive AUD yield curve

QUESTION 29: TOPIC: Foreign exchange Theory

WHICH ONE OF THE FOLLOWING BULLION COINS HAS A 999.9/1000 GOLD PURITY (.9999 FINENESS)?

A: the American "Gold Eagle"

B: the Canadian "Maple Leaf"

C: the United Kingdom "Sovereign"

D: the South African "Krugerand"

QUESTION 30: TOPIC: Foreign exchange Theory

IF THE DIFFERENTIAL BETWEEN 3-MONTH USD INTEREST RATES AND 3-MONTH GBP INTEREST RATES WIDENS, WHAT HAPPENS TO THE 3-MONTH GBP/USD FORWARD POINTS...

A: cannot say

B: they widen

C: depends on the spot rate

D: they narrow

QUESTION 31: TOPIC: Foreign exchange Calculations

IF SPOT GBP/CHF IS QUOTED 1.4275-80 AND THE 3-MONTH FORWARD OUTRIGHT IS 1.4254-61, WHAT ARE THE FORWARD POINTS?

A: 0.21/0.19

B: 19/21

C: 2.1/1.9

D: 21/19

QUESTION 32: TOPIC: Foreign exchange Calculations

USING STRAIGHT LINE INTERPOLATION AND FROM THE FOLLOWING RATES: 3 MONTHS USD/CHF SWAP: 83/80, 6 MONTHS USD/CHF SWAP 125/119. WHAT IS THE PRICE FOR 5 MONTHS USD/CHF SWAP? (ASSUME 30 DAY MONTHS).

A: 118/113

B: 97/93

C: 115/110

D: 111/106

QUESTION 33: TOPIC: Foreign exchange Calculations

GIVEN THE FOLLOWING RATES, WHAT IS THE THEORETICAL 3-MONTH (91-DAY) FORWARD OUTRIGHT ON THE RIGHT-HAND SIDE FOR GBP/USD? GBP/USD SPOT: 1.6345-49, USD 3 MONTHS: 3.84-3.94 P.C., GBP 3 MONTHS: 5.93-6.03 P.C.

A: 1.6264

B: 1.6270

C: 1.6272

D: 1.6287

QUESTION 34: TOPIC: Foreign exchange Calculations

YOUR SPOT USD/JPY DEALER SEEMS TO HAVE SUFFERED TODAY. HE SAYS HE HAS LOST "25 POINTS ON 5 DOLLARS". HOW MUCH HAS HE LOST?

A: JPY 1,250,000

B: USD 1,250,000

C: USD 125,000

D: JPY 125,000

QUESTION 35: TOPIC: Foreign exchange Calculations

YOUR SPOT EUR/USD DEALER CLOSE OF BUSINESS POSITION IS SHORT EUR 10,000,000 AT 1.3787. THE MARKET CLOSING RATE IS 1.3755 AND THE POSITION IS REVALUED OVERNIGHT IN THE BANK'S BOOKS AT THIS OFFICIAL CLOSING RATE (MID POINT). WHICH OF THE FOLLOWING IS THE CORRECT OFFICIAL P AND L FIGURE?

A: Profit USD 32,000.00

B: Loss USD 32,000.00

C: Profit EUR 32,000.00

D: Loss USD 23,000.00

QUESTION 36: TOPIC: Foreign exchange Calculations

MID SPOT USD/CHF: 1.0000, 1 MONTH MID USD/CHF: 7 PTS USD DISCOUNT. MID SPOT GBP/USD: 1.6500, 1 MONTH MID GBP/USD: 35 PTS GBP DISCOUNT. CALCULATE THE MID MARKET 1 MONTHS GBP/CHF SWAP POINTS.

A: +47 pts

B: 47 pts GBP Premium

C: 47 pts GBP Discount

D: -470 pts

QUESTION 37: TOPIC: Fwd/fwds, FRAs, Money market Futures and Swaps

HOW IS VARIATION MARGIN ON THE SHORT STERLING FUTURES CONTRACT CALCULATED?

A: Revaluation against GBP LIBOR fixing

B: A fixed margin per contract

C: Revaluation against a weighted average price

D: Revaluation against the closing price on the exchange

QUESTION 38: Fwd/fwds, FRAs, Money market Futures and Swaps

AN INTEREST RATE SWAP IS...

A: an OTC instrument to swap interest rate payments or receipts

B: none of these

C: an off balance sheet instrument quoted on a recognized exchange to hedge long term interest rate risk

D: an off balance sheet instrument to hedge short-term interest rate risk

QUESTION 39: TOPIC: Fwd/fwds, FRAs, Money market Futures and Swaps

IT IS SEPTEMBER 201X AND YOU ARE THE FIXED RATE PAYER IN A 5 YEAR GBP INTEREST RATE SWAP NOMINAL PRINCIPAL GBP 100 MILLION FIXED V. 6 MONTHS LIBOR. THE FIXED RATE IS 2.25 P.C. TODAY'S LIBOR IS CONFIRMED AS 1.50 P.C. AND BACK IN MARCH 201X THE 6 MONTHS LIBOR WAS QUOTED AT 2.00 P.C. WHAT NET INTEREST PAYMENT IS MADE ON THIS MONTH'S RE-RATING DATE? (ASSUME 30 DAY MONTHS).

A: You will receive GBP 123,287.67

B: You will pay GBP 125,000

C: You will pay GBP 123,287.67

D: You will receive GBP 125,000

QUESTION 40: TOPIC: Fwd/fwds, FRAs, Money market Futures and Swaps

A CORPORATE TREASURER HAS A 3 MONTH USD LIABILITY AT LIBOR PLUS 0.50 WHICH IS TO BE RE-RATED IN EXACTLY 1 MONTH'S TIME. USD FRA PRICES ARE QUOTED AS FOLLOWS: 1X3: 1.85-1.90 P.C., 1X4: 2.05-2.10 P.C., 1X6: 2.25-2.30 P.C. HE IS CONCERNED THAT INTEREST RATES WILL RISE. WHAT SHOULD HE DO TO HEDGE THIS POSITION?

A: buy a 1X4 USD FRA at 2.05 p.c.

B: buy a 1X3 USD FRA at 1.90 p.c.

C: sell a 1X4 USD FRA at 2.05 p.c.

D: buy a 1X4 USD FRA at 2.10 p.c.

QUESTION 41: TOPIC: Fwd/fwds, FRAs, Money market Futures and Swaps

ASSUMING ALL DATES ARE GOOD BUSINESS DAYS A USD FRA FOR THE PERIOD 25/3/1X-25/6/1X WILL HAVE ITS LIBOR SETTLEMENT RATE FIXED ON...

A: 23rd March 201X

B: 25th March 201X

C: 23rd June 201X

D: 25th June 201X

QUESTION 42: TOPIC: Fwd/fwds, FRAs, Money market Futures and Swaps

VARIATION MARGIN FOR AN EXCHANGE TRADED INSTRUMENT IS SETTLED...

A: only at settlement

B: daily

C: only when a loss is incurred following daily revaluation

D: only on trade date

QUESTION 43: TOPIC: Fwd/fwds, FRAs, Money market Futures and Swaps

HOW ARE SHORT STERLING STIR FUTURES CONTRACTS QUOTED ON NYSE EURONEXT.LIFFE?

A: on the variation margin payable

B: as a forward-forward interest rate

C: on the same basis as a bond price

D: 100 minus the implied forward-forward interest rate

QUESTION 44: TOPIC: Fwd/fwds, FRAs, Money market Futures and Swaps

IT IS MARCH 201X. WHICH OF THE FOLLOWING WOULD BE VALID ARBITRAGE POSITION?

A: Short June ED futures, short 3s v. 6s USD FRA

B: Long June ED futures, short 3s v. 6s USD FRA

C: Short June ED futures, Long 3s v. 6s USD FRA

D: Short June ED futures, short 6s v. 9s USD FRA

QUESTION 45: Fwd/fwds, FRAs, Money market Futures and Swaps

WHICH OF THE FOLLOWING BEST DESCRIBES A PLAIN VANILLA INTEREST RATE SWAP?

A: an exchange of cash flows spot against 2 year forward

B: an exchange of floating USD for floating EUR interest payments over a 2 year period

C: an exchange of fixed for floating interest flows over a 2 year period

D: an exchange of floating USD for floating EUR principal amounts over a 2 year period

QUESTION 46: TOPIC: Fwd/fwds, FRAs, Money market Futures and Swaps

WHICH OF THE FOLLOWING IS NOT NEGOTIABLE, TRADABLE NOR ASSIGNABLE?

A: CHF Bankers Acceptances

B: GBP Certificate of Deposit

C: EUR FRA

D: US Treasury Bill

QUESTION 47: TOPIC: Fwd/fwds, FRAs, Money market Futures and Swaps

IT IS FEBRUARY 201X. WHICH OF THE FOLLOWING TRANSACTIONS PERMIT A PROFITABLE ARBITRAGE POSITION TO BE SET UP?

A: March ED futures 98.00 ask, 1X4 USD FRAs Offered at 1.95 p.c.

B: March ED futures 98.00 bid, 1X4 USD FRAs Offered at 2.05 p.c.

C: March ED futures 98.00 bid, 1X4 USD FRAs Offered at 1.95 p.c.

D: March ED futures 98.00 ask, 1X4 USD FRAs Offered at 2.05 p.c.

QUESTION 48: TOPIC: Fwd/fwds, FRAs, Money market Futures and Swaps

IF YOU ARE CONCERNED ABOUT EUR INTEREST RATES RISING AND ARE CURRENTLY RECEIVING A FIXED INCOME FROM A 3 YEAR BOND HOLDING, WHICH SWAP STRUCTURE WOULD BEST SUIT YOU?

A: pay EONIA, receive 3 year fixed

B: receive LIBOR floating, pay 3 year fixed

C: pay LIBOR floating, receive 3 year fixed

D: receive EONIA, pay 7 day fixed

QUESTION 49: TOPIC: Options

IF A CORPORATE TREASURER WANTS TO HEDGE AGAINST THE CHF APPRECIATING AGAINST THE USD, HE SHOULD...

A: Buy a USD Put/CHF Call

B: Sell a CHF Call/USD Put

C: Buy a CHF Swaption

D: Sell Euroswiss STIR Futures

QUESTION 50: TOPIC: Options

IF YOU ARE SHORT GBP PUTS / USD CALLS STRIKE 1.7500 AND THE DELTA OF THE POSITION PREVIOUSLY 0.45 MOVES TO 0.60 WHAT DOES THIS MEAN?

A: the options have moved OTM and you should hold 40% of the position in cash as a delta hedge

B: the options have moved ITM and you should sell 15% of the position as a delta hedge

C: the options have moved ITM and you should hold 60% of the position in cash as a delta hedge

D: the options have moved OTM and you should hold 15% of the position as a delta hedge

QUESTION 51: TOPIC: Options

THE CURRENT 3-MONTH EUR/USD FORWARD OUTRIGHT IS 1.3650. A EUROPEAN-STYLE 3-MONTH EUR CALL/USD PUT OPTION WITH A STRIKE OF 1.3600 HAS A PREMIUM OF 100 POINTS. WHAT IS THE BREAK-EVEN OF THIS OPTION?

A: 1.3500

B: 1.3600

C: 1.3650

D: 1.3700

QUESTION 52: TOPIC: Options

WHAT IS A ZERO-COST COLLAR?

A: Long cap and long floor at zero premium

B: Long cap and short floor at same strike

C: Long cap and short floor at zero premium

D: Long cap and long floor at same strike

QUESTION 53: TOPIC: Options

YOU HAVE PURCHASED A EUR 10 MILLION EUR CALL / USD PUT WITH A STRIKE PRICE OF 1.37 00 FOR WHICH YOU HAVE PAID USD 15,000.00. WHAT IS THE BREAK EVEN OF THIS OPTION?

A: 1.3685

B: 1.3720

C: 1.3715

D: 1.3750

QUESTION 54: TOPIC: Options

WHICH OF THE FOLLOWING IS THE CORRECT WAY TO CONSTRUCT A SYNTHETIC SHORT POSITION IN USD AGAINST JPY?

A: buy a USD Put / JPY Call and sell a USD Call / JPY Put at the same strike price with the same expiry

B: buy a USD Put / JPY Call at one strike price and sell a USD Call / JPY Put at a higher strike price with the same expiry

C: sell a USD Put / JPY Call at one strike price and buy a USD Call / JPY Put at a higher strike price with the same expiry

D: sell a USD Put / JPY Call and buy a USD Call / JPY Put at the same strike price with the same expiry

QUESTION 55: TOPIC: Principles of ALM

A SOLD JUN 3-MONTH STIR-FUTURE SHOULD BE REPORTED IN THE GAP REPORT AS OF 22 MAY...

A: as a taken deposit with a term of one month

B: as a given deposit with a term of one month and a taken deposit with a term of four months

C: as a taken deposit with a term of one month and a given deposit with a term of four months

D: as a given deposit with a term of four months

QUESTION 56: TOPIC: Principles of ALM

A BANK EXPECTS INTEREST RATES TO FALL WITH A PARALLEL DOWNWARD SHIFT IN THE YIELD CURVE. WHAT ACTION SHOULD THE BANK TAKE IF IT WANTS TO BENEFIT FROM THIS VIEW?

A: run a zero gap

B: reduce the maturity of its asset portfolio

C: lengthen the maturity of its asset portfolio

D: increase the maturity of its liabilities

QUESTION 57: TOPIC: Principles of ALM

WHICH OF THE FOLLOWING IS PART OF THE TYPICAL SCOPE OF ASSET LIABILITY MANAGEMENT (ALM)?

A: Planning the liability structure and net funding requirements arising from trading book assets carried at amortized cost.

B: Making sure that fixed assets are depreciated according to the applicable tax code.

C: Planning the maturity structure and net funding requirements arising from banking book and trading book transactions.

D: Selling distressed assets and investing in bank liabilities trading at distressed levels.

QUESTION 58: TOPIC: Principles of ALM

WHICH DUTIES ARE ASSIGNED TO THE ALCO (ASSET AND LIABILITY COMMITTEE)?

A: balance sheet analysis and allocation of corporate credit limits

B: the specification and management of the bank's market risk

C: the supervision of financial control and accounting processes

D: the management of the bank's customer business

QUESTION 59: TOPIC: Principles of ALM

ALCO REPORTAGE FOR THE 3-6 MONTH TIME BUCKET IDENTIFIES THAT THE BANK HAS GBP 1 BILLION IN LIABILITIES THAT WILL BE MATURING AND GBP 800 MILLION IN ASSETS THAT WILL BE MATURING. THE REPORTED GAP FOR THIS PERIOD IS THEREFORE...

A: A funding gap of GBP 200 million

B: A positive gap of GBP 0.2 billion

C: A negative gap of GBP 200 million

D: A negative gap of GBP 1 billion

QUESTION 60: TOPIC: Principles of ALM

IN ADDITION TO THE LIQUIDITY COVERAGE RATIO AND THE NET STABLE FUNDING RATIO, BASEL III INTRODUCES...

A: a minimum 7.5 % leverage ratio

B: a maximum 7.5 % leverage ratio

C: a minimum 3.0 % leverage ratio

D: a maximum 3.0 % leverage ratio

QUESTION 61: TOPIC: Principles of ALM

WHICH OF THE FOLLOWING IS A VALID REASON TO DISCONTINUE ACCOUNTING FOR A TRANSACTION AS A HEDGE?

A: correlation between the underlying risk and the hedge transaction improves

B: on advice from the dealer to do so

C: the underlying risk is confirmed as being certain to occur

D: if an anticipated underlying risk is no longer certain to occur

QUESTION 62: TOPIC: Principles of ALM

WITH RESPECT TO THE INSTITUTION'S AVAILABLE-FOR-SALE PORTFOLIO, WHICH OF THE FOLLOWING SITUATIONS GIVES RISE TO A NEGATIVE MARK TO MARKET AS THE YIELD CURVE STEEPENS?

A: lending long, borrowing short

B: match-funded commercial roll-over loans

C: buying CP, issuing bonds

D: lending short, borrowing long

You selected the CORRECT option - A: lending long, borrowing short

QUESTION 63: TOPIC: Principles of Risk

HOW IS THE HOLDING PERIOD IN VAR CALCULATIONS DEFINED?

A: the time the portfolio or position is not altered or sold

B: the time between the moment that the risk manager monitors a limit break and the moment that a trader is ordered to close his position

C: the time that a trader normally holds his position

D: the time between the opening of a position and the moment that the position is first monitored by the risk manager

QUESTION 64: TOPIC: Principles of Risk

FOR BASEL CAPITAL PURPOSES OPERATIONAL RISK IN FOREIGN EXCHANGE INVOLVES...

A: problems with pre-settlement risk and market replacement risk

B: problems with processing, product pricing, and valuation

C: problems with delivery risk, credit assessment, and clearing risk

D: problems with basis, reciprocation and reputational risk

QUESTION 65: TOPIC: Principles of Risk

WHICH OF THE FOLLOWING IS AN EXAMPLE OF CREDIT RISK IN THE NAME OF MAJOR BANK?

A: a sale of a currency option to Major Bank (premium received)

B: a deposit accepted from Major Bank in JPY

C: a futures trade effected with Major Bank via the CME Group open outcry market

D: a purchase of a USD CD from Mega Bank originally issued by Major Bank

QUESTION 66: TOPIC: Principles of Risk

UNDER BASEL RULES THE MEANING OF CCF IS...

A: Credit Contribution Factor

B: Credit Collateralization Factor

C: Currency Conversion Factor

D: Credit Conversion Factor

QUESTION 67: TOPIC: Principles of Risk

UNDER BASEL III WHICH OF THE FOLLOWING ARE REQUIRED?

A: a minimum common equity capital ratio of 5.5 % and a capital conservation buffer of 2.5 %

B: a minimum common equity capital ratio of 4.5 % and a capital conservation buffer of 1.5 %

C: a minimum common equity capital ratio of 2.5 % and a capital conservation buffer of 4.0 %

D: a minimum common equity capital ratio of 4.5 % and a capital conservation buffer of 2.5 %

QUESTION 68: TOPIC: Principles of Risk

WHICH RISKS ARE INCREASED BY TAKING COLLATERAL?

A: operational risk

B: legal risk

C: liquidity risk

D: all of these

QUESTION 69: TOPIC: Principles of Risk

WHAT TYPE OF RISK IS FRAUD GENERALLY CONSIDERED TO BE?

A: Market

B: Operational

C: Legal

D: None of these

QUESTION 70: TOPIC: Principles of Risk

WHAT ARE THE BIS BASEL GUIDELINES FOR VAR MODELS?

A: 95% confidence level and 10-day holding period.

B: 99% confidence level and 20-day holding period.

C: 95% confidence level and 20-day holding period.

D: 99% confidence level and 10-day holding period.

End of Mock examination No. 3

ACI Dealing Certificate - MOCK EXAMINATION No. 4

(Please note that in the examination proper topic titles are not advised.)

QUESTION 1: TOPIC: Basic Interest Rate Calculations

WITH SPOT EUR/GBP QUOTED 0.7000 (MID-POINT), CALCULATE THE LEVEL OF THE 180 DAY EUR/GBP OUTRIGHT PRICE IF THE VARIABLE CURRENCY IS QUOTED 3.80 P.C. AND THE BASE CURRENCY IS QUOTED 2.90 P.C.

A: 0.6960

B: 0.7029

C: 0.6971

D: 0.7040

QUESTION 2: TOPIC: Basic Interest Rate Calculations

THERE IS CURRENTLY A FLATTISH YIELD CURVE IN USD. WHICH OF THE FOLLOWING DATA ELEMENTS DO YOU REQUIRE TO CALCULATE A 2 1/2 MONTHS DEPOSIT RATE?

A: 2 v. 3 months forward-forward interest rate

B: 2 and 3 months cross currency forward swap points

C: 1 and 3 months standard period interest rates

D: 2 and 3 months standard period interest rates

QUESTION 3: TOPIC: Basic Interest Rate Calculations

IF SHORT-TERM CASH RATES ON 3RD APRIL 201X RANGE FROM T/N 5.55 P.C. THROUGH 3 MONTHS 5.00 P.C. TO 12 MONTHS 4.25 P.C. AND A MONTH LATER ON 3RD MAY 201X THE SHORT TERM RATES RANGE FROM T/N 4.00 P.C. THROUGH 3 MONTHS 4.12 P.C. TO 12 MONTHS 4.25 P.C. I) DESCRIBE THE SHAPE OF THE SHORT-TERM SEGMENT OF THE YIELD CURVE ON 3RD APRIL AND II) 3RD MAY USING STANDARD MARKET TERMINOLOGY.

A: i) 03/04 inverted, ii) 03/05 positive

B: i) 03/04 inverted, ii) 03/04 flat

C: i) 03/04 positive, ii) 03/05 inverted

D: i) 03/04 positive, ii) 03/05 negative

QUESTION 4: TOPIC: Basic Interest Rate Calculations

WHICH OF THE FOLLOWING DATA ELEMENTS DO YOU REQUIRE TO PLOT A SPOT YIELD CURVE?

A: 1X2, 2X3, 3X6, 6X12 months forward-forward interest rates

B: 1 to 12 months cross currency forward swap points

C: 1 to 6 months standard periods and 6 to 12 months forward-forward interest rate

D: 1 to 12 months standard period interest rates

QUESTION 5: TOPIC: Basic Interest Rate Calculations

EURIBOR IS THE...

A: Another name for EUR LIBOR

B: Daily fixing for EUR interbank money market rates in the European market

C: The official repo rate quoted by the ECB

D: Daily fixing for EUR interbank money market rates in the London market

QUESTION 6: TOPIC: Basic Interest Rate Calculations

A NEGATIVE YIELD CURVE INDICATES THAT...

A: market sentiment is that over time interest rates will rise

B: market sentiment is that over time interest rates will fall

C: forward FX rates are at a premium

D: longer term interest rates are higher than short term

QUESTION 7: TOPIC: Cash Money markets Theory

YOU HAVE BOUGHT A PRIMARY ISSUE JPY LONDON CERTIFICATE OF DEPOSIT FROM BANK OF FUTURAMA LONDON WITH AN ISSUE RATE OF 1.95 P.C. ON THE SAME DAY, TO MAKE A TRADING PROFIT AT WHICH RATE WOULD YOU HAVE TO SELL IT?

A: 1.85 p.c.

B: 1.95 p.c.

C: 2.25 p.c.

D: 2.00 p.c.

QUESTION 8: TOPIC: Cash Money markets Theory

THE IMPLIED REPO RATE IS...

A: the rate offered by the central bank in repo transactions

B: the break-even rate at which it is possible to buy a bond, repo it out and sell a futures contract

C: the repo rate applicable to special collateral

D: none of these

QUESTION 9: TOPIC: Cash Money markets Theory

WHICH OF THE FOLLOWING IS A EUROCURRENCY DEPOSIT?

A: A 3-month deposit of GBP 10,000,000.00 offered by the UK branch of a US bank in London

B: A 3-month deposit of USD 10,000,000.00 offered by a US bank in London

C: A 3-month deposit of USD 10,000,000.00 offered by the US branch of a UK bank in New York

D: A 3-month deposit of USD 10,000,000.00 offered by a US bank in New York

QUESTION 10: TOPIC: Cash Money markets Theory

WHICH OF THE FOLLOWING GROUPS OF MONEY MARKET INSTRUMENTS ALL TYPICALLY PAY RETURN IN THE FORM OF A DISCOUNT TO FACE VALUE?

A: US BA, US T-bill, US CP

B: GBP Deposit, US T-Bond, GBP CD

C: US T-bill, USD ECP, UK Gilt

D: USD Deposit, USD classic repo, USD CD

QUESTION 11: TOPIC: Cash Money markets Theory

WHAT ADVANTAGE IS THERE TO THE PURCHASER OF A CERTIFICATE OF DEPOSIT COMPARED TO THE PLACING OF A FIXED DEPOSIT?

A: It is a negotiable instrument

B: There is no advantage

C: It eliminates counterparty risk

D: It normally pays a higher rate of interest

QUESTION 12: TOPIC: Cash Money markets Theory

THE LATEST VERSION OF THE GLOBAL MASTER REPURCHASE AGREEMENT...

A: makes Sell/buy backs the same as a "Classic Repo"

B: is a replacement for IFEMA

C: prohibits Sell/buy backs

D: provides Sell/buy backs with a legal framework

QUESTION 13: TOPIC: Cash Money markets Calculations

AS AN INVESTOR, WHICH OF THE FOLLOWING PRICES WOULD YOU EXPECT TO PAY FOR A USD DOMESTIC COMMERCIAL PAPER ISSUED IN THE AMOUNT OF USD 10 MILLION FOR 92 DAYS AT 2.00 P.C.?

A: USD 10,000,000.00

B: USD 9,948,888.89

C: USD 9,949,148.80

D: USD 10,051,111.11

QUESTION 14: TOPIC: Cash Money markets Calculations

A CD WITH A FACE VALUE OF USD 50 MILLION AND A COUPON OF 4.50 PERCENT WAS ISSUED AT PAR FOR 90 DAYS AND IS NOW TRADING AT 4.50 PERCENT WITH 30 DAYS REMAINING TO MATURITY. WHAT IS NOW THE GAIN OR LOSS IN SECONDARY MARKET PROCEEDS COMPARED TO THE ISSUE PRICE?

A: a loss of USD 1,400.99

B: a gain of USD 186,099.00

C: zero

D: a gain of USD 373,599.00

QUESTION 15: TOPIC: Cash Money markets Calculations

What initial consideration does a dealer receive against GBP 50 million collateral in a 3-day repo at a rate of 4.10 p.c. if the GMRA permits him to charge an initial margin of 2.50%?

A: GBP 50,000,000.00

B: GBP 51,000,000.00

C: GBP 51,250,000.00

D: GBP 51,050,000.00

QUESTION 16: TOPIC: Cash Money markets Calculations

WHAT SALE PROCEEDS WOULD YOUR CORPORATE CUSTOMER RECEIVE FOR 1 MONTH ECP WITH FACE VALUE OF USD 20 MILLION ISSUED THROUGH YOU TODAY AT LIBOR PLUS 20 BP. TODAY'S 1 MONTH LIBOR IS FIXED AT 6.00 P.C. (ASSUME 30 DAY MONTHS).

A: USD 19,898,082.19

B: USD 19,896,666.67

C: USD 19,897,197.81

D: USD 19,898,598.92

QUESTION 17: TOPIC: Cash Money markets Calculations

TWO BANKS IN THE INTERBANK MARKET QUOTE YOU FOR 1 MONTH (30 DAYS) EUR BAS. BLAIR BANK PARIS QUOTES 2.50-2.55 P.C. AND MEGA BANK BRUSSELS QUOTES 2.47-2.52 P.C. YOU ARE A BUYER OF EUR 5 MILLION 1 MONTH BAS. WITH WHOM DO YOU DEAL AND WHAT PRICE DO YOU PAY?

A: Mega Bank Brussels, EUR 4,989,708.33

B: Mega Bank Brussels, EUR 4,989,500.00

C: Blair Bank Paris, EUR 4,989,375.00

D: Blair Bank Paris, EUR 4,989,583.33

QUESTION 18: TOPIC: Cash Money markets Calculations

TRADITIONAL BROKERS LIMITED LONDON QUOTE YOU 3 7/8-3 3/4 P.C. IN 3 MONTHS (91 DAYS) GBP SECONDARY CDS. YOU HAVE AN INTEREST TO SELL CDS AND HAVING CHECKED THE DELIVERY RISK LIMIT IN THE NAME OF BLAIR BANK (THE BUYER) AND YOU DEAL ON THE BROKER'S PRICE SELLING GBP 20 MILLION CDS ORIGINALLY ISSUED FOR 181 DAYS AT 3.75 P.C. BY MAJOR BANK, LONDON. HOW MUCH DO YOU RECEIVE?

A: GBP 20,176,988.75

B: GBP 20,183,218.54

C: GBP 20,174,546.44

D: GBP 20,084,523.24

QUESTION 19: TOPIC: Foreign exchange Theory

A 6 MONTHS GBP/USD SWAP IS QUOTED 79-75. USD INTEREST RATES ARE EXPECTED TO RISE WITH GBP INTEREST RATES REMAINING STABLE. WHAT EFFECT WOULD YOU EXPECT THIS TO HAVE ON THE FORWARD PRICE?

A: it will move towards 8-12

B: it will move towards par

C: it will remain unchanged

D: insufficient information to decide

QUESTION 20: TOPIC: Foreign exchange Theory

IF A 6 MONTH EUR/GBP SWAP IS QUOTED 197-203, WHICH OF THE FOLLOWING STATEMENTS WOULD YOU CONSIDER TO BE MOST ACCURATE?

A: 6 months EUR rates are higher than 6 months GBP rates

B: Spot EUR/GBP will be higher by approximately 2 big figures in 6 months time

C: GBP yield curve is positive whilst the EUR curve is negative

D: 6 months EUR rates are lower than 6 months GBP rates

QUESTION 21: TOPIC: Foreign exchange Theory

IF DURING A TELEPHONE CONVERSATION THE DEALER QUOTING A SPOT FX PRICE CAUTIONS THE MARKET USER "YOUR RISK" WHAT DOES THIS MEAN?

A: any transaction ensuing is at the risk of the market user

B: if not dealt on immediately, the price is subject to change and should be rechecked before dealing

C: the price is not firm at all and is for indication only

D: advice given alongside the price quote is subject to local regulatory authority guidelines

QUESTION 22: TOPIC: Foreign exchange Theory

WHICH OF THE FOLLOWING IS A FOREIGN EXCHANGE CONTRACT INVOLVING PHYSICAL SETTLEMENT OF THE CURRENCY AMOUNTS ON ONE OR MORE VALUE DATES?

A: A time/delivery forward contract

B: A non-deliverable forward

C: An Exchange traded currency contract

D: An out-of-the-money OTC currency option

QUESTION 23: TOPIC: Foreign exchange Theory

WHAT IS THE FUNCTION OF AN AUTOMATIC TRADING SYSTEM (ATS) OR ELECTRONIC BROKER IN THE SPOT FX MARKET?

A: a screen-based communications system for professional spot traders

B: a screen-based anonymous dealing system for professional spot traders

C: a screen-based position keeping system for professional spot traders

D: a screen-based spot rates information system

QUESTION 24: TOPIC: Foreign exchange Theory

VOICE-BROKERS IN SPOT FX ARE REMUNERATED WITH...

A: A fee paid by the seller

B: Commission paid by both parties at rates agreed beforehand

C: The Bid/offer spread

D: A share of the bid/offer spread

QUESTION 25: TOPIC: Foreign exchange Theory

TODAY IS FIXING DATE FOR A GBP/USD NON-DELIVERABLE FORWARD. WHAT HAPPENS?

A: if the original n-d-f exchange rate is in the money it becomes a live spot foreign exchange contract

B: the original n-d-f exchange rate is compared with the current spot and the difference is settled today

C: the original n-d-f exchange rate is compared with the current spot and the difference is settled on value date

D: if the original n-d-f exchange rate is out of the money it expires worthless (no further action)

QUESTION 26: TOPIC: Foreign exchange Theory

IF THE MID-POINT SPOT EUR/JPY IS QUOTED: 108.00 AND 6 MONTHS FORWARD SWAP IS QUOTED: 100 POINTS EUR DISCOUNT, HOW CAN THE OUTRIGHT RATE BE DESCRIBED?

A: Big figure = 107, points adjustment = +1.00

B: Big figure = 107, points adjustment -1.00

C: Big figure = 109, points adjustment = +1.00

D: Big figure = 108, points adjustment = -1.00

QUESTION 27: TOPIC: Foreign exchange Theory

IN PRECIOUS METALS TRADING WHAT IS 'BACKWARDATION'?

A: A reversal of a Gold lease transaction one or more days after establishment

B: An adjustment to the Gold Fixing price based on historic price trends

C: A market situation where prices for future delivery are higher than the spot price

D: A market situation where prices for future delivery are lower than the spot price

QUESTION 28: TOPIC: Foreign exchange Theory

IF THE CURRENT SPOT DATE IS FRIDAY 27TH FEBRUARY, WHAT IS THE FIXED 1-MONTH DATE IN FOREIGN EXCHANGE?

A: 28th March

B: 1st April

C: 27th March

D: 31st March

QUESTION 29: TOPIC: Foreign exchange Theory

WHICH OF THE FOLLOWING CHARACTERISTICS DOES NOT APPLY TO A FX SWAP?

A: it can replace a pair of money market transactions

B: it eliminates credit risk with the counterparty

C: it consists of a pair of transactions, usually one spot and one for a forward date

D: it can be used to exploit arbitrage opportunities

QUESTION 30: TOPIC: Foreign exchange Theory

YOUR FORWARD FX BROKER 'VOICE BROKERS LIMITED' IS QUOTING THE ONE MONTH EUR/USD 23-27. YOU ARE INTERESTED IN BUYING SPOT AND SELLING FORWARD EUR AT 25 POINTS YOUR FAVOUR. YOU ADVISE THE BROKER OF THIS INTEREST AND PUT HIM ON OFFERING FORWARD EUR AT 25 POINTS. WHAT IS THE BROKER'S NEW PRICE TO THE MARKET?

A: 23-25

B: 25-27

C: 25-23

D: 27-25

QUESTION 31: TOPIC: Foreign exchange Calculations

YOUR FORWARD DEALER HAS JUST QUOTED WOOLWORTHS PLC, A CORPORATE CLIENT, A 3 MONTHS OUTRIGHT GBP/USD OF 1.6500 (BANK SELLS OUTRIGHT GBP). IF THE 3 MONTHS GBP/USD SWAP IS CURRENTLY QUOTED 110-105 WHAT IS THE SPOT RATE ON WHICH THE OUTRIGHT WAS BASED?

A: 1.6395

B: 1.6605

C: 1.6390

D: 1.6610

QUESTION 32: TOPIC: Foreign exchange Calculations

YOUR CORPORATE CLIENT SEOUL INTERNATIONAL INDUSTRIES IS HOLDING A N-D-F LONG USD 10 MILLION AT 1090.00 AGAINST KRW TO BE FIXED TODAY AT 11.00 A.M. WHAT WILL BE THE CASH AMOUNT TO BE SETTLED AND IN WHOSE FAVOUR IS THE PAYMENT IF THE COMPARATOR SPOT RATE IS FIXED AT 1091.00 (ASSUME SETTLEMENT IN KRW)?

A: KRW 1,000,000 payable to the bank

B: KRW 1,000,000 payable to Seoul International Industries

C: KRW 10,000,000 payable to the bank

D: KRW 10,000,000 payable to Seoul International Industries

QUESTION 33: TOPIC: Foreign exchange Calculations

IF SPOT USD/CHF IS QUOTED 1.0000-12 AND T/N IS QUOTED 3/4-1/2 WHAT IS YOUR PRICE TO A CUSTOMER WHO WANTS TO BUY CHF VALUE TOMORROW?

A: 1.00995

B: 1.000075

C: 1.009925

D: 1.00005

QUESTION 34: TOPIC: Foreign exchange Calculations

AT THE END OF THE DAY YOU ARE SHORT EUR 1.2 MILLION AGAINST JPY AT 146.60. YOU ARE ASKED TO REVALUE YOUR POSITION AT 146.00 WHAT IS THE RESULTING PROFIT OR LOSS IN JPY?

A: Loss JPY 720,000

B: Profit JPY 720,000

C: Loss JPY 77,200

D: Profit JPY 77,200

QUESTION 35: TOPIC: Foreign exchange Calculations

SPOT GBP/USD IS QUOTED 1.6600 (MID POINT). IF 6 MONTHS (180 DAYS) USD INTEREST RATES ARE QUOTED 1.75 P.C. AND SAME PERIOD GBP INTEREST RATES ARE QUOTED 4.25 P.C. (MID RATES) WHAT IS THE APPROXIMATE LEVEL OF GBP/USD SWAP POINTS IN THIS PERIOD?

A: 198 pts GBP discount

B: 19.8 pts GBP discount

C: 19.8 pts GBP premium

D: 198 pts GBP premium

QUESTION 36: TOPIC: Foreign exchange Calculations

FROM THE FOLLOWING RATES: SPOT GBP/USD: 1.6210/15. T/N GBP/USD SWAP: -0.3/+0.2. WHAT IS THE THEORETICAL QUOTE FOR GBP/USD OUTRIGHT VALUE TOMORROW?

A: 1.620998/1.621503

B: 1.62098/1.62153

C: 1.62097/1.62152

D: 1.62102/1.62147

QUESTION 37: TOPIC: Fwd/fwds, FRAs Money market Futures and Swaps

ON THURSDAY 12TH MAY 201X, YOU SELL A 1X4 FRA IN USD. THE START AND END DATES OF THE FRA PERIOD ARE THURSDAY 16TH JUNE AND FRIDAY 16TH SEPTEMBER. WHICH DATE'S LIBOR WILL BE USED FOR THE FRA SETTLEMENT CALCULATION?

A: 18th June

B: 16th June

C: 16th September

D: 14th June

QUESTION 38: TOPIC: Fwd/fwds, FRAs Money market Futures and Swaps

IT IS MARCH 201X. IF SEPTEMBER EUR STIR FUTURES ARE QUOTED 98.02 AND EUR DECEMBER STIR FUTURES ARE QUOTED 97.70, HOW WOULD THE MID-RATE 6s V. 12s EUR FRA BE QUOTED? (ASSUME 30 DAY MONTHS).

A: 2.12 p.c.

B: 2.27 p.c.

C: 2.54 p.c.

D: 2.15 p.c.

QUESTION 39: TOPIC: Fwd/fwds, FRAs Money market Futures and Swaps

PRINCIPALS WHO ENTER INTO AN INTEREST RATE SWAP WITH THE INTENTION OF SHORTLY AFTERWARDS ASSIGNING OR TRANSFERRING THE SWAP TO A THIRD PARTY...

A: should only reveal any such intentions after the confirmations have been exchanged

B: should never reveal their future dealing intentions to their counterparties

C: should agree upon the method of assignment before transacting

D: should make clear their intention to do so when initially negotiating the deal

QUESTION 40: TOPIC: Fwd/fwds, FRAs Money market Futures and Swaps

IT IS APRIL 201X. OF THESE CHOICES, WHICH IS THE BEST METHOD TO HEDGE A SHORT GBP 20 MILLION CASH POSITION JUNE TO DECEMBER 201X AT 2.20 P.C.?

A: sell 40 Short Sterling June at 97.90 and sell 40 Short Sterling September contracts at 97.87

B: buy 40 Short Sterling June at 97.90 and buy 40 Short Sterling September contracts at 97.87

C: sell 20 Short Sterling June at 97.90 and sell 20 Short Sterling September contracts at 97.87

D: buy a 2s v. 10s GBP 20,000,000.00 FRA at 2.15 p.c.

QUESTION 41: TOPIC: Fwd/fwds, FRAs Money market Futures and Swaps

YOU RECEIVE A MARGIN CALL ON A SHORT STERLING FUTURES POSITION, YOU BOUGHT 10 CONTRACTS YESTERDAY AT 96.20. THIS INDICATES THAT...

A: the futures price closed below the previous close

B: the futures price closed below 96.20

C: the futures price closed above the previous close

D: the futures price closed above 96.20

QUESTION 42: TOPIC: Fwd/fwds, FRAs Money market Futures and Swaps

HOW IS A USD OVERNIGHT INDEXED SWAP (OIS) SETTLED?

A: Two days after maturity by net payment

B: Periodic exchange of fixed and floating payments up to and including maturity

C: At maturity by net payment

D: After maturity by exchange of fixed and floating payments

QUESTION 43: TOPIC: Fwd/fwds, FRAs Money market Futures and Swaps

TODAY IS THE FIXING DATE FOR 6/9 USD FRA WHICH YOU SOLD AT 5.50 P.C. FOR WHICH THE FRABBA LIBOR IS FIXED TODAY AT 6.00 P.C. WHICH OF THE FOLLOWING IS TRUE?

A: There will be no exchange whatsoever

B: Your counterparty will pay you on settlement date

C: You will pay the counterparty on fixing date

D: You will pay the counterparty on settlement date

QUESTION 44: TOPIC: Fwd/fwds, FRAs Money market Futures and Swaps

IT IS NOVEMBER 201X, YOU ARE OVER-LENT 3 MONTHS STARTING IN 7 MONTHS' TIME (IMM DATES). THE CORRESPONDING FRA IS QUOTED 1.31-1.36 P.C. AND THE APPROPRIATE FUTURES ARE PRICED AT 98.62-98.64. YOU ARE WORRIED ABOUT INTEREST RATES RISING. WHAT IS THE BEST WAY TO HEDGE YOUR RISK?

A: Sell the FRA at 1.31 p.c.

B: Buy the FRA at 1.36 p.c.

C: Buy the futures at 98.64

D: Sell the futures at 98.62

QUESTION 45: TOPIC: Fwd/fwds, FRAs Money market Futures and Swaps

A GBP FRA FOR DATES 25/1/1X- 25/4/1X WILL HAVE ITS LIBOR SETTLEMENT RATE FIXED ON...

A: 25th January 201X

B: 23rd April 201X

C: 25th April 201X

D: 23rd January 201X

QUESTION 46: TOPIC: Fwd/fwds, FRAs Money market Futures and Swaps

IF A DEALER HAS ENTERED INTO AN OIS IN EUR 50 MILLION PAYING 7 DAYS FIXED AT 3.00 P.C. AND RECEIVING EURONIA AND THE NET PAYMENT AT MATURITY IS CALCULATED AS EUR 4,861.11 IN THE DEALER'S FAVOUR WHAT WAS THE AVERAGE COMPOUNDED EURONIA FOR THE PERIOD?

A: 2.50 p.c.

B: 3.50 p.c.

C: 3.25 p.c.

D: 4.00 p.c.

QUESTION 47: TOPIC: Fwd/fwds, FRAs Money market Futures and Swaps

IF THE MID MARKET 1 MONTH USD INTEREST RATE IS QUOTED 2.15 P.C. AND THE MID MARKET 3 MONTHS USD IS QUOTED 1.75 P.C. (ASSUME 30 DAY MONTHS), WHAT IS THE LEVEL OF THE 1s V. 3s FORWARD/FORWARD USD INTEREST RATE?

A: 2.00 p.c.

B: 1.82 p.c.

C: 1.66 p.c.

D: 1.55 p.c.

QUESTION 48: TOPIC: Fwd/fwds, FRAs Money market Futures and Swaps

WHAT IS THE OVERNIGHT INDEX USED FOR GBP OIS?

A: GBP LIBOR

B: GBP repo rate

C: EONIA

D: SONIA

QUESTION 49: TOPIC: Options

THE PAYOFF OF A SHORT CALL CAN BE DESCRIBED AS WHICH OF THE FOLLOWING...?

A: Limited profit, limited loss

B: Unlimited profit, unlimited loss

C: Unlimited profit, limited loss

D: Limited profit, unlimited loss

QUESTION 50: TOPIC: Options

WHAT ARE THE COMPONENTS OF THE PREMIUM ON A DEEPLY OUT-OF-THE-MONEY OPTION WITH ONE MONTH TO EXPIRY?

A: zero intrinsic value + zero time value

B: intrinsic value + zero time value

C: zero intrinsic value + small time value

D: intrinsic value + large time value

QUESTION 51: TOPIC: Options

WHAT IS THE PRINCIPAL DIFFERENCE BETWEEN AN INTEREST RATE GUARANTEE AND AN FRA?

A: an interest rate guarantee is a contract for difference, an FRA is an option product

B: an interest rate guarantee involves an up-front premium payable, an FRA does not

C: an interest rate guarantee is based on the current fwd/fwd interest rate, the buyer chooses the price of an FRA

D: there is no difference between an interest rate guarantee and an FRA

QUESTION 52: TOPIC: Options

WHICH OF THE FOLLOWING IS THE CORRECT WAY TO CONSTRUCT A SHORT STRADDLE?

A: sell a Put and buy a Call at the same ATM strike price with the same expiry

B: sell a Call at one strike price and sell a Call at a higher strike price with the same expiry

C: sell a Put and sell a Call at the same ATM strike price with the same expiry

D: sell a Put at one strike price and sell a Call at a higher strike price with the same expiry

QUESTION 53: TOPIC: Options

A CLIENT WISHES TO PURCHASE 10 OPTION CONTRACTS ON THE JUNE IMM EURODOLLAR FUTURES CONTRACT (NOMINAL USD 1,000,000). THE PREMIUM IS QUOTED AS 0.12. HOW MUCH MUST THE CLIENT PAY?

A: USD 300.00

B: USD 30,000.00

C: Depends on the current price of the futures contract

D: USD 3,000.00

QUESTION 54: TOPIC: Options

A DEALER SIMULTANEOUSLY SELLS A GBP PUT/CHF CALL AT 1.3700 AND SELLS A GBP CALL/CHF PUT AT 1.4200 FOR THE SAME PERIOD AND EQUAL PREMIUMS. HOW WOULD YOU DESCRIBE THIS STRATEGY?

A: A long strangle

B: A long collar

C: A short strangle

D: A long cylinder

QUESTION 55: TOPIC: Principles of ALM

A SOLD JUN 3-MONTH STIR-FUTURE SHOULD BE REPORTED IN THE GAP REPORT AS OF 22 MAY...

A: as a taken deposit with a term of one month

B: as a given deposit with a term of one month and a taken deposit with a term of four months

C: as a taken deposit with a term of one month and a given deposit with a term of four months

D: as a given deposit with a term of four months

QUESTION 56: TOPIC: Principles of ALM

WHICH OF THE FOLLOWING STATEMENTS IS TRUE FOR THE BASEL III LCR?

A: Assets and Liabilities are assessed currency by currency.

B: The LCR only regulates a bank's local currency liquidity position

C: The LCR only regulates a bank's foreign currencies liquidity positions

D: Assets and Liabilities are assessed on an overall total portfolio basis (all currencies).

QUESTION 57: TOPIC: Principles of ALM

WHICH OF THE FOLLOWING IS AN ACCURATE DESCRIPTION OF ASSET AND LIABILITY MANAGEMENT IN THE DEALING ROOM?

A: the process to generate a balance sheet

B: a strategic management tool to manage interest rate risk and liquidity risk

C: running a matched book

D: a technique used in short-term nostro cash management

QUESTION 58: TOPIC: Principles of ALM

WHICH ONE OF THE FOLLOWING STATEMENTS ABOUT INTEREST RATE MOVEMENTS IS TRUE?

A: An upward parallel shift of interest rates will cause a loss of income if the rate-sensitivity of a bank's liabilities is higher than the rate-sensitivity of its assets.

B: A bank will lose income if it has more rate-sensitive liabilities than rate-sensitive assets.

C: Falling interest rates will always result in mark-to-market profits on short positions in fixed rate securities.

D: Rising interest rates can result in mark-to-market losses on fixed-rate assets.

QUESTION 59: TOPIC: Principles of ALM

HOW WOULD A 3s V. 6s PURCHASED FRA APPEAR IN THE BANK'S GAP REPORTAGE?

A: as an asset maturing in 3 months time only

B: as a liability maturing in 3 months time and an asset maturing in 6 months time

C: as a liability maturing in 6 months time only

D: as an asset maturing in 3 months time and a liability maturing in 6 months time

QUESTION 60: TOPIC: Principles of ALM

WHAT IS THE MAXIMUM POSSIBLE MACAULAY DURATION OF AN FRN RESETTING AT 6 MONTHS LIBOR?

A: 3 months

B: zero

C: 6 months

D: 1 year

QUESTION 61: TOPIC: Principles of ALM

WHAT DO BASEL RULES RECOMMEND THAT STRESS TESTS SHOULD COVER?

A: all time horizons which are relevant to banks' maturity profiles

B: both short and longer term horizons up to 12 months

C: short-term (e.g. four-week) period only

D: longer term (e.g. 12-month horizon) only

QUESTION 62: TOPIC: Principles of ALM

WHAT IS FUNDS TRANSFER PRICING?

A: another name for a bank's 'Base rate' to corporate customers

B: the minimum return on an asset in VaR calculations

C: a method for the dealers to maximise their margin above cost of funds

D: a means to allocate inter-divisional profits in an equitable fashion

QUESTION 63: TOPIC: Principles of Risk

WHAT IS MEANT BY THE TERM "MARK TO MARKET"?

A: The setting of open position limits in foreign currencies

B: The revaluation using appropriate current market rates of dealing risk positions

C: The recording of current rates in position keeping systems

D: The agreement of outstanding deal details with a broker

QUESTION 64: TOPIC: Principles of Risk

WHICH OF THE FOLLOWING RISKS ARE LEAST LIKELY TO BE A CONCERN WHEN TRANSACTING A FORWARD EXCHANGE CONTRACT?

A: Counterparty risk

B: Settlement risk

C: Basis risk

D: Market risk

QUESTION 65: TOPIC: Principles of Risk

UNDER BASEL SECURITISATION RULES THE HIGHEST POTENTIAL RISK WEIGHT IS...

A: 350%

B: 750%

C: 1500%

D: 1250%

QUESTION 66: TOPIC: Principles of Risk

Under Basel rules, what is the meaning of RWA?

A: Risk Weighted Average

B: Recovery Weighted Assets

C: Risk Weighted Adjustments

D: Risk Weighted Assets

QUESTION 67: TOPIC: Principles of Risk

WHICH OF THE FOLLOWING IS NOT A USUAL WAY OF DESCRIBING AN APPROACH TO VAR CALCULATION?

A: Forward price simulation

B: Monte Carlo simulation.

C: Historical simulation.

D: Variance-covariance approach.

QUESTION 68: TOPIC: Principles of Risk

A CUSTOMER BASED IN THE UK EXPORTS AUTOMOTIVE PARTS TO THE US. HIS MAIN COMPETITOR IS IN FRANCE. WHAT TYPE OF EXPOSURE TO CURRENCY RISK IS POSED BY MOVEMENTS IN EUR/USD?

A: None

B: Economic exposure

C: Transaction exposure

D: Translation exposure

QUESTION 69: TOPIC: Principles of Risk

TRANSACTION RISK IS SUFFERED BY...

A: a corporate treasurer assessing exposure in USD with the company balance sheet in GBP

B: a euro zone based importer being invoiced in EUR

C: an exporter invoicing goods and services in USD with its cost base in GBP

D: an exporter losing business due to exchange rate advantages enjoyed by competitor producers

QUESTION 70: TOPIC: Principles of Risk

TODAY, YOU SELL A 3X6 FRA IN USD 1 MILLION. TOMORROW ALL INTEREST RATES RISE BY 1%. APPROXIMATELY WHAT IS YOUR CREDIT RISK ON THE FRA COUNTERPARTY AT CLOSE OF BUSINESS TOMORROW?

A: USD 10,000

B: USD 1,000

C: USD 2,500

D: zero

End of Mock examination No. 4

ACI Dealing Certificate - MOCK EXAMINATION No. 5

(Please note that in the examination proper topic titles are not advised.)

QUESTION 1: TOPIC: Basic Interest Rate Calculations

ACCORDING TO THE LIQUIDITY PREFERENCE THEORY WHICH ONE OF THE FOLLOWING STATEMENTS IS CORRECT?

A: under normal economic and market conditions longer term interest rates are lower than short term

B: investors lending funds for longer periods expect to earn a higher interest rate

C: investors lending funds for longer periods prefer instant access to their money to higher interest rates

D: none of these

QUESTION 2: TOPIC: Basic Interest Rate Calculations

A 6-MONTH (182-DAY) INVESTMENT OF CHF 15.5 MILLION YIELDS A RETURN OF CHF 100,000. WHAT IS THE RATE OF RETURN?

A: 1.32 p.c.

B: 1.28 p.c.

C: 1.29 p.c.

D: 0.65 p.c.

QUESTION 3: TOPIC: Basic Interest Rate Calculations

CONVERT A USD INTEREST RATE OF 4.00 P.C. QUOTED ON A MONEY MARKET BASIS TO A BOND BASIS.

A: 4.055 p.c.

B: 3.945 p.c.

C: 3.960 p.c.

D: 4.040 p.c.

QUESTION 4: TOPIC: Basic Interest Rate Calculations

WHAT IS THE DAY COUNT/ANNUAL BASIS CONVENTION FOR EUROYEN DEPOSITS IN THE INTERNATIONAL MARKETS?

A: Actual/actual

B: Actual/360

C: 30E/360

D: Actual/365

QUESTION 5: TOPIC: Basic Interest Rate Calculations

A 3 MONTH (90 DAY) DEPOSIT OF USD 25 MILLION IS MADE AT 2.25 P.C. AT MATURITY, IT IS ROLLED OVER THREE TIMES AT 2.55 P.C. FOR 91 DAYS, 2.15 P.C. FOR 92 DAYS AND 2.19 P.C. FOR 92 DAYS. WHAT IS THE EQUIVALENT ANNUAL RATE (2 DECIMAL PLACES) PAID ON THIS DEPOSIT?

A: 2.26 p.c.

B: 2.19 p.c.

C: 2.25 p.c.

D: 2.30 p.c.

QUESTION 6: TOPIC: Basic Interest Rate Calculations

IF TODAY IS THURSDAY 27TH JANUARY 201X WHICH OF THE FOLLOWING ARE THE CORRECT DATES FOR A SPOT/NEXT USD DEPOSIT TAKEN IN LONDON?

A: 31st January to 1st February 201X

B: 1st February to 2nd February 201X

C: 30th January to 31st January 201X

D: 29th January to 30th January 201X

QUESTION 7: TOPIC: Cash Money markets Theory

COVERED INTEREST ARBITRAGE IS POSSIBLE WHEN...

A: you can raise the currency more cheaply via the FX swap than in the money market

B: the interest rate differential widens rather than narrows

C: there is a large swing in the spot rate

D: the low interest rate currency depreciates

QUESTION 8: TOPIC: Cash Money markets Theory

IN AN INTEREST ARBITRAGE OPERATION TO RAISE THE BASE CURRENCY FOR 6 MONTHS AS A MARKET USER YOU MUST...

A: buy and sell the base currency on the market maker's 6 mos BID FX swap and borrow the variable currency

B: buy and sell the base currency on the market maker's 6 mos OFFER FX swap and borrow the variable currency

C: sell and buy the base currency on the market maker's 6 mos OFFER FX swap and lend the variable currency

D: sell and buy the variable currency on the market maker's 6 mos BID FX swap and borrow the variable currency

QUESTION 9: TOPIC: Cash Money markets Theory

WHICH OF THE FOLLOWING STATEMENTS IS TRUE OF US T-BILLS? THEY ARE...

A: yield based instruments using the Actual/360 annual basis

B: discount paying instruments using the Actual/360 annual basis

C: yield based instruments using the Actual/Actual annual basis

D: discount paying instruments using the Actual/Actual annual basis

QUESTION 10: TOPIC: Cash Money markets Theory

UNDER NORMAL CIRCUMSTANCES WHICH OF THE FOLLOWING INSTRUMENTS IS NOT NEGOTIABLE?

A: USD Bankers Acceptance

B: GBP Eligible Bill

C: JPY Certificate of Deposit

D: CHF Money Market Deposit

QUESTION 11: TOPIC: Cash Money markets Theory

IN RESPECT OF THE PURCHASE OF A US T-BILL IN THE SECONDARY MARKET WHICH OF THE FOLLOWING ARE DESCRIPTIONS OF THE CASH FLOWS INVOLVED IN THIS TRANSACTION IN THE MARKET?

A: secondary market price OUT on value date, principal plus interest IN on maturity date

B: secondary market price OUT on value date, face value IN on maturity date

C: secondary market price OUT on value date, face value less discount IN on maturity date

D: face value OUT on value date, face value plus interest IN on maturity date

QUESTION 12: TOPIC: Cash Money markets Theory

WHICH OF THE FOLLOWING IS MOST ATTRACTIVE TO A DEALER LONG OF CASH AND LOOKING TO INVEST FOR ONE YEAR?

A: 8 p.c. annual bond yield

B: 8 p.c. semi annual money market yield

C: 8 p.c. annual money market yield

D: 8 p.c. semi-annual bond yield

QUESTION 13: TOPIC: Cash Money markets Calculations

IF THE COLLATERAL RECEIVED BY YOUR CUSTODY AGENT AGAINST USD 20 MILLION ADVANCED IN CASH IN A 3-DAY TRI-PARTY REVERSE REPO AT A RATE OF 3.00 P.C. IS VALUED AT USD 19,656,019.65 (YOU ARE CHARGED A 1.75% MARGIN), WHAT IS THE MATURITY CONSIDERATION OF THIS TRANSACTION?

A: USD 19,670,846.69

B: USD 20,000,000.00

C: USD 20,004,914.00

D: USD 20,005,000.00

QUESTION 14: TOPIC: Cash Money markets Calculations

YOU BUY US DOMESTIC COMMERCIAL PAPER ISSUED BY BUSH INVESTMENTS INC. FACE VALUE USD 20,000,000 30 DAYS AT 4.00 P.C. WHAT AMOUNT DO YOU PAY FOR THIS CP?

A: USD 20,000,000.00

B: USD 19,933,333.33

C: USD 19,933,554.82

D: USD 19,934246.58

QUESTION 15: TOPIC: Cash Money markets Calculations

90 DAY GBP BANKERS ACCEPTANCES ARE QUOTED AT A DISCOUNT RATE OF 4.00 P.C. WHAT IS THE TRUE YIELD?

A: 4.00 p.c.

B: 3.96 p.c.

C: 4.04 p.c.

D: 4.02 p.c.

QUESTION 16: TOPIC: Cash Money markets Calculations

WHAT IS THE TRUE YIELD OF US COMMERCIAL PAPER: ISSUER: OBAMA INDUSTRIES INC. FACE VALUE USD 12,000,000.00, PURCHASE RATE: 2.75 P.C. 60 DAYS TO MATURITY.

A: 2.75 p.c.

B: 2.76 p.c.

C: 2.73 p.c.

D: 2.69 p.c.

QUESTION 17: TOPIC: Cash Money markets Calculations

YOU ARE QUOTED 3.875-4.00 P.C. IN 3 MONTHS (90 DAYS) EUR SECONDARY MARKET CDS. YOU PURCHASE CDS WITH A FACE VALUE OF EUR 10 MILLION ORIGINALLY ISSUED AT A RATE OF 4 P.C. FOR 180 DAYS. WHAT IS THE PURCHASE PRICE?

A: EUR 10,099,009.40

B: EUR 10,100,749.69

C: EUR 10,102,135.56

D: EUR 10,000,000.00

QUESTION 18: TOPIC: Cash Money markets Calculations

YOUR DEALER REPOS USD 10 MILLION US T-NOTES 5.50% 201Y WITH A DIRTY PRICE OF 9,581,000 ON A 2 MONTH (61 DAYS), REPO RATE AT 4.25 P.C. WHAT IS THE REPO INTEREST ON THIS REPO?

A: USD 10,068,051.35

B: USD 10,068,996.51

C: USD 68,996.51

D: USD 68,051.35

QUESTION 19: TOPIC: Foreign exchange Theory

IF THE SPOT EUR/USD IS QUOTED TO YOU BY FOUR DIFFERENT BANKS AS FOLLOWS, WHICH IS THE BEST RATE FOR YOU TO BUY USD?

A: 1.37 28/33

B: 1.37 30/35

C: 1.37 31/36

D: 1.37 34/39

QUESTION 20: TOPIC: Foreign exchange Theory

IF A SPOT DEALER STATES HIS POSITION IS "THREE LONG IN CABLE". WHAT IS HIS ACTUAL POSITION?

A: None of these

B: Overbought USD 3 million against GBP

C: Overbought GBP 3 million against USD

D: Overbought GBP 3 million against EUR

QUESTION 21: TOPIC: Foreign exchange Theory

IF SPOT GBP/USD IS QUOTED 1.50 95-00 AND EUR/USD IS QUOTED 1.41 00-05. AS MARKET USER WHAT TRANSACTION CAN YOU EFFECT AT 0.9338?

A: You can buy EUR against GBP

B: You can buy GBP against EUR

C: You can sell GBP against EUR

D: insufficient information to decide

QUESTION 22: TOPIC: Foreign exchange Theory

TO CALCULATE THE RATE AT WHICH YOU WOULD BUY GBP AGAINST CHF AS MARKET MAKER YOU WOULD...

A: multiply the GBP/USD Offer by the USD/CHF Offer

B: multiply the GBP/USD Bid by the USD/CHF Bid

C: multiply the GBP/USD Offer by the USD/CHF Bid

D: multiply the GBP/USD Bid by the USD/CHF Offer

QUESTION 23: TOPIC: Foreign exchange Theory

WHAT IS THE RELATIONSHIP OF THE STERLING EXCHANGE RATE TO THE EURO?

A: it is a legacy currency as defined in the Delors Plan

B: it varies within a 2.25 percent range either side of its parity

C: it is irrevocably fixed against the Euro

D: it is freely floating

QUESTION 24: TOPIC: Foreign exchange Theory

HOW DO YOU CALCULATE A FWD/FWD OFFERED FX SWAP RATE 3s/6s.

A: Longer term BID minus Shorter term OFFER

B: Longer term OFFER divided by Shorter term BID

C: Longer term OFFER minus Shorter term BID

D: Longer term OFFER plus Shorter term BID

QUESTION 25: TOPIC: Foreign exchange Theory

A DEALER WISHES TO ROLL A LONG USD/JPY FOREIGN EXCHANGE POSITION IN THE TOM-NEXT. WHICH OF THE FOLLOWING STATEMENTS IS TRUE?

A: The dealer must buy USD/JPY for value today and sell USD/JPY for value tomorrow

B: The dealer must sell USD/JPY for value tomorrow and buy USD/JPY for value spot

C: The dealer must buy USD/JPY for value tomorrow and sell USD/JPY for value spot

D: The dealer must sell USD/JPY for value today and buy USD/JPY for value tomorrow

QUESTION 26: TOPIC: Foreign exchange Theory

WHICH OF THE FOLLOWING BEST DESCRIBES TARGET2?

A: the system used by the Euro Bankers Association to clear cross border Euro denominated securities

B: the pan-Europe netting system used for reducing credit risk in respect of derivatives transactions

C: the system used in Germany for settling high value domestic securities transactions

D: the interlinking mechanism that connects national RTGS payments systems in EU member states

QUESTION 27: TOPIC: Foreign exchange Theory

A 1 MONTH GBP/USD SWAP IS QUOTED 18-15. IF US INTEREST RATES FALL AND GBP INTEREST RATES REMAIN STABLE WHAT EFFECT WOULD YOU EXPECT ON THE FORWARD RATE?

A: GBP premium would increase

B: insufficient information to decide

C: USD discount would reduce

D: GBP discount would increase

QUESTION 28: TOPIC: Foreign exchange Theory

IF THE 3 MONTHS FORWARD GBP/USD SWAP MOVES FROM A 5 POINT GBP PREMIUM TO A 3 POINT GBP DISCOUNT AND USD INTEREST RATES REMAIN THE SAME, WHAT HAS HAPPENED TO GBP INTEREST RATES?

A: GBP interest rates are now higher than USD

B: GBP interest rates are now lower than USD

C: GBP interest rate remain the same

D: GBP interest rates have fallen

QUESTION 29: TOPIC: Foreign exchange Theory

WHAT IS THE PRINCIPAL DIFFERENCE BETWEEN PRECIOUS METALS TRADING FOR PHYSICAL DELIVERY AND BOOK ENTRY?

A: for physical delivery an institution must be located in London

B: for physical delivery an institution must be a member of the Gold fixing panel

C: for physical delivery an institution must hold a LOCO account

D: for physical delivery an institution must be a member of LBMA

QUESTION 30: TOPIC: Foreign exchange Theory

AS A BUYER OF USD 1,000,000 WHICH OF THE FOLLOWING USD/CHF SPOT QUOTES MADE BY FOUR DIFFERENT MARKETS MAKING BANKS BEST SUITS YOU?

A: 0.90 98-03

B: 0.91 00-05

C: 0.91 01-06

D: 0.90 99-04

QUESTION 31: TOPIC: Foreign exchange Calculations

MID SPOT USD/JPY: 76.00, 3 MONTHS MID USD/JPY: -33 POINTS. MID SPOT GBP/USD: 1.5500, 3 MONTHS MID GBP/USD: -97 POINTS. CALCULATE THE MID MARKET 3 MONTHS GBP/JPY SWAP POINTS.

A: +125

B: +12.5

C: -125

D: -12.5

QUESTION 32: TOPIC: Foreign exchange Calculations

YOU HAVE JUST DEALT WITH YOUR CORPORATE CLIENT ENRON INC. WHO HAS BOUGHT EUR AGAINST USD OUTRIGHT SIX MONTHS AT 1.4115. YOU DECIDE TO COVER THIS POSITION AND CALL TWO BANKS. BANK A QUOTES SPOT: 1.40 47-52 AND 6 MONTHS: 52-57 AND BANK B QUOTES SPOT: 1.20 50-55 AND 6 MONTHS SWAP: 50-55. WITH WHICH BANK OR BANKS AND AT WHAT RATES WILL YOU DEAL TO COVER THE POSITION AT THE MOST FAVOURABLE PRICE FOR YOU?

A: Buy spot EUR from Bank A at 1.4052 and sell and buy EUR/USD with Bank A spot ag 6 mths at 57 pts

B: Buy spot EUR from Bank A at 1.4052 and sell and buy EUR/USD with Bank B spot ag 6 mths at 52 pts

C: Buy spot EUR from Bank A at 1.4055 and sell and buy EUR/USD with Bank B spot ag 6 mths at 55 pts

D: Buy spot EUR from Bank A at 1.4052 and sell and buy EUR/USD with Bank B spot ag 6 mths at 55 pts

QUESTION 33: TOPIC: Foreign exchange Calculations

GIVEN THE FOLLOWING MARKET RATES CALCULATE A BROKEN DATE RATE AT WHICH YOU CAN BUY EUR FROM A CUSTOMER AGAINST USD OUTRIGHT 1 1/2 MONTHS FORWARD. SPOT EUR/USD: 1.3700-05, 1 MONTH EUR/USD: 12-10, 2 MONTHS EUR/USD: 26-22, 3 MONTHS EUR/USD: 36-32, 6 MONTHS EUR/USD: 65-60. ASSUME 30 DAY MONTHS.

A: 1.3686

B: 1.3619

C: 1.3719

D: 1.3681

QUESTION 34: TOPIC: Foreign exchange Calculations

YOU QUOTE A CORPORATE CUSTOMER SPOT GBP/EUR SPOT: 1.1195/00. WHAT IS THE RECIPROCAL QUOTE?

A: 0.8933-38

B: 0.8921/25

C: 0.8923-28

D: 0.8928-33

QUESTION 35: TOPIC: Foreign exchange Calculations

YOU ARE QUOTED A SPOT AUD/USD RATE OF 1.03 27-32 BY AUSTRALIAN OUTBACK BANK. HOW MANY US DOLLARS WILL YOU RECEIVE VALUE SPOT IF YOU SELL AUD 1,000,000?

A: USD 1,033,200.00

B: USD 968,335.43

C: USD 1,032,700.00

D: USD 967,866.82

QUESTION 36: TOPIC: Foreign exchange Calculations

YOU ARE SHORT GBP 3 MILLION AT A RATE OF 1.6500 AGAINST USD AND THE EXCHANGE RATE HAS NOW MOVED TO 1.6650. IF YOU WERE TO SQUARE YOUR POSITION AT THIS LEVEL HOW MUCH PROFIT OR LOSS WOULD YOU MAKE?

A: LOSS GBP 4,500

B: PROFIT GBP 45,000

C: PROFIT USD 4,500

D: LOSS USD 45,000

QUESTION 37: TOPIC: Fwd/fwds, FRAs, Money market Futures and Swaps

THREE MONTHS AGO YOU WERE ANTICIPATING GBP INTEREST RATES WERE GOING TO FALL AND THEREFORE TOOK A TRADING POSITION USING A 3V6 FRA FOR GBP 10 MILLION WHICH WAS QUOTED TO YOU AT THAT TIME AS 2.23-2.35 P.C. THE 3V6 PERIOD IS 90 DAYS. AT SETTLEMENT, GBP LIBOR IS FIXED AT 2.28 P.C. WHAT IS THE SETTLEMENT AMOUNT?

A: You receive GBP 1,225.98

B: You pay GBP 1,242.921

C: You pay GBP 1,225.98

D: You receive GBP 1,242.92

QUESTION 38: TOPIC: Fwd/fwds, FRAs, Money market Futures and Swaps

YOU ARE TOLD THAT 3s V. 6s USD FRAS ARE QUOTED AT 4.50 P.C. AND SPOT AGAINST 3 MONTHS USD ARE QUOTED AT 4.00 P.C. (BOTH MID RATES). WHAT IS THE MID RATE FOR SPOT AGAINST 6 MONTHS? (ASSUME 30 DAY MONTHS)

A: 4.88 p.c.
B: 4.27 p.c.
C: 4.00 p.c.
D: 4.55 p.c.

QUESTION 39: TOPIC: Fwd/fwds, FRAs, Money market Futures and Swaps

IT IS MID FEBRUARY 201X. YOU ARE SHORT USD FOR A THREE MONTH PERIOD MARCH TO JUNE 201X. IF YOU ARE WORRIED ABOUT INTEREST RATES RISING WHAT IS THE BEST HEDGE FOR YOUR POSITION?

A: sell March ED contracts on NYSE Euronext.liffe

B: buy June ED contracts on NYSE Euronext.liffe

C: sell June ED contracts on NYSE Euronext.liffe

D: buy March ED contracts on NYSE Euronext.liffe

QUESTION 40: TOPIC: Fwd/fwds, FRAs, Money market Futures and Swaps

WHICH OF THE FOLLOWING IS TRUE?

A: the minimum price movement for the Short Sterling futures contract on NYSE Euronext.liffe is 0.005

B: the Euroyen futures contract traded on NYSE Euronext.liffe has a nominal value of JPY 100,000,000

C: the Eurodollar futures contract traded on CME Group is non-fungible

D: the value of one tick on the NYSE Euronext.liffe Euribor futures contract is EUR 10.00

QUESTION 41: TOPIC: Fwd/fwds, FRAs, Money market Futures and Swaps

WHAT IS THE NAME OF THE ELECTRONIC TRADING PLATFORM ON THE CME GROUP CHICAGO FUTURES MARKET?

A: IMM

B: CONNECT

C: CLEARSTREAM

D: GLOBEX

QUESTION 42: TOPIC: Fwd/fwds, FRAs, Money market Futures and Swaps

INTEREST RATE SWAPS UNDER ISDA TERMS CAN BE FIXED RATE V. FLOATING. DEALING IN LONDON, ON WHICH MARKET RATE IS THIS FLOATING RATE MOST FREQUENTLY BASED?

A: UK Clearing banks' Base rate

B: US banks' Prime rate

C: a rate agreed between bank and counterparty at re-rating dates

D: LIBOR

QUESTION 43: TOPIC: Fwd/fwds, FRAs, Money market Futures and Swaps

IF YOU FUNDED YOUR FIXED-INCOME INVESTMENT PORTFOLIO WITH SHORT-TERM DEPOSITS, HOW WOULD YOU HEDGE YOUR INTEREST RATE EXPOSURE WITH INTEREST RATE SWAPS?

A: Pay floating and receive fixed through swaps for the term of the portfolio

B: You cannot: the maturity of the swaps would be longer than that of the deposits

C: You should not: there would be too much basis risk

D: Pay fixed and receive floating through swaps for the term of the portfolio

QUESTION 44: TOPIC: Fwd/fwds, FRAs, Money market Futures and Swaps

IT IS JUNE 201X. SEPTEMBER EURODOLLAR STIR FUTURES ARE TRADING AT 97.50-52. THE BROKER IS LOOKING FOR AN IMM SEPTEMBER 1X PRICE. WHAT IS HE LOOKING FOR?

A: a better FRA offer than the current September futures price

B: a better FRA bid than the current September futures price

C: a 3s v. 6s 90 day FRA 'bid-offer' price coinciding with the Sept 1X futures nominal dates

D: a 90 day cash market 'bid-offer' price

QUESTION 45: TOPIC: Fwd/fwds, FRAs, Money market Futures and Swaps

A CORPORATE TREASURER IS CONCERNED ABOUT INTEREST RATES RISING AND WANTS TO HEDGE HIS LONGER TERM FUNDING. WHICH OF THE FOLLOWING TRANSACTIONS BEST SUITS HIS REQUIREMENTS?

A: sell a strip of FRAs

B: pay fixed and receive floating on an interest rate swap

C: receive fixed and pay floating on an interest rate swap

D: buy a strip of futures

QUESTION 46: TOPIC: Fwd/fwds, FRAs, Money market Futures and Swaps

YOU ARE THE FIXED RATE PAYER IN A 5 YEAR GBP INTEREST RATE SWAP NOMINAL PRINCIPAL GBP 100 MILLION FIXED V. 6 MONTHS LIBOR. THE FIXED RATE IS 2.25 P.C. ON TODAY'S RE-RATING YOU WILL PAY GBP 123,287.67. WHAT WAS THE LIBOR FIXING USED ON THE FLOATING SIDE OF THE SWAP ON ITS LAST RE-RATING DATE?

A: 2.125 p.c.

B: 2.00 p.c.

C: 2.75 p.c.

D: 2.50 p.c.

QUESTION 47: TOPIC: Fwd/fwds, FRAs, Money market Futures and Swaps

IT IS DECEMBER 1X. STIR ED FUTURES ARE TRADING MARCH 1Y: 93.22 AND JUNE 1Y: 93.13. USING THIS INFORMATION CALCULATE A MID-MARKET RATE FOR A 3s V. 9s USD FRA (ROUNDED TO 2 DEC PLACES).

A: 6.82 p.c.

B: 6.78 p.c.

C: 6.88 p.c.

D: 7.00 p.c.

QUESTION 48: TOPIC: Fwd/fwds, FRAs, Money market Futures and Swaps

IF YOU MAKE A CALLING BANK EUR FRA PRICES OF 2s V. 3s: 3.70-3.74 AND 3s V. 4s: 3.74-3.78 THE COUNTERPARTY DEALER SAYS HE WANTS TO BUY AT 3.74 P.C. WHAT HAVE YOU DONE?

A: you have bought a 3s v. 4s EUR FRA

B: you have sold a 3s v. 4s EUR FRA

C: you have sold a 2s v. 3s EUR FRA

D: you have bought a 2s v. 3s EUR FRA

QUESTION 49: TOPIC: Options

'THE PURCHASE OF A PUT AND SALE OF A CALL AT THE SAME STRIKE PRICE AND SAME EXPIRY' WHAT OPTION STRATEGY IS BEING DESCRIBED HERE?

A: A synthetic short position

B: A short Straddle

C: A long Straddle

D: A synthetic long position

QUESTION 50: TOPIC: Options

WHAT IS AN INTEREST RATE GUARANTEE?

A: A cap

B: A floor

C: A collar

D: An option to enter into an FRA

QUESTION 51: TOPIC: Options

IF A SOLD USD CALL / CHF PUT OPTION GOES "IN THE MONEY", IN RESPECT OF THIS OUTSTANDING TRANSACTION THE OPTIONS TRADER WILL BE...

A: increasing his long USD delta hedge position

B: increasing his short USD delta hedge position

C: reducing his long USD delta hedge position

D: reducing his short USD delta hedge position

QUESTION 52: TOPIC: Options

WHAT IS THE CASH PRICE FOR A BRITISH POUND OPTION ON THE IMM (GBP FUTURES NOMINAL SIZE = GBP 62,500) QUOTED AS 1.5600...

A: GBP 1,100.00

B: USD 975.00

C: GBP 1,760.00

D: USD 2,200.00

QUESTION 53: TOPIC: Options

ONE OF THE FOLLOWING INTEREST RATE RISK MANAGEMENT PRODUCTS INVOLVES PAYMENT OF AN UP-FRONT PREMIUM, WHICH ONE?

A: all of these

B: Swaption

C: FRA

D: Interest rate swap

QUESTION 54: TOPIC: Options

WHAT ARE THE COMPONENTS OF THE PREMIUM OF AN IN-THE-MONEY OPTION WITH THREE MONTH TO EXPIRY?

A: intrinsic value + time value

B: zero intrinsic value + time value

C: intrinsic value + zero time value

D: zero intrinsic value + zero time value

QUESTION 55: TOPIC: Principles of ALM

USING REPRICING GAP ANALYSIS, A BANK'S BALANCE SHEET IS CONSIDERED ASSET-SENSITIVE TO MARKET INTEREST RATE CHANGES, IF...

A: more liabilities than assets have variable rates or short residual maturities

B: more assets than liabilities will be repriced in the near term

C: non-interest bearing liabilities are greater than non-interest bearing assets

D: more liabilities than assets will be repriced in the near term

QUESTION 56: TOPIC: Principles of ALM

WHICH OF THE FOLLOWING BEST DESCRIBE THE PROCESS OF HEDGING?

A: off-setting risk in one market with protection in a closely correlated market

B: using a derivative product with low correlation to the underlying risk

C: having a contractual obligation to complete a cash transaction

D: buying Futures when your view is that interest rates are rising

QUESTION 57: TOPIC: Principles of ALM

WHAT WOULD HAPPEN TO A BANK'S NET INTEREST INCOME IF IT RAN A ZERO GAP IN AN ENVIRONMENT OF DECREASING INTEREST RATES?

A: Net interest income would increase considerably.

B: Net interest income would increase slightly.

C: Net interest income would hardly change at all.

D: Net interest income would decrease.

QUESTION 58: TOPIC: Principles of ALM

WHEN CONSIDERING CREDIT DERIVATIVES BASEL RULES REGARD THE SALE OF CREDIT PROTECTION AS...?

A: providing a matching interest rate swap

B: an unmatured forward exchange transaction

C: the same as taking collateral against a loan

D: providing a guarantee

QUESTION 59: TOPIC: Principles of ALM

WHAT IS A HEDGE?

A: A means of cancelling a deal

B: A riskless transaction

C: A means by which to reduce a risk

D: An equal and opposite risk

QUESTION 60: TOPIC: Principles of ALM

IT IS APRIL 201X. YOU HAVE A COMMITMENT TO LEND GBP 10 MILLION FOR THREE MONTHS COMMENCING IN TWO MONTHS TIME AND ARE CONCERNED ABOUT GBP INTEREST RATES RISING IN THE MEANTIME. WHICH OF THE FOLLOWING BEST MEETS YOUR HEDGE REQUIREMENT?

A: buy a 2s v. 5s GBP 10 million FRA

B: Sell 10 June Short Sterling contracts

C: Sell 20 September Short Sterling contracts

D: buy a 2s v. 3s GBP 10 million FRA

QUESTION 61: TOPIC: Principles of ALM

WHICH OF THE FOLLOWING IS A FUNCTION OF ASSET AND LIABILITY MANAGEMENT (ALM)?

A: monitoring credit quality of assets and establishing an early warning system

B: running a matched trading book

C: managing the financial risk of the bank by protecting it from the adverse effects of changing interest rates

D: coordinated limit management of a financial institution's credit portfolio

QUESTION 62: TOPIC: Principles of ALM

WHAT IS A SYNTHETIC CDO?

A: a credit default swap traded to gain exposure to a portfolio of derivatives

B: a total return swap based on floating rate derivative instruments

C: an interest rate swap based on managed rates

D: a form of CDO that invests in credit default swaps or other non-cash assets to gain exposure to a portfolio of fixed income assets

QUESTION 63: TOPIC: Principles of Risk

YOU HAVE DEALT TODAY FOR AN OUTRIGHT FX TRANSACTION VALUE 3 MONTHS FORWARD WITH YOUR CORPORATE CLIENT MADOFF INVESTMENTS. WHAT RISKS DO YOU RUN?

A: Collateral risk only

B: Delivery risk only

C: Delivery risk and Market replacement risk

D: Delivery risk and Collateral risk

QUESTION 64: TOPIC: Principles of Risk

CLOSE-OUT NETTING IS WHERE COUNTERPARTIES HAVE...

A: multiple FX transactions value any day in the future which can be cancelled

B: signed a master agreement agreeing to net identified certain transactions between them

C: multicurrency assets and liabilities maturing in the future replaced with as a single net figure

D: multiple offsetting FX contracts which can be agreed to be netted in event of default

QUESTION 65: TOPIC: Principles of Risk

GAP ANALYSIS IS AN APPROACH...

A: to reduce credit risk

B: to remove the possibility of Nostro overdrafts

C: to manage foreign exchange risk

D: to assess interest rate risk

QUESTION 66: TOPIC: Principles of Risk

WHICH OF THE FOLLOWING TECHNIQUES IS USED TO ASSESS MARKET RISK UNDER ABNORMAL MARKET CONDITIONS?

A: Scenario analysis only

B: Market replacement cost

C: Back testing only

D: Stress testing only

QUESTION 67: TOPIC: Principles of Risk

YOU AND A TRADING COUNTERPARTY HAVE AN AGREEMENT TO MAKE ONE SINGLE DAILY PAYMENT AND RECEIPT THAT WILL BE THE SUM OF ALL PAYMENTS AND RECEIPTS DUE IN A PARTICULAR CURRENCY BETWEEN YOURSELVES DURING THAT TRADING DAY. OF WHAT IS THIS AN EXAMPLE?

A: Delivery vs payment

B: Bilateral netting

C: Multilateral netting

D: Open delivery

QUESTION 68: TOPIC: Principles of Risk

CALCULATE YOUR BANK'S DELIVERY RISK (IN USD) FOR THE FOLLOWING DEALS OUTSTANDING WITH BLAIR BANK PLC, LONDON. ALL DEALS VALUE TODAY'S SPOT DATE: MATURING FORWARD PURCHASE OF USD 5 MILLION AGAINST CHF, SPOT SALE USD 7.5 MILLION AGAINST DKK AND SPOT PURCHASE OF USD 10 MILLION AGAINST JPY.

A: USD 15 million

B: USD 17.5 million

C: USD 7.5 million

D: USD 22.5 million

QUESTION 69: TOPIC: Principles of Risk

THE RISK THAT AN INSTITUTION WILL EXPERIENCE A LOSS ON A TRADE OR A POSITION DUE TO AN ADVERSE EXCHANGE/INTEREST RATE MOVEMENT IS BEST DESCRIBED AS...

A: Systemic Risk

B: Operational Risk

C: Market risk

D: Credit Risk

QUESTION 70: TOPIC: Principles of Risk

WHICH OF THE FOLLOWING IS THE MOST ACCURATE DESCRIPTION OF THE DIFFERENCE BETWEEN HEDGING AND ARBITRAGE?

A: hedging offsets an existing risk in one market, arbitrage is simultaneous trading for profit

B: hedging ensures a profit is made on all positions, arbitrage frequently provides a riskless profit

C: hedging removes risk completely, arbitrage leaves some risk for P and L purposes

D: none of these

End of Mock examination No. 5

ACI Dealing Certificate - MOCK EXAMINATION No. 6

(Please note that in the examination proper topic titles are not advised.)

QUESTION 1: TOPIC: Basic Interest Rate Calculations

WITH SPOT EUR/USD QUOTED 1.3500 (MID-POINT), CALCULATE THE LEVEL OF THE 180 DAY EUR/USD FX SWAP PRICE IF 6 MONTHS USD INT RATE IS 4.00 p.c. AND 6 MONTHS EUR INT RATE IS 3.00 p.c.

A: +665 pts

B: -665 pts

C: -66.5 pts

D: +66.5 pts

QUESTION 2: TOPIC: Basic Interest Rate Calculations

THE RATE OF DISCOUNT ON A DISCOUNT-PAYING MONEY MARKET INSTRUMENT IS ALWAYS...

A: numerically lower than its equivalent yield

B: numerically higher than its equivalent yield

C: numerically equal to its equivalent yield

D: none of these apply

QUESTION 3: TOPIC: Basic Interest Rate Calculations

CALCULATE THE 6 MONTHS EUR INTEREST RATE FROM THE 3 MONTHS (91 DAYS) EUR INTEREST RATE OF 2.90 p.c. AND THE 3s v. 6s FORWARD-FORWARD (92 DAYS) EUR INTEREST RATE OF 3.7187 p.c.

A: 3.3094 p.c.

B: 3.0625 p.c.

C: 3.325 p.c.

D: 4.6446 p.c.

QUESTION 4: TOPIC: Basic Interest Rate Calculations

WHAT IS EONIA?

A: Volume-weighted average overnight EUR deposit rate

B: Volume-weighted average overnight EUR LIBOR

C: ECB overnight lending rate

D: Arithmetic average overnight EUR deposit rate

QUESTION 5: TOPIC: Basic Interest Rate Calculations

1 MONTH (30 DAYS) USD BID RATE: 3.90 P.C., 2 MONTHS (61 DAYS) USD BID RATE: 4.00 P.C., 3 MONTHS (91 DAYS): 4.35 P.C. CALCULATE (THROUGH STRAIGHT LINE INTERPOLATION) A USD INTEREST RATE QUOTE FOR A 2 1/2 MONTHS DEPOSIT OFFERED BY A CUSTOMER.

A: 4.17 p.c.

B: 4.35 p.c.

C: 4.00 p.c.

D: 5.06 p.c.

QUESTION 6: TOPIC: Basic Interest Rate Calculations

IF IN LONDON, YOU ACCEPT A JPY DEPOSIT FOR 19 MONTHS, WHEN IS THE INTEREST PAYABLE?

A: at the end of the first month, then every six months

B: at maturity only

C: quarterly, then balance at maturity

D: annually, then balance at maturity

QUESTION 7: TOPIC: Cash Money markets Theory

WHEN CONSIDERING YIELD AND DISCOUNT RATES WHICH OF THE FOLLOWING WILL GIVE THE BEST RETURN TO AN INVESTOR?

A: GBP 3 month fixed deposit at 2.97 p.c.

B: GBP T-Bills yielding 2.97 p.c.

C: GBP 3 months Bankers Acceptance purchased at 2.97 p.c.

D: GBP 3 month CD issued at 2.97 p.c.

QUESTION 8: TOPIC: Cash Money markets Theory

WHEN CALCULATING THE INTEREST ON A CASH DRIVEN GILT REPO TRANSACTION WHAT IS THE MARKET CONVENTION FOR THE DAY COUNT / ANNUAL BASIS USED?

A: 30/365

B: Actual/365

C: 30/360

D: Actual/360

QUESTION 9: TOPIC: Cash Money markets Theory

WHICH TYPE OF REPO IS THE LEAST RISKY FOR THE BUYER?

A: HIC repo

B: There is no real difference

C: Delivery repo

D: Tri-party repo

QUESTION 10: TOPIC: Cash Money markets Theory

WHICH OF THE FOLLOWING MONEY MARKET INSTRUMENTS ARE QUOTED AT A DISCOUNT RATE IN THE INTERBANK MARKET?

A: US T-Bills

B: USD BAs

C: ECP

D: UK T-Bills

QUESTION 11: TOPIC: Cash Money markets Theory

WHICH OF THE FOLLOWING IS ALWAYS A COLLATERALISED TRANSACTION?

A: Repo

B: Interbank deposit

C: ECP

D: CD

QUESTION 12: TOPIC: Cash Money markets Theory

WHICH OF THE FOLLOWING INSTRUMENTS IS NORMALLY QUOTED ON A YIELD BASIS?

A: USD Money Market deposit

B: US Treasury Bill

C: US Domestic Commercial Paper

D: US Bankers Acceptance

QUESTION 13: TOPIC: Cash Money markets Calculations

WHAT IS THE TRUE YIELD OF US DOMESTIC COMMERCIAL PAPER ISSUED BY GETTY CHEMICAL INDUSTRIES INC., FACE VALUE USD 15,000,000.00, ISSUE RATE: 3.15 p.c., 61 DAYS TO MATURITY.

A: 3.3129 p.c.

B: 3.1539 p.c.

C: 3.1500 p.c.

D: 3.1669 p.c.

QUESTION 14: TOPIC: Cash Money markets Calculations

IN A CASH DRIVEN REPO TRANSACTION A DEALER REPOS GBP 10 MILLION UK GILTS 5.50% TREASURY 201Y WITH AN INITIAL CONSIDERATION OF GBP 9,581,000 FOR 30 DAYS AT A RATE OF 5.25 p.c. WHAT IS THE MATURITY CONSIDERATION REPAID BY HIM?

A: GBP 9,622,342.67

B: GBP 9,581,000.00

C: GBP 10,000,000.00

D: GBP 10,041,342.67

QUESTION 15: TOPIC: Cash Money markets Calculations

A DEALER REPOS OUT EUR 10,565,503.42 OF THE 5.25% DBR 201Y FOR 7 DAYS AT A RATE OF 2.75 p.c. WHAT ARE THE START AND TOTAL FINAL CASH FLOWS THROUGH THIS REPO?

A: EUR 10,565,503.42, EUR 10,575,075.64

B: EUR 10,565,503.42, EUR 10,571,153.03

C: EUR 10,565,000.00, EUR 10,570,649.34

D: EUR 10,565,510.42, EUR 10,571,160.03

QUESTION 16: TOPIC: Cash Money markets Calculations

WHAT INITIAL CONSIDERATION DOES A DEALER RECEIVE AGAINST EUR 100 MILLION COLLATERAL (6% OAT 201Y) IN A 7-DAY REPO AT A RATE OF 1.75 P.C. IF THE DIRTY PRICE OF THE COLLATERAL IS 96.90 AND UNDER THE GMRA THE REPOER CHARGES A 1% MARGIN?

A: EUR 95,940,594.06

B: EUR 101,000,000.00

C: EUR 99,009,900.99

D: EUR 97,869,000.00

QUESTION 17: TOPIC: Cash Money markets Calculations

YOU INVEST USD 10,000,000.00 FOR 3 MONTHS (92 DAYS) AT 4.50 p.c. AFTER 3 MONTHS, YOU REINVEST PRINCIPAL PLUS INTEREST AT 4.57 p.c. FOR THE SUBSEQUENT THREE MONTHS (91 DAYS). AFTER 6 MONTHS, YOU DO THE SAME AGAIN AT 4.62 p.c. (FOR 90 DAYS). AFTER 9 MONTHS, YOU DO THE SAME AGAIN AT 4.65 p.c. (FOR 92 DAYS). WHAT IS YOUR OVERALL INVESTMENT RETURN (INTEREST RATE) FOR THE 12 MONTHS?

A: 4.6654 p.c.

B: 4.6075 p.c.

C: 4.6286 p.c.

D: 4.5972 p.c.

QUESTION 18: TOPIC: Cash Money markets Calculations

WHAT IS THE VALUE AT MATURITY OF A NEW 3-MONTH (91-DAY) CD WITH A FACE VALUE OF GBP 200 MILLION AND A COUPON OF 4 p.c.?

A: GBP 200,000,000.00

B: GBP 202,022,222.22

C: GBP 201,994,520.55

D: GBP 198,025,173.61

QUESTION 19: TOPIC: Foreign exchange Theory

SPOT EUR/USD IS QUOTED BY THE BROKER 1.38 50-55. YOU HAVE AN INTEREST TO BUY EUR AT 1.38 52 AND PUT HIM ON AT THAT LEVEL. WHAT DOES THIS MAKE HIS NEW TWO WAY PRICE TO THE MARKET?

A: 1.38 50-52

B: 1.38 55-52

C: 1.38 50-55

D: 1.38 52-55

QUESTION 20: TOPIC: Foreign exchange Theory

ASSUMING A FLAT YIELD CURVE IN BOTH CURRENCIES, WHEN QUOTING A 1-TO 2-MONTH FORWARD FX TIME OPTION PRICE IN A CURRENCY PAIR TRADING AT A DISCOUNT TO A CUSTOMER...

A: you would take as bid rate the bid side of the 2-month forward and as offered rate the offered side of the 1-month forward

B: you would take as bid rate the offered side of the 2-month forward and as offered rate the bid side of the 1-month forward

C: you would take as bid rate the offered side of the 1-month forward and as offered rate the offered side of the 2-month forward

D: you would take as bid rate the bid side of the 1-month forward and as offered rate the bid side of the 2-month forward

QUESTION 21: TOPIC: Foreign exchange Theory

YOU HAVE QUOTED SPOT USD/CHF AT 0.9423-26.YOUR CUSTOMER SAYS "I TAKE 5".WHAT DOES HE MEAN?

A: He buys CHF 5,000,000.00 at 0.9426

B: He buys USD 5,000,000.00 at 0.9423

C: He buys CHF 5,000,000.00 at 0.9423

D: He buys USD 5,000,000.00 at 0.9426

QUESTION 22: TOPIC: Foreign exchange Theory

HOW MUCH IS A BIG FIGURE WORTH PER MILLION OF BASE CURRENCY IF EUR/JPY IS 79.50?

A: EUR 795.00

B: EUR 100,000

C: JPY 13,050

D: JPY 1,000,000

QUESTION 23: TOPIC: Foreign exchange Theory

IF TODAY'S DATE IS TUESDAY 27TH FEBRUARY 201X (A LEAP YEAR), WHAT WOULD THE TWO MONTHS MATURITY DATE FROM SPOT FOR FORWARD FOREIGN EXCHANGE DEALING BE?

A: Wednesday 1st May 201X

B: Friday 26th April 201X

C: Tuesday 30th April 201X

D: Monday 29th April 201X

QUESTION 24: TOPIC: Foreign exchange Theory

TO WHAT DOES THE TERM 'LONDON GOOD DELIVERY' REFER IN PRECIOUS METALS TRADING?

A: none of these

B: the specification of a gold bar to meet the requirements of the LBMA

C: the reconciliation process following gold and silver transfers in LOCO London

D: the physical delivery of Gold to a purchasing institution

QUESTION 25: TOPIC: Foreign exchange Theory

SPOT CABLE IS QUOTED 1.5575/80 AND YOU SAY '5 YOURS!' TO THE BROKER. HAVE YOU...

A: bought GBP 5 million at 1.5580

B: bought USD 5 million at 1.5580

C: sold GBP 5 million at 1.5575

D: sold USD 5 million at 1.5575

QUESTION 26: TOPIC: Foreign exchange Theory

IF YOU ARE DEALING IN THE INTERNATIONAL AUD/USD SPOT MARKET, BY MARKET CONVENTION MOST INTERBANK TRANSACTIONS WOULD BE EFFECTED IN ROUND AMOUNTS OF...

A: US Dollars

B: it depends on the counterparty bank

C: it depends on the dealing centre

D: Australian Dollars

QUESTION 27: TOPIC: Foreign exchange Theory

EUR/GBP IS QUOTED 0.87 00-05. IF GBP INTEREST RATES ARE QUOTED AT 2.00 P.C. IN 3 MONTHS AND THE SAME PERIOD EUR INTEREST RATES ARE QUOTED AT 3.00 P.C. HOW WOULD YOU EXPECT FORWARD EUR TO BE DESCRIBED AND QUOTED AGAINST STERLING IN PARIS?

A: at a forward Discount

B: at a forward Premium

C: around PAR

D: 2-3

QUESTION 28: TOPIC: Foreign exchange Theory

WHICH ONE OF THE FOLLOWING STATEMENTS IS THE BEST DEFINITION OF FX SWAP RATES?

A: There is insufficient information to decide

B: They indicate the market's expectation of future spot rates

C: They are equal to the difference in the inflation rates of two countries

D: They reflect the interest rate differential between two currencies

QUESTION 29: TOPIC: Foreign exchange Theory

USD/CAD 1 MONTH SWAP POINTS ARE QUOTED 41-37. WHICH OF THE FOLLOWING STATEMENTS IS CORRECT?

A: USD is worth more CAD forward than spot

B: USD interest rates are higher than CAD

C: USD interest rates are lower than CAD

D: Insufficient information to decide

QUESTION 30: TOPIC: Foreign exchange Theory

IF YOU ARE TOLD THAT GBP INTEREST RATES ARE MARGINALLY HIGHER THAN USD BUT IN THE 3 MONTHS THE GBP/USD FX SWAP BID IS QUOTED AT PAR, HOW WOULD YOU EXPECT THEM TO BE DISPLAYED ON A DEALER'S RATES SCREEN?

A: insufficient information to decide

B: 4-Par

C: Par-4

D: +2-2 around PAR

QUESTION 31: TOPIC: Foreign exchange Calculations

YOU ARE QUOTED THE FOLLOWING RATES: SPOT GBP/USD: 1.6250/55. O/N SWAP: 1.50/1.45. T/N SWAP: 1.35/1.25. S/N SWAP: 1.60/1.55. WHERE CAN YOU SELL GBP AGAINST USD FOR VALUE TOMORROW?

A: 1.625635

B: 1.625125

C: 1.624875

D: 1.625375

QUESTION 32: TOPIC: Foreign exchange Calculations

SPOT USD/SGD IS TRADING AT 1.7500/10. THE 30-DAY SWAP IS QUOTED 100/90 AND THE 60-DAY SWAP IS 160/150. WHAT RATE SHOULD I QUOTE FOR A 35-DAY SWAP?

A: 120/110

B: 105/95

C: 115/105

D: 110/100

QUESTION 33: TOPIC: Foreign exchange Calculations

CURRENT MID-MARKET RATES, SPOT EUR/GBP: 0.8500, 3 MONTHS EUR INT: 2.00 p.c., 3 MONTHS GBP INT: 1.00 p.c. WHAT IS THE 3 MONTHS FORWARD OUTRIGHT EUR/GBP MID RATE? ASSUME 30 DAY MONTHS.

A: 0.8500

B: 0.8482

C: 0.8521

D: 0.8479

QUESTION 34: TOPIC: Foreign exchange Calculations

IF 3 MONTHS OUTRIGHT FORWARD EUR/USD IS 0.90 20-30 AND THREE MONTHS FORWARD SWAP POINTS ARE QUOTED 20-15, WHAT IS THE CURRENT SPOT USD/CHF?

A: 0.90 40-45

B: 0.91 05-00

C: 0.90 45-40

D: 0.90 00-05

QUESTION 35: TOPIC: Foreign exchange Calculations

SPOT GBP/USD: 1.6000-05, S/WEEK SWAP: 7-6.5. YOU HAVE JUST BEEN DEALT WITH ON A SPOT AGAINST 7 DAYS FIXED SWAP IN GBP 10 MILLION AT 7 POINTS YOUR FAVOUR AND FIXED THE RATES AT 1.6005 AND 1.5998. YOU ARE UPDATING YOUR CASHFLOWS. WHAT IMPACT ON GBP AND USD CASHFLOWS WILL THE TRANSACTION HAVE?

A: Spot: + GBP 10,000,000, - USD 16,050,000, 7 days: - GBP 10,000,000, + USD 15,998,000

B: Spot: - GBP 10,000,000, + USD 16,988,000, 7 days: - GBP 10,000,000, + USD 16,005,000

C: Spot: - GBP 10,000,000, - USD 16,005,000, 7 days: + GBP 10,000,000, + USD 15,998,000

D: Spot: - GBP 10,000,000, + USD 16,005,000, 7 days: + GBP 10,000,000, - USD 15,998,000

QUESTION 36: TOPIC: Foreign exchange Calculations

THE BROKER IS QUOTING SPOT USD/CHF 0.90 55-60 AND A COMMERCIAL CUSTOMER CALLS AND ASKS YOU TO SELL HIM CHF 5 MILLION. YOU ARE REQUIRED TO CHARGE A SPREAD (OR MARGIN) OF 5 POINTS ON ALL EXCHANGE DEALS FOR THIS NAME. WHAT DO YOU QUOTE HIM AND HOW MANY USD WILL HE PAY YOU VALUE SPOT?

A: 0.9050, USD 5,524,861.87

B: 0.9060, USD 5,518,763.80

C: 0.9050, USD 4,425,000.00

D: 0.9055, USD 5,521,811.15

QUESTION 37: TOPIC: Fwd/fwds, FRAs Money market Futures and Swaps

WHICH OF THE FOLLOWING IS TRUE?

A: NYSE Euronext.liffe Euribor nominal amount EUR 1,000,000, minimum price movement = 1 tick

B: NYSE Euronext.liffe Euroswiss delivery months are March, June, Sept and Dec

C: CME Group Eurodollar nominal amount USD 1,000,000, 0.005 tick value = USD 12.50

D: all of these

QUESTION 38: TOPIC: Fwd/fwds, FRAs Money market Futures and Swaps

ONE OF THE STANDARD LEGAL DOCUMENTS FOR INTEREST RATE SWAPS USED IN LONDON IS...

A: BBAIRS

B: ISMA

C: ICOM

D: TBMA/ISMA

QUESTION 39: TOPIC: Fwd/fwds, FRAs Money market Futures and Swaps

IT IS MAY 201X, HOW WOULD YOU SET UP AN ARBITRAGE POSITION IN FUTURES AND FRAS?

A: Sell 1-3 FRAs, Sell June Futures

B: Sell 1-3 FRAs, Buy June Futures

C: Sell 1-4 FRAs, Sell June Futures

D: Buy 1-4 FRAs, Sell June Futures

QUESTION 40: TOPIC: Fwd/fwds, FRAs Money market Futures and Swaps

IN A PLAIN VANILLA INTEREST RATE SWAP, THE "FIXED-RATE PAYER"...

A: has established the price sensitivities of a longer-term fixed-rate asset and a floating-rate liability

B: has established the price sensitivities of a longer-term fixed-rate liability and a floating-rate asset

C: receives fixed in the swap

D: pays floating in the swap

QUESTION 41: TOPIC: Fwd/fwds, FRAs Money market Futures and Swaps

YOU EXPECTED USD INTEREST RATES TO RISE AND THEREFORE TOOK A SPECULATIVE POSITION USING A 3 v 6 FRA FOR USD 20 MILLION WHICH WAS QUOTED TO YOU AS 2.30-2.35 p.c. THE 3 v 6 PERIOD IS 90 DAYS. AT SETTLEMENT, USD LIBOR IS FIXED AT 3.00 p.c. WHAT IS THE SETTLEMENT AMOUNT AND DO YOU PAY OR RECEIVE?

A: You receive USD 38,213.39

B: You pay USD 31,819.41

C: You receive USD 32,258.06

D: You pay USD 32,258.06

QUESTION 42: TOPIC: Fwd/fwds, FRAs Money market Futures and Swaps

A TOTAL RETURN SWAP...

A: permits the full amount of receivables on a loan to be hedged

B: permits the maturity of a swap to be continuously adjusted by reference to a regularly available benchmark

C: is an insurance policy similar to a credit derivative

D: permits the risk and return on an asset to be achieved without actually owning it

QUESTION 43: TOPIC: Fwd/fwds, FRAs Money market Futures and Swaps

IF YOU SOLD DECEMBER FUTURES AT 98.70 AND AT THE END OF THE DAY YOUR MARGIN ACCOUNT IS CREDITED, WOULD THE END-OF-DAY SETTLEMENT PRICE HAVE BEEN...

A: More than 98.70

B: less than 98.70

C: None of these

D: 98.70

QUESTION 44: TOPIC: Fwd/fwds, FRAs Money market Futures and Swaps

YOU HAVE JUST HEARD THAT THE INITIAL MARGIN ON THE 3 MONTH SHORT STERLING CONTRACT ON NYSE EURONEXT.LIFFE HAS BEEN INCREASED. WHICH OF THE FOLLOWING STATEMENTS WOULD BEST EXPLAIN THE INCREASE?

A: Too many contracts have been traded

B: The sterling money markets have lost liquidity

C: Not enough contracts have been traded

D: Sterling interest rates are more volatile

QUESTION 45: TOPIC: Fwd/fwds, FRAs Money market Futures and Swaps

WHICH OF THE FOLLOWING RATES IS USED AS THE FLOATING RATE IN A US DOLLAR 7 DAY OIS?

A: Federal Funds Effective rate compounded

B: EONIA compounded

C: 3 months BBA USD LIBOR

D: Overnight USD settled daily

QUESTION 46: TOPIC: Fwd/fwds, FRAs Money market Futures and Swaps

WHICH OF THE FOLLOWING IS NOT AN INDEX OR BASIS SWAP?

A: 3 month USD LIBOR against 6 month USD LIBOR

B: USD CD rate against USD Commercial Paper Rate

C: 6 month USD LIBOR against 5 year US Treasuries

D: 12 month USD LIBOR against Prime Rate

QUESTION 47: TOPIC: Fwd/fwds, FRAs Money market Futures and Swaps

YOU HAVE SOLD 10 SHORT STERLING FUTURES CONTRACTS AT 93.50 AND THE MARKET CLOSED AT 93.35. WHAT VARIATION MARGIN WILL BE CALCULATED AND ADVISED TO YOU ON THIS OPEN POSITION?

A: You must pay GBP 3,750.00

B: You must pay GBP 1,875.00

C: You will receive GBP3,750.00

D: You will receive GBP 1,875.00

QUESTION 48: TOPIC: Fwd/fwds, FRAs Money market Futures and Swaps

BASIS RISK ON A FUTURES CONTRACT IS...

A: The risk of an adverse change in the spread between futures and cash prices

B: The progressive illiquidity of a futures contract as it approaches expiry

C: The risk of a divergence between the futures price and the final fixing of the underlying interest rate

D: The risk of an adverse change in the futures price

QUESTION 49: TOPIC: Options

WHAT IS THE PREMIUM OF A EUROPEAN STYLE OTC CURRENCY OPTION?

A: the price of the option - payable on deal date

B: the price at which the option may be exercised

C: the difference between the spot rate and the strike price at expiry

D: the profit or loss on an option at expiry

QUESTION 50: TOPIC: Options

IF THE PREMIUM OF AN OTC CURRENCY OPTION USD CALL/JPY PUT IS CALCULATED TO BE 2.5% WHAT WOULD THE BUYER PAY ON PURCHASE OF THE OPTION ON AN UNDERLYING AMOUNT OF USD 1 MILLION?

A: JPY 25,000

B: USD 2,500

C: JPY 2,500

D: USD 25,000

QUESTION 51: TOPIC: Options

IF A CURRENCY OPTION IS DESCRIBED AS "OUT OF THE MONEY", THE DELTA...

A: tends towards zero

B: tends towards 1

C: is equal to zero

D: tends towards 0.5

QUESTION 52: TOPIC: Options

A LONG STRANGLE (THE PURCHASE OF A PUT AT ONE STRIKE PRICE AND THE PURCHASE OF A CALL AT A HIGHER STRIKE PRICE - BOTH WITH THE SAME EXPIRY) CAN BE DESCRIBED AS...

A: a directional trade

B: a risk reversal

C: a synthetic forward

D: a volatility trade

QUESTION 53: TOPIC: Options

THE PREMIUM FOR A EUR/GBP OPTION IS QUOTED AS 0.023. THE NOMINAL VALUE OF THE OPTION IS EUR 3 MILLION. HOW MUCH IS THE PREMIUM?

A: EUR 69,000.00

B: GBP 6,900.00

C: GBP 23,000.00

D: GBP 69,000.00

QUESTION 54: TOPIC: Options

YOUR CUSTOMER HAS JUST BOUGHT AN INTEREST RATE COLLAR. PREMIUM ON CAP PURCHASED EQUALS THE PREMIUM ON THE FLOOR SOLD. HOW MIGHT THIS BE DESCRIBED?

A: Risk free investment

B: Arbitrage

C: A Strangle

D: Zero cost Collar

QUESTION 55: TOPIC: Principles of ALM

HOW COULD A LONG HEDGE POSITION IN A 6X9 FRA FOR USD 10 MILLION BE CONSIDERED WHEN PERFORMING A GAP ANALYSIS?

A: a 6-month liability and a 9-month liability, both for USD 5 million

B: a 9-month asset and a 6-month asset, both for USD 5 million

C: a 6-month liability and a 9-month asset, both for USD 10 million

D: a 9-month liability and a 6-month asset, both for USD 10 million

QUESTION 56: TOPIC: Principles of ALM

WHICH OF THE FOLLOWING REPRESENTS A WEAKNESS OF A TRADITIONAL APPROACH TO GAP ANALYSIS?

A: It does not capture foreign exchange risk

B: all of these

C: Gap analysis uses only outstanding trade data

D: Gap analysis ignores interest flows and the associated reinvestment risk

QUESTION 57: TOPIC: Principles of ALM

AMONGST OTHER ASSETS, WHAT CONSTITUTES LEVEL 1 ASSETS IN THE TWO CATEGORIES UNDER THE LCR UNDER BASEL RULES

A: 100% of qualifying bank reserves and 100% of domestic sovereign or central bank debt in domestic currency

B: 100% of qualifying bank reserves and 85% of sovereign or central bank assets with 20% risk weighting

C: 85% of sovereign or central bank assets with 20% risk weighting and 85% of qualifying corporate bonds rated AA- or higher

D: 100% of qualifying bank reserves and 100% qualifying corporate bonds rated AA- or higher

QUESTION 58: TOPIC: Principles of ALM

THE CREDIT PROTECTION SELLER IN A CDS...

A: assumes the credit risk from the buyer in exchange for a single up-front fee, and is obliged to pay compensation only in the event of the buyer

B: assumes the credit risk on a bond from the issuer in exchange for a periodic protection fee similar to an insurance premium, and is obliged to pay only if a negative credit event occurs

C: assumes the credit risk on a reference bond from the issuer in exchange for a periodic protection fee similar to an insurance premium, and is obliged to pay only if a negative credit event occurs

D: assumes the credit risk on a reference bond from the buyer in exchange for a periodic protection fee similar to an insurance premium, and is obliged to pay only if a negative credit event occurs

QUESTION 59: TOPIC: Principles of ALM

UNDER BASEL RULES WHEN DISCUSSION THE LEVERAGE RATIO, WHAT CONSTITUTES 'ADJUSTED ASSETS'?

A: 3% of tier 1 and tier 2 capital

B: tier 1 and tier 2 capital divided by adjusted assets

C: tier 1 minus tier 2 capital

D: total assets minus intangible assets

QUESTION 60: TOPIC: Principles of ALM

IT IS JUNE 1X. WHICH OF THE FOLLOWING SEQUENCES BEST DESCRIBES THE MECHANICS USED BY THE ALM DEALERS OF USING FINANCIAL FUTURES TO HEDGE A SHORT 3s v. 6s FORWARD-FORWARD USD INTEREST RATE RISK IN THE CASH MARKET?

A: sell Sept 1X STIR ED futures, receive/pay profit/loss daily, sell back futures, lend cash

B: buy Sept 1X STIR ED futures, receive/pay profit/loss daily, sell back futures, take cash

C: buy Sept 1X STIR ED futures, receive/pay profit/loss daily, sell back futures, lend cash

D: sell Sept 1X STIR ED futures, receive/pay profit/loss daily, buy back futures, take cash

QUESTION 61: TOPIC: Principles of ALM

WHEN IS A BANK DEEMED TO BE INTEREST RATE SENSITIVE IN A PARTICULAR MATURITY BUCKET?

A: when its assets subject to re-pricing exceed its fixed rate assets in that time bucket

B: when its liabilities subject to re-pricing exceed its assets subject to re-pricing in a different time bucket

C: when its fixed rate liabilities subject to re-pricing exceed its fixed rate assets in a different time bucket

D: when its liabilities subject to re-pricing exceed its assets subject to re-pricing in that time bucket

QUESTION 62: TOPIC: Principles of ALM

WHAT IS MEANT BY LOSS GIVEN DEFAULT?

A: a parameter used in the calculation of Economic Capital or Regulatory Capital under Basel rules for a banking institution

B: the amount of a loss resulting from collateral depreciation

C: the bank's best assessment of a bad debt

D: exposure on the bank's default

QUESTION 63: TOPIC: Principles of Risk

UNDER BASEL RULES THE RISK WEIGHT FOR CLAIMS ON UNRATED SOVEREIGNS AND THEIR CENTRAL BANKS IN THE STANDARDIZED APPROACH IS...

A: 350%

B: 150%

C: 100%

D: 75%

QUESTION 64: TOPIC: Principles of Risk

UNDER BASEL RULES, EXPECTED CREDIT LOSS IS A FUNCTION OF WHICH OF THE FOLLOWING SETS OF PARAMETERS?..

A: 1 minus recovery rate, probability of default and exposure at default

B: loss given default, 1 minus recovery rate and exposure at default

C: exposure at origination, recovery rates and probability of default

D: exposure at origination, exposure at default and loss given default

QUESTION 65: TOPIC: Principles of Risk

THE VARIANCE / CO-VARIANCE VAR METHODOLOGY RELIES ON WHICH OF THE FOLLOWING CONCEPTS...

A: GANN

B: Simple historic volatility

C: BIS risk weighting

D: zero coupon yield curve

QUESTION 66: TOPIC: Principles of Risk

IF THE DAILY 90% CONFIDENCE LEVEL VAR OF A PORTFOLIO IS ESTIMATED TO BE USD 10,000.00, WHAT DOES THIS INDICATE?

A: in 1 out of 90 days it is expected that the portfolio value will decline by USD 10,000.00 or more.

B: in 1 out of 10 days it is expected that the portfolio value will decline by USD 10,000.00 or more.

C: in 1 out of 90 days it is expected that the portfolio value will decline by USD 10,000.00 or less.

D: in 1 out of 10 days it is expected that the portfolio value will decline by USD 10,000.00 or less.

QUESTION 67: TOPIC: Principles of Risk

WHICH OF THE FOLLOWING IS NOT AN OBJECTIVE OF POSITION-KEEPING?

A: Measuring market exposure

B: Calculating average book rate

C: Monitoring counterparty credit risk

D: Calculating Profit and Loss

QUESTION 68: TOPIC: Principles of Risk

WHO SHOULD AUTHORISE THE SET UP OF COUNTERPARTY (CREDIT) LIMITS?

A: the dealers

B: the processing department on receipt of instructions from the broker

C: the processing department in response to a request from the bank concerned

D: an independent credit assessment department

QUESTION 69: TOPIC: Principles of Risk

UNDER THE FOUNDATION APPROACH, THE BIS PRESCRIBES FIXED LOSS GIVEN DEFAULT RATIOS FOR CERTAIN CLASSES OF UNSECURED EXPOSURES. WHICH OF THE FOLLOWING ATTRACTS A 75% LGD?

A: senior claims on sovereigns not secured by recognized collateral

B: senior claims on corporates not secured by recognized collateral

C: senior claims on banks not secured by recognized collateral

D: all subordinated claims on corporates, sovereigns and banks

QUESTION 70: TOPIC: Principles of Risk

WHICH ONE OF THE FOLLOWING BEST DESCRIBES EXPECTED SHORTFALL / CONDITIONAL VALUE-AT-RISK AT THE 95% LEVEL?

A: the expected loss on the portfolio in the worst 95% of cases

B: the maximum loss in those cases where the loss exceeds the VaR at the 95% level

C: the expected loss in those cases where the loss exceeds the VaR at the 5% level

D: the expected loss in those cases where the loss exceeds the VaR at the 95% level

End of Mock examination No. 6

Chapter 5

Mock examinations Nos. 1 – 6

Answers and brief explanations

QUESTION 1: TOPIC: Basic Interest Rate Calculations

ANSWER: A: gently upwards sloping

According to some textbooks on investment a normal yield curve is positive or gently upwards sloping.

QUESTION 2: TOPIC: Basic Interest Rate Calculations

ANSWER: B: 3.470 p.c.

ACI formulae page 2 Data: annual int rate: 0.035. ANSWER: 3.470 p.c.

QUESTION 3: TOPIC: Basic Interest Rate Calculations

ANSWER: C: 3.960 p.c.

ACI formulae page 2 Data: bond coupon: 0.04, ANSWER: 3.960 p.c.

QUESTION 4: TOPIC: Basic Interest Rate Calculations

ANSWER: C: a semi-annual money market rate of 4.00 p.c.

A semi-annual money market rate of 4.00 p.c. (interest calculated on an Actual/360 annual basis and paid twice a year) gives you the best return.

QUESTION 5: TOPIC: Basic Interest Rate Calculations

ANSWER: C: 4.875 p.c.

ACI formulae (not included) Data: 2 months (61 days): 0.045, 2s v. 6s fwd/fwd (122 days): 0.050247, annual basis: Act/365. ANSWER: 4.875 p.c.

QUESTION 6: TOPIC: Basic Interest Rate Calculations

ANSWER: A: Inverted

A yield curve where shorter term interest rates are higher than longer term rates is described as inverted or negative.

QUESTION 7: TOPIC: Cash Money markets Theory

ANSWER: D: paid to the owner of the bonds as a manufactured dividend

Gilt coupon payments made during the life of a classic repo are paid to the original owner of bond as a manufactured dividend.

QUESTION 8: TOPIC: Cash Money markets Theory

ANSWER: B: all of these

All these are descriptions of how custody arrangements for repos can be made. HIC = Hold in Custody.

QUESTION 9: TOPIC: Cash Money markets Theory

ANSWER: D: 0.01 p.c.

Basis points are a means to quote interest rates to two decimal places rather than the traditional method of fractions in the money markets. 1 Basis point = 1/100 of 1 p.c. or 0.01 p.c.

QUESTION 10: TOPIC: Cash Money markets Theory

ANSWER: A: sell and buy the base currency on the market maker's 3 mos OFFER FX swap and borrow the base currency

In an interest arbitrage operation to raise the variable currency for 3 months as a market user you must buy and sell the variable currency (sell and buy the base currency) on the right hand side of the swap (the forward OFFER of the base currency) and borrow the base currency.

QUESTION 11: TOPIC: Cash Money markets Theory

ANSWER: C: Collateral illiquidity and counterparty risk

With illiquid collateral it may be difficult to sell so the margin gives some comfort in the event of default of the counterparty. A reverse repoer will take more collateral from a less credit-worthy counterparty (more likely to default).

QUESTION 12: TOPIC: Cash Money markets Theory

ANSWER: B: More than the face value

Buying a CD in the secondary market after interest rates have fallen from the level at issue will mean the CD will be traded for more than face value.

QUESTION 13: TOPIC: Cash Money markets Calculations

ANSWER: A: 4.00 p.c.

Simple int formula: The price = face value less discount amount. The discount rate is calculated by reversing the simple interest formula: discount rate = (face value minus discount amount) multiplied by 360 X 100 divided by (face value multiplied by No. of days).

QUESTION 14 : TOPIC: Cash Money markets Calculations

ANSWER: A: USD 991,916.67

ACI formulae page 3 Data: face value: USD 1,000,000.00, discount rate (60 days): 0.0485, annual basis: Act/360. ANSWER: USD 991,916.67.

QUESTION 15: TOPIC: Cash Money markets Calculations

ANSWER: D: make a profit of 0.125 p.c.

Buying UK T-Bills is like making a loan and selling them in the secondary market is like taking a deposit. Therefore if you buy T-Bills at 4.00 p.c. (like lending the cash at a yield of 4.00 p.c.) and then sell them at 3.875 p.c. (like borrowing the cash) you will make a profit of 0.125 p.c. over the 90 days.

QUESTION 16: TOPIC: Cash Money markets Calculations

ANSWER: B: USD 5,047,298.98

ACI formulae page 3 Data: principal: USD 5,000,000.00, issue rate (90 days): 0.055, yield (30 days): 0.051, annual basis: Act/360. ANSWER: USD 5,047,298.98.

QUESTION 17: TOPIC: Cash Money markets Calculations

ANSWER: A: GBP 39,920.84 Profit

ACI formulae page 3 Data: principal: GBP 5,000,000.00, issue rate (90 days): 0.0475, Sec CD yield (30 days): 0.045, annual basis: Act/365. ANSWER: GBP 39,920.84 Profit (ignoring funding costs = GBP 5,039,920.84 less 5,000,000.00).

QUESTION 18: TOPIC: Cash Money markets Calculations

ANSWER: D: 6.98 p.c.

ACI formulae page 3 Data: discount rate (95 days): 0.0685, annual basis: Act/360. ANSWER: 6.9761 rounded here to 6.98 p.c.

QUESTION 19: TOPIC: Foreign exchange Theory

ANSWER: B: two business days after deal date

The official value date for settlement of spot gold or silver transactions versus the US Dollar is two business days after deal date where a good business day is defined as one in which banks are open in London for delivery of the gold and in New York for settlement of the US Dollars.

QUESTION 20: TOPIC: Foreign exchange Theory

ANSWER: C: I pay 23 points my favour for 3 million in the three months

The correct way of advising the voice broker of your interest (your order) to sell and buy GBP 3 million is 'I pay (bid) 23 points my favour for 3 million in the three months'. (Model Code Chapter XI) this makes the broker's new price 23-20 (improving his bid from 25 to 23).

QUESTION 21: TOPIC: Foreign exchange Theory

ANSWER: A: All of these

The extension of a contract at off-market rates gives rise to credit risk implications and can permit the counterparty to defer a profit or a loss to a future accounting period. The previously available Model Code recommends that this practice should be avoided.

QUESTION 22: TOPIC: Foreign exchange Theory

ANSWER: B: Overbought USD 5 million against ZAR

USD/ZAR is quoted to a USD base and dealers tend to describe their positions in terms of the base currency therefore in this case the dealer is confirming his open position as overbought USD 5 million against ZAR.

QUESTION 23: TOPIC: Foreign exchange Theory

ANSWER: A: to match interbank buyers with sellers in the spot and forward FX markets

The role of a voice broker in the foreign exchange market is to match interbank buyers with sellers in the spot and forward FX markets.

QUESTION 24: TOPIC: Foreign exchange Theory

ANSWER: A: 'High-Low'

If the base currency of a foreign exchange rate quotation (here the USD) is described as being at a forward DISCOUNT then the numbers in the swap bid-offer spread are quoted and displayed "High - Low (international terminology) or to put it another equally correct way: the quoted currency (here ZAR) is described as being at a forward PREMIUM in relation to the base currency (London terminology).

QUESTION 25: TOPIC: Foreign exchange Theory

ANSWER: B: the interest differential between GBP and USD to widen

Dealing as a market user at 104 GBP Discount points against you means that your view must be that the interest differential between GBP and USD will widen (e.g. GBP int rates up USD same and swap points increase).

QUESTION 26: TOPIC: Foreign exchange Theory

ANSWER: A: LBMA

It is the London Bullion Market Association which regulated precious metals trading in London.

QUESTION 27: TOPIC: Foreign exchange Theory

ANSWER: A: you have sold and bought GBP 10 million Spot against 3 mths at 35 pts against you

If, on your quote of 3 months GBP/USD FX swap of 35-38, the calling counterparty asks to do 10 million at 35 points (your bid for forward GBP) you have sold and bought the base currency, here GBP 10 million Spot against 3 months and this price is described as being 35 points against you.

QUESTION 28: TOPIC: Foreign exchange Theory

ANSWER: A: 1.11 08/13

You are buying GBP (Selling EUR). You must therefore deal to pay as few EUR as possible. The best rate for you therefore is 1.1113 (the 08/13 quote). The EUR based quotes are not as good.

QUESTION 29: TOPIC: Foreign exchange Theory

ANSWER: B: Spot Bid for GBP, O/N Offer of GBP and T/N Offer of GBP

You need the Spot Bid for GBP (1.5520), O/N Offer of GBP (-1.75 pts) and T/N Offer of GBP (-1.40 pts) and you can buy GBP from a client value today at 1.551685.

QUESTION 30: TOPIC: Foreign exchange Theory

ANSWER: C: USD interest rates have fallen

If the spot EUR/USD rate and EUR interest rates do not change but the forward EUR/USD points move from 2-5 (EUR Premium) to 6-1 (through parity, now a EUR Discount) this indicates that USD interest rates have fallen and are now lower than EUR.

QUESTION 31: TOPIC: Foreign exchange Calculations

ANSWER: C: -119

ACI formula page 7 Data: Spot EUR/CHF = 1.005, CHF int rate (180 days): 0.0125, EUR int rate (180 days): 0.0345, annual basis (both ccies): Act/360. ANSWER: 119 pts EUR Discount (negative.)

QUESTION 32: TOPIC: Foreign exchange Calculations

ANSWER: C: 1.625125

The method to calculate an ante spot outright is to add/subtract the benefit or cost of bringing the cashflows back from the spot date to the desired ante spot date. Here add the 1.25 pts benefit of selling and buying Tom/next GBP against USD to the spot rate of 1.6250 = 1.625125.

QUESTION 33: TOPIC: Foreign exchange Calculations

ANSWER: A: 89.90

The outright is 89.75. The forward points are quoted 20-15 therefore the points are subtracted from the spot to achieve the outright quote. The bank is selling USD so the dealer uses the Spot offer (of USD) and the Offered points -15, meaning that the Spot rate must be 89.75 + 0.15 = 89.90.

QUESTION 34: TOPIC: Foreign exchange Calculations

ANSWER: D: loss USD 14,682.25

Buy JPY 500,000,000 at 109.00 cost USD 4,587,155.96 revalued at 109.35 is equal to USD 4,572,473.71. USD has gone up in value and we are short USD (long JPY) therefore a loss of USD 14,682.25.

QUESTION 35: TOPIC: Foreign exchange Calculations

ANSWER: D: 215-210

If Spot EUR/GBP is 0.88 75-80 and three months forward outright EUR/GBP is 0.86 60-70, subtract the forward outright from the spot rate to achieve the points as 215-210.

QUESTION 36: TOPIC: Foreign exchange Calculations

ANSWER: A: 1.6040

Spot 1.6020/25 and 1 month forward 20/25, you add the left hand points to left hand spot arrive at the buying rate for USD (non base currency) as a market user, here 1.6040.

QUESTION 37: TOPIC: Fwd/fwds, FRAs, Money market Futures and Swaps

ANSWER: B: 3s v.6s GBP interest rates have risen during the day

If the September 1X Short Sterling Futures price on NYSE Euronext.liffe closes lower this means that the 3s v.6s GBP interest rates have risen over the day.

QUESTION 38: TOPIC: Fwd/fwds, FRAs, Money market Futures and Swaps

ANSWER: B: all of these

All these are advantages of financial futures over the cash market forward-forward alternative.

QUESTION 39: TOPIC: Fwd/fwds, FRAs, Money market Futures and Swaps

ANSWER: D: 3.47 p.c.

ACI formula sheet (page 4): long int rate (180 days offer): 0.03, short int rate (90 days bid): 0.0325, annual basis: Act/360. ANSWER: 3.47(3945) p.c. you buy from customer.

QUESTION 40: TOPIC: Fwd/fwds, FRAs, Money market Futures and Swaps

ANSWER: A: LIBOR Actual/360

The floating rate of an ISDA based 5 year USD interest rate swap is always LIBOR on an Actual/360 annual basis.

QUESTION 41: TOPIC: Fwd/fwds, FRAs, Money market Futures and Swaps

ANSWER: A: Yes, you receive EUR 44,143.14

ACI formula sheet (page 4): FRA: 150,000,000.00, FRA rate (89 days): 0.0315, EUR LIBOR 0.0327, annual/basis: Act/360 ANSWER: EUR 44,143.14 in your favour as you were correct in that EUR int rate have risen.

QUESTION 42: TOPIC: Fwd/fwds, FRAs, Money market Futures and Swaps

ANSWER: A: to switch the risk from 3 months fixed to overnight

Of the choices listed the only appropriate answer is "to switch the risk from 3 months fixed to overnight."

QUESTION 43: TOPIC: Fwd/fwds, FRAs, Money market Futures and Swaps

ANSWER: C: GBP 12.50

The value of 1 tick on the Short Sterling futures contract on NYSE Euronext.liffe is GBP 12.50.

QUESTION 44: TOPIC: Fwd/fwds, FRAs, Money market Futures and Swaps

ANSWER: B: USD 1,875.00 to the seller

Movement of 7.5 on 10 contracts and each 0.01 movement is worth USD 25.00 = USD 1,875.00 variation margin payable to the seller (you) by 10.00 a.m. tomorrow.

QUESTION 45: TOPIC: Fwd/fwds, FRAs, Money market Futures and Swaps

ANSWER: A: The CME EURODOLLAR futures contract has a minimum price interval of one-quarter basis point value (0.0025) for the nearest contract

The CME EURODOLLAR futures contract has a minimum price interval of one-quarter basis point value (0.0025) for the nearest contract.

QUESTION 46: TOPIC: Fwd/fwds, FRAs, Money market Futures and Swaps

ANSWER: C: agreed to be netted and paid on each re-rating date

If an interest rate swap includes synchronisation and netting, the interest payments are agreed to be netted and paid on each re-rating date.

QUESTION 47: TOPIC: Fwd/fwds, FRAs, Money market Futures and Swaps

ANSWER: D: pay SONIA receive GBP 1 week fixed

An example of an OIS (Overnight index swap) is where the parties agree to swap interest payments based on paying SONIA (Sterling Overnight Index Average) and receiving GBP 1 week fixed.

QUESTION 48: TOPIC: Fwd/fwds, FRAs, Money market Futures and Swaps

ANSWER: A: You receive USD 1,574.84

ACI formula sheet (page 4): principal: 10,000,000.00, FRA rate (92 days): 0.055, LIBOR (92 days): 0.055625, annual basis: Act/360. ANSWER: USD 1,574.84 - you receive from the seller.

QUESTION 49: TOPIC: Options

ANSWER: D: When the option is just before expiry

An at the money option premium exhibits the greatest theta, all other things being equal, when just before expiry.

QUESTION 50: TOPIC: Options

ANSWER: B: a combination of buying a Cap and selling a Floor at different strike prices

An interest rate Collar is a combination of buying a Cap and Selling a Floor at different strike prices with a view to reducing the overall cost of the hedging strategy.

QUESTION 51: TOPIC: Options

ANSWER: A: when it is out-of-the money

An option has no intrinsic value when it is out-of-the money.

QUESTION 52: TOPIC: Options

ANSWER: D: Black and Scholes

The most frequently encountered pricing model used for Currency options in the OTC market is the Black and Scholes model originally developed in the 1970s for stock market option pricing by the two named US mathematics professors and Nobel prize winners.

QUESTION 53: TOPIC: Options

ANSWER: D: Bermudan

This is a description of a Bermudan option.

QUESTION 54: TOPIC: Options

ANSWER: B: a fund manager worried about falling interest rates

Of these choices a fund manager worried about falling interest rates is most likely to use an interest rate floor.

QUESTION 55: TOPIC: Principles of ALM

ANSWER: C: negative

Borrowing short and lending long has a negative impact on the bank's overall liquidity.

QUESTION 56: TOPIC: Principles of ALM

ANSWER: A: the Macaulay duration of a coupon paying bond is always lower than its maturity

The Macaulay duration is the weighted average life of all cashflows meaning that the Macaulay duration of a coupon paying bond will always be lower than its maturity.

QUESTION 57: TOPIC: Principles of ALM

ANSWER: A: Securitisation is the financial practice of pooling various types of contractual debt in the form of bonds to investors

Securitisation is the financial practice of pooling various types of contractual debt in the form of bonds to investors.

QUESTION 58: TOPIC: Principles of ALM

ANSWER: C: an agreement whereby the seller will compensate the buyer in the event of a specified loan default or other credit event

A Credit Default Swap (CDS)is an agreement whereby the seller will compensate the buyer in the event of a specified loan default or other credit event.

QUESTION 59: TOPIC: Principles of ALM

ANSWER: B: compliance

Compliance is not the responsibility of ALCO.

QUESTION 60: TOPIC: Principles of ALM

ANSWER: D: structuring a bank's portfolio so that its net interest revenue and/or the market value of its portfolio will not be adversely affected by changes in interest rates

Interest rate immunisation in ALM is structuring a bank's portfolio so that its net interest revenue and/or the market value of its portfolio will not be adversely affected by changes in interest rates.

QUESTION 61: TOPIC: Principles of ALM

ANSWER: C: A positive gap of GBP 200 million

With maturing assets greater than liabilities in the 12 month time bucket the gap for this period can be described as being 'a positive gap of GBP 200 million'.

QUESTION 62: TOPIC: Principles of ALM

ANSWER: D: Asset and liability at 3 years, asset at 3 months

If you buy a 3 year bond and enter into a USD payer's swap against 3 months LIBOR these transactions would be returned in the bank's gap reportage as an asset and liability at 3 years and an asset at 3 months.

QUESTION 63: TOPIC: Principles of Risk

ANSWER: A: the bank itself

It is the bank itself which sets economic capital levels.

QUESTION 64: TOPIC: Principles of Risk

ANSWER: B: Delivery Risk

Having sold a secondary market USD 5 million CD originally issued by Mega Bank to Major Bank value spot. Your risk on Major Bank is Delivery Risk.

QUESTION 65: TOPIC: Principles of Risk

ANSWER: B: 45%

The loss-given default (LGD) for senior claims on corporates, sovereigns and banks not secured by recognised collateral is 45%.

QUESTION 66: TOPIC: Principles of Risk

ANSWER: D: Operational

If the payments system your bank is using to settle a market transaction fails this would be described as Operational risk.

QUESTION 67: TOPIC: Principles of Risk

ANSWER: B: to estimate potential economic losses in abnormal markets

Stress testing is intended to estimate potential economic losses in abnormal markets.

QUESTION 68: TOPIC: Principles of Risk

ANSWER: C: VaR limits attempt to indicate the level of market risk before its economic consequences are realised

VaR limits attempt to indicate the level of market risk before its economic consequences are realised.

QUESTION 69: TOPIC: Principles of Risk

ANSWER: D: It permits aggregation of market risks across asset classes

A VaR-based approach to measuring market risk permits aggregation of market risks across asset classes.

QUESTION 70: TOPIC: Principles of Risk

ANSWER: B: Raise interest rates

Whilst the level of USD interest rates may influence the value of the US Dollar, there are many other factors which could give rise to the dealer being "squeezed". Of these possible answers the Fed Reserve raising interest rates would make the covering of a short USD position more expensive.

End of Mock examination No. 1

QUESTION 1: TOPIC: Basic Interest Rate Calculations

ANSWER: C: 4.85 p.c.

Simple int formula Data: Principal GBP 5,500,000.00, interest (181 days): 132,278.77, annual basis: Act/365. ANSWER: 4.85 p.c.

QUESTION 2: TOPIC: Basic Interest Rate Calculations

ANSWER: B: 4.142 p.c.

ACI formulae page 2 Data: annual bond coupon: 0.042, semiannual result rounded to 4.142 p.c.

QUESTION 3: TOPIC: Basic Interest Rate Calculations

ANSWER: A: after one year and at maturity

Interest on fixed deposits with a maturity over one year is paid annually on their anniversary and at maturity.

QUESTION 4: TOPIC: Basic Interest Rate Calculations

ANSWER: B: USD 13,052,822.61

ACI formulae (not included) Data: USD 10,000,000.00, annual interest rate: 0.027 for 10 years, annual basis: Act/360 = 13,052,822.61.

QUESTION 5: TOPIC: Basic Interest Rate Calculations

ANSWER: A: EONIA

EONIA (Euro Overnight Index Average) is the benchmark interest rate average for overnight EUR funds traded in the Eurozone, calculated daily by the ECB (European Central Bank) from data supplied by banks on the EURIOBOR contributor panel. EURONIA is a similar average but produced in London for all transactions through the London brokers market.

QUESTION 6: TOPIC: Basic Interest Rate Calculations

ANSWER: D: 4.242 p.c.

ACI formulae (not included) Data: Principal: GBP 10,000,000.00, int rate1 (90 days): 0.04, int rate2 (91 days): 0.041, int rate3 (92 days): 0.0425, int rate4 (92 days): 0.0435 p.c. ANSWER: int 424,198.48 applied to principal of GBP 10 million for 365 days = 4.242 p.c.

QUESTION 7: TOPIC: Cash Money markets Theory

ANSWER: D: US Treasury Bills

US Treasury Bills are quoted and traded at a discount. The majority of instruments traded in the international money markets are interest bearing (simple interest formula). The exceptions to this rule must be learnt.

QUESTION 8: TOPIC: Cash Money markets Theory

ANSWER: A: ECP is traded as a discount-paying instrument quoted as a yield

Of the statements available the only one accurately describing the main features of the Euro Commercial Paper market in the UK and Europe is that ECP is traded as a discount-paying instrument and quoted as a yield.

QUESTION 9: TOPIC: Cash Money markets Theory

ANSWER: A: Sterling CDs pay a return at maturity calculated as a yield using the simple interest formula

Of the statements available the only one accurately describing the main features of the Sterling CD market in London is that Sterling CDs pay a return at maturity calculated as a yield using the simple interest formula.

QUESTION 10: TOPIC: Cash Money markets Theory

ANSWER: C: Actual/Actual

All GBP short term money market have interest calculated on an Actual / 365 annual basis but UK Government securities (UK Gilts) follow the Actual / Actual annual basis convention.

QUESTION 11: TOPIC: Cash Money markets Theory

ANSWER: B: the party charging the initial margin

The counterparty to a repo charging the initial margin can make a margin call as agreed in the bi-lateral GMRA signed between the parties prior to any transactions being effected.

QUESTION 12: TOPIC: Cash Money markets Theory

ANSWER: D: Money market deposit

Money market deposits/loans are not normally negotiable.

QUESTION 13: TOPIC: Cash Money markets Calculations

ANSWER: A: USD 25,000,000.00

US CP is a discount paying instrument quoted at a rate of discount and repays the face value at maturity = USD 25,000,000.00.

QUESTION 14: TOPIC: Cash Money markets Calculations

ANSWER: B: USD 32,666.96

ACI formulae page 3 Data: principal: 15,000,000.00, issue rate (180 days): 0.02, Sec CD yield (40 days): 0.012, annual basis: Act/360. ANSWER: 15,129,826.89 less 15,097,159.94 = EUR 32,666.96.

QUESTION 15: TOPIC: Cash Money markets Calculations

ANSWER: D: 4.17 p.c.

ACI formulae page 3 Data: discount rate (90 days): 0.04125, annual basis: Act/365. ANSWER: 4.1674 p.c. - rounded to 4.17 p.c.

QUESTION 16: TOPIC: Cash money market Calculations

ANSWER: C: GBP 9,581,000.00

The initial consideration of a special making the dirty price GBP 9,581,325.60. As this is a cash driven trade there is no margin (haircut) and the final consideration is rounded to the nearest 2 dec places i.e. 95.81 making the initial consideration GBP 9,581,000.

QUESTION 17: TOPIC: Cash Money markets Calculations

ANSWER B: EUR 10,200,000.00

Simple int formula (not included) Data: principal EUR 10,000,000.00, yield (90 days): 0.04, annual basis: Act/360 = 200,000.00 so EUR 10,000,000 plus 200,000.00 interest (simple interest formula) is the maturity value of the CD.

QUESTION 18: TOPIC: Cash Money markets Calculations

ANSWER: A: GBP 201,370,272.70

ACI formulae page 3 Data: principal: GBP 200,000,000.00, issue rate (91 days): 0.04, yield (31 days remaining): 0.0365, annual basis: Act/365. ANSWER: GBP 201,370,272.70.

QUESTION 19: Foreign exchange Theory

ANSWER: A: it is freely floating

Sterling remains freely floating against all other currencies (unless local exchange controls in the overseas centre come into play).

QUESTION 20: Foreign exchange Theory

ANSWER: A: a differential between interest rates and forward FX swap points in a currency pair

A covered interest arbitrage profitable position might arise if there is a differential between interest rates and forward FX swap points in a currency pair.

QUESTION 21: Foreign exchange Theory

ANSWER: C: at least 995/1000 pure gold; weight between 350 and 430 fine ounces

LBMA requirements for a "good delivery bar" are at least 995/1000 pure gold; weight between 350 and 430 fine ounces.

QUESTION 22: Foreign exchange Theory

ANSWER: A: lending 3 months EUR, buying and selling EUR against USD in a FX swap spot against 3 months and borrowing USD for 3 months

Ignoring any risk on uncovered interest flows, an example of a covered interest arbitrage transaction is lending 3 months EUR, buying and selling EUR against USD in a FX swap spot against 3 months and borrowing USD for 3 months.

QUESTION 23: Foreign exchange Theory

ANSWER: A: 1, 2, 3, 6 and 12 months.

The standard periods for a full 'run through' of forward EUR/USD swap quotations in the interbank market are 1, 2, 3, 6 and 12 months.

QUESTION 24: Foreign exchange Theory

ANSWER: A: 1.54 01

On a spot quote of 1.54 01-06 you can buy USD (sell GBP) at 1.54 01 the best spot bid for GBP (offer for USD) available

QUESTION 25: Foreign exchange Theory

ANSWER: A: High-Low

In forward exchange terminology, the currency with the higher interest rate can be described as being at a forward discount and if this currency is the base currency (the GBP) in an indirect currency pair (here the GBP/USD), then the numbers in the forward swap points will be quoted "High-Low".

QUESTION 26: Foreign exchange Theory

ANSWER: C: you have bought GBP spot against SEK and sold GBP 3 months forward against SEK

If on a quote of 370/350 the customer deals on your forward Offer of GBP of at 350 you have bought GBP spot against SEK and sold GBP 3 months forward against SEK.

QUESTION 27: Foreign exchange Theory

ANSWER: A: They sold you GBP 2,000,000 at 1.5720

The FX market talks in terms of the base currency – here GBP therefore on this quote the caller has sold you GBP 2 million.

QUESTION 28: Foreign exchange Theory

ANSWER: D: All of these

The incentives for market-making in the Foreign exchange market is the favourable Bid/offer spread, gaining market intelligence on the level of the currency and to engender good interbank and corporate dealing relationships, therefore 'all of these'.

QUESTION 29: Foreign exchange Theory

ANSWER: A: 6 months EUR rates are lower than 6 months GBP rates

The only thing you can positively identify from this quote is that the EUR is at a Premium (GBP is at a Discount) therefore EUR interest rates are lower than GBP in the 6 months period.

QUESTION 30: Foreign exchange Theory

ANSWER: A: 6 months EUR rates are higher than 6 months USD rates

The only thing you can positively identify from this quote is that the EUR is at a Discount (USD is at a Premium) therefore EUR interest rates are higher than USD in the 6 months period.

QUESTION 31: TOPIC: Foreign exchange Calculations

ANSWER: C: EUR 4,836,369.50

The base currency in EUR/USD quote is EUR therefore divide the USD amount by 1.2406 (Bid for USD/Offer of EUR) to find the amount of EUR you receive when selling USD 6 million (here EUR 4,836,369.50).

QUESTION 32: TOPIC: Foreign exchange Calculations

ANSWER: A: a) client pays Bank USD 7,326.00, b) 54.10

With the comparator rate fixed at 55.00 the n-d-f will settle in favour of the bank and the client will pay USD 7,326.00 (40 points). The client then covers his exchange requirement at 54.90 - a further cost of 10 points making a total of 50 points cost reducing his all-in rate achieved to 54.10 (54.60 less 0.40 less 0.10).

QUESTION 33: TOPIC: Foreign exchange Calculations

ANSWER: B: 1.5471

Spot 1.5500 less 0.0029 points (GBP Discount) ANSWER: 1.5471.

QUESTION 34: TOPIC: Foreign exchange Calculations

ANSWER: D: 89.0175

For the bank's outright sale of currency to a customer on a date before spot (ante spot) the spot rate must be adjusted by the cost of the short date cover. If the short date quote is "High-Low" then standard forward logic appears to be reversed with the right hand points value of the short date swap (Tom/next) being be added to the bank's left hand selling rate for JPY against USD. Here the Tom/next swap points of 1.75 are added to the left hand of the spot rate to achieve the required outright rate value tomorrow (89.0175).

QUESTION 35: TOPIC: Foreign exchange Calculations

ANSWER: D: 131.90

Data: Spot GBP/JPY: 132.00, GBP int rate (30 days): 0.01125, annual basis: Act/365, JPY int rate (30 days): 0.0025, annual basis: Act/360 = 131.90.

QUESTION 36: TOPIC: Foreign exchange Calculations

ANSWER: A: 121.00 and 120.76

Data: Spot EUR/USD: 1.3750, Spot USD/JPY: 88.00. EUR int rate (30 days): 0.02875, JPY int rate (30 days): 0.0050, annual basis (both currencies): Act/360. ANSWER: 121.00, 120.76.

QUESTION 37: TOPIC: Fwd/fwds, FRAs, Money market Futures and Swaps

ANSWER: D: If Settlement rate higher than FRA contractual rate - Seller pays Buyer

The correct rule regarding payment direction on settlement of a USD FRA under the ISDA bridge (FRABBA) agreement is that if the Settlement rate is higher than the FRA contractual rate then the Seller reimburses the Buyer.

QUESTION 38: TOPIC: Fwd/fwd, FRAs, Money market Futures and Swaps (Money market Swaps)

ANSWER: C: sell a strip of 6x12, 12x18 and 18x24 FRAs

To hedge the remaining life of this IRS you would sell a strip of 6x12, 12x18 and 18x24 FRAs.

QUESTION 39: TOPIC: Fwd/fwds, FRAs, Money market Futures and Swaps

ANSWER: C: IMM and NYSE Euronext.liffe

The 3 month Eurodollar contract is traded on the IMM, the International Monetary Market of CME Group Chicago, SGX in Singapore and NYSE Euronext.liffe in London.

QUESTION 40: TOPIC: Fwd/fwds, FRAs, Money market Futures and Swaps

ANSWER: A: Sell 3x7

To lock into a lending rate (you are overborrowed for 4 months in 3 months time) you must sell a 3x7 GBP FRA.

QUESTION 41: TOPIC: Fwd/fwds, FRAs, Money market Futures and Swaps

ANSWER: A: on any day the total number of futures contracts that have not yet expired, or fulfilled by delivery

Open interest is the total number of futures contracts that have not yet expired or fulfilled by delivery measured on any day in a futures market.

QUESTION 42: TOPIC: Fwd/fwds, FRAs, Money market Futures and Swaps

ANSWER: A: 4.65 p.c.

ACI formula sheet (not provided): spot ag 3 months (90 days): 0.047, 3s/6s (90 days): 0.045466, annual basis: Act/360 = 4.65 p.c.

QUESTION 43: TOPIC: Fwd/fwds, FRAs, Money market Futures and Swaps

ANSWER: D: the interest payments are agreed to be netted and paid on each re-rating date

If an interest rate swap includes synchronisation and netting, the interest payments are agreed to be netted and paid on each re-rating date

QUESTION 44: TOPIC: Fwd/fwds, FRAs, Money market Futures and Swaps

ANSWER: C: sell June ED futures at 98.00, sell 3X6 USD FRA at 2.07 p.c.

The only profitable arbitrage position of these would be to sell June ED futures at 98.00 (equivalent to a borrowing cost of 2.00 p.c.) and sell 3X6 USD FRA at 2.07 p.c. (equivalent to lending at 2.07 p.c.)

QUESTION 45: TOPIC: Fwd/fwds, FRAs, Money market Futures and Swaps

ANSWER: D: Monday 19th March 201X

US Dollars are a currency traded from Spot therefore the forward/forward period hedged by this FRA is three months commencing on Monday 19th March 201X.

QUESTION 46: TOPIC: Fwd/fwds, FRAs, Money market Futures and Swaps

ANSWER: A: all of these

All these statements correctly identify the differences between OTC IRS, FRAs and exchange traded futures.

QUESTION 47: TOPIC: Fwd/fwds, FRAs, Money market Futures and Swaps

ANSWER: D: Forward Rate Agreement (FRA) and Non Deliverable Forward (NDF)

The two examples of contracts for difference are the FRA and the NDF.

QUESTION 48: TOPIC: Fwd/fwds, FRAs, Money market Futures and Swaps

ANSWER: C: USD 5,000.00

ACI Formula sheet (not provided). Data: 100 contracts, not current front month contract therefore tick value: 0.005, 2 'points' profit (USD 25.00 per point), ANSWER: USD 5,000.00.

QUESTION 49: TOPIC: Options

ANSWER: A: unlimited downside risk, limited profit potential

As a writer or seller you are obliged to complete the contract if exercised (at the buyer's option). The buyer will only exercise if the option is In the money (for him) meaning a loss to you. The only profit you will make is the Premium received, much of which will be needed to delta hedge the risk position. A sold option therefore gives unlimited risk limited profit.

QUESTION 50: TOPIC: Options

ANSWER: D: CHF 60,000

Premium of this option is 0.02 X USD 3,000,000 = CHF 60,000.00.

QUESTION 51: TOPIC: Options

ANSWER: D: to reduce the market risk by an offsetting cash position

Delta hedging is an options hedging strategy that aims to reduce the market risk associated with price movements in the underlying market by an offsetting cash position to the percentage indicated by the delta.

QUESTION 52: TOPIC: Options

ANSWER: B: As part of the daily variation margin

The premium for exchange-traded options is normally paid as part of the daily variation margin.

QUESTION 53: TOPIC: Options

ANSWER: B: the price at which the option may be exercised

The strike price of an OTC currency option is the price at which the option may be exercised.

QUESTION 54: TOPIC: Options

ANSWER: D: Vega

Vega (not a true Greek letter) is an estimate of how much the theoretical value of an option changes when volatility changes by 1.00%.

QUESTION 55: TOPIC: Principles of ALM

ANSWER: D: the difference between the duration of assets and liabilities

A Duration gap is the difference between the duration of assets and liabilities.

QUESTION 56: TOPIC: Principles of ALM

ANSWER: A: Modern matched-maturity systems differentiate transfer prices by the maturity of the commitment and also apply a marginal funding cost perspective

Modern matched-maturity systems differentiate transfer prices by the maturity of the commitment and also apply a marginal funding cost perspective.

QUESTION 57: TOPIC: Principles of ALM

ANSWER: D: >20% of regulatory capital

Losses of up to 20% of regulatory capital would generally be considered excessive

QUESTION 58: TOPIC: Principles of ALM

ANSWER: B: Rising CHF interest rates

A customer sells a 3-month Euro Swiss Franc (EUROSWISS) futures contract to hedge against CHF interest rates rising.

QUESTION 59: TOPIC: Principles of ALM

ANSWER: B: hedging a long US Government bond position with a USD payer's swap involves basis risk

Hedging a long US Government bond position with a USD payer's swap is an asset swap and involves basis risk.

QUESTION 60: TOPIC: Principles of ALM

ANSWER: D: Effective Expected Positive Exposure

Under Basel rules EEPE is Effective Expected Positive Exposure.

QUESTION 61: TOPIC: Principles of ALM

ANSWER: A: interest rate risk

The principal risk identified by Gap (Mismatch) management reportage is interest rate risk.

QUESTION 62: TOPIC: Principles of ALM

ANSWER: C: by imposing minimum reserve requirements

Central banks in many financial centres seek to control a local bank's liquidity position by imposing minimum reserve requirements.

QUESTION 63: TOPIC: Principles of Risk

ANSWER: D: The risk your position might change in value because of a move in the rate/price

Market risk is best defined as the risk your position might change in value (P&L) because of a move in the rate/price of a position. No position = No risk.

QUESTION 64: TOPIC: Principles of Risk

ANSWER: A: the time the portfolio or position is not altered or sold

The holding period used in any VaR calculation is defined as being the time the portfolio or position is not altered or sold.

QUESTION 65: TOPIC: Principles of Risk

ANSWER: A: Equity

In assessing Market Risk in the Trading Book of those items mentioned only Equity counts as Tier One capital.

QUESTION 66: TOPIC: Principles of Risk

ANSWER: D: IFXCO

IFXCO – the international foreign exchange and currency options master agreement including 'close-out netting' is a means to mitigate market replacement risk by bi-lateral agreement.

QUESTION 67: TOPIC: Principles of Risk

ANSWER: C: Required Stable Funding

Under Basel III rules the meaning of RSF is Required Stable Funding.

QUESTION 68: TOPIC: Principles of Risk

ANSWER: D: to pay for unexpected losses

The purpose of Risk Capital is to pay for unexpected losses.

QUESTION 69: TOPIC: Principles of Risk

ANSWER: A: Mark-to-model valuation refers to prices determined by financial models, rather than actual market prices.

Under the Advanced internal rated based (A-IRB) approach mark-to-model valuation refers to prices determined by financial models, rather than actual market prices.

QUESTION 70: TOPIC: Principles of Risk

ANSWER: C: Operational

Fraud is generally considered to be an Operational risk.

End of Mock examination No. 2

ACI Dealing Certificate MOCK EXAMINATION No. 3 - ANSWERS

QUESTION 1: TOPIC: Basic Interest Rate Calculations

ANSWER: D: 3.325 p.c.

ACI formulae (not included) Data: 3 months (91 days): 0.029, 3s v. 6s fwd/fwd (92 days): 0.037187, annual basis: Act/360. ANSWER: 3.325 p.c.

QUESTION 2: TOPIC: Basic Interest Rate Calculations

ANSWER: A: WMBA

The WMBA (Wholesale Market Brokers Association) in London is responsible for calculating and announcing the daily SONIA (Sterling OverNight Index Average) fixing.

QUESTION 3: TOPIC: Basic Interest Rate Calculations

ANSWER: C: USD 8,626,087.84

ACI formulae (not included) Data: FV: 10,000,000.00, 5 year int rate: 0.03. ANSWER: USD 8,626,087.84.

QUESTION 4: TOPIC: Basic Interest Rate Calculations

ANSWER: A: 1.327 p.c.

ACI formulae (not included) Data: 3 months (90 days): 0.015, 3s v. 6s fwd/fwd (90 days): 0.0115, annual basis: Act/360. ANSWER: 1.327156 (rounded to 1.327 p.c.)

QUESTION 5: TOPIC: Basic Interest Rate Calculations

ANSWER: D: 2 5/16 p.c.

The nearest fractions equivalent to 1/16 p.c. either side of the rate of 2.30 p.c. are either 2 1/4 (2.25) or 2 5/16 (2.3125). Rounding UP to the nearest fraction means that 2 5/16 p.c. is the correct solution.

QUESTION 6: TOPIC: Basic Interest Rate Calculations

ANSWER: B: Positive

If long term rates are higher than short term rates the yield curve will slope upwards from left to right and will be described as being "Positive".

QUESTION 7: TOPIC: Cash Money markets Theory

ANSWER: D: a Repo trade (of a maturity over one day) with a fixed end or maturity date

According to the Bank of England Gilt Repo Code of best practice a term Repo is a Repo trade (of a maturity over one day) with a fixed end or maturity date.

QUESTION 8: TOPIC: Cash Money markets Theory

ANSWER: D: US Domestic CP is quoted on a discount rate and ECP is quoted on a true yield basis

The major difference between US Domestic Commercial Paper and ECP (Euro Commercial Paper) issued in London denominated in US Dollars is that US Domestic Commercial Paper is quoted on a discount rate and ECP (Euro Commercial Paper) is quoted on a yield basis.

QUESTION 9: TOPIC: Cash Money markets Theory

ANSWER: C: principal invested OUT on value date, principal plus interest IN on maturity date

The purchase of a GBP Certificate of Deposit at issue (to be held to maturity) gives rise to the following cash flows: principal invested OUT on value date, principal plus interest IN on maturity date.

QUESTION 10: TOPIC: Cash Money markets Theory

ANSWER: D: Semi-annual money market yield of 2.50 p.c.

The more frequently interest is paid the better the return. Here a semiannual rate provides the best return and a money market basis on a full year (actual/360) is always better than the bond basis (30/360).

QUESTION 11: TOPIC: Cash Money markets Theory

ANSWER: A: BA or bank bill

Bankers Acceptances (BAs) and Bank Bills (Bills of Exchange) are often referred to as "two-named paper" as the issuer and the acceptor are connected with the instrument.

QUESTION 12: TOPIC: Cash Money markets Theory

ANSWER: D: the Japanese Government

If you deal a single currency Repo in which the collateral is a JGB, then you have dealt in collateral issued by the Japanese Government. (JGB = Japanese Government Bond).

QUESTION 13: TOPIC: Cash Money markets Calculations

ANSWER: A: GBP 14,941,666.10

ACI formulae page 3 Data: face value: 15,000,000.00, yield (30 days): 0.0475 (LIBOR 4.00 plus 0.75), annual basis: Act/365. ANSWER: GBP 14,941,666.10.

QUESTION 14: TOPIC: Cash Money markets Calculations

ANSWER: A: USD 10,049,689.44.

ACI formulae page 3 Data: principal: 10,000,000.00, issue rate (180 days coupon): 0.0225, Sec CD yield (90 days): 0.025 (market maker's offer), annual basis: Act/360. ANSWER: USD 10,049,689.44.

QUESTION 15: TOPIC: Cash Money markets Calculations

ANSWER: C: EUR 5,072,874.16

ACI formulae page 3 Data: principal: 5,000,000.00, issue rate (182 days): 0.03, Sec CD yield (7 days): 0.03, annual basis: Act/360. ANSWER: EUR 5,072,874.16.

QUESTION 16: TOPIC: Cash Money markets Calculations

ANSWER: C: A 90 day CD for USD 5 million at an issue rate of 3 p.c. is worth USD 5,037,500.00 at maturity

Simple int formula Data: principal: USD 5 million, issue (coupon) rate of 0.03, annual basis: Act/360. ANSWER: USD 5,037,500.00 (principal plus int).

QUESTION 17: TOPIC: Cash Money markets Calculations

ANSWER: C: EUR 9,886,308.36

The dirty price of the bunds is EUR 10,008,219.18 and as repoer, the dealer is charged 1.25% margin (haircut) meaning the cash he receives is EUR 9,884,660.92 on which he pays repo interest of EUR 1,647.44 (9,884,660.92 X 0.02 X 3 / 360) and so the maturity consideration repaid is EUR 9,886,308.36.

QUESTION 18: TOPIC: Cash Money markets Calculations

ANSWER: A: USD 24,961,111.11

ACI formulae page 3 Data: face value: USD 25,000,000.00, discount rate(14 days): 0.04, annual basis: Act/360. ANSWER: USD 24,961,111.11

QUESTION 19: TOPIC: Foreign exchange Theory

ANSWER: D: the differential between the interest rates in the two currencies for that period

In all forward dealing the discount or premium between the spot and the forward price of one currency against another is directly proportionate to the difference in interest rates between the two currencies involved for the period in question in the Eurocurrency money markets (provided both are freely convertible currencies.)

QUESTION 20: TOPIC: Foreign exchange Theory

ANSWER: B: as FX swap points

Forward foreign exchange rates quoted in the interbank market are expressed as FX swap points – equivalent to the interest differential between the two currencies.

QUESTION 21: TOPIC: Foreign exchange Theory

ANSWER: C: an electronic deal matching system for Spot FX markets

An electronic deal matching system can be described as a system requiring participants to enter into a restricted access database their credit limits permitting them to deal either as market makers inputting their bid, offer or two way dealing prices or market users.

QUESTION 22: TOPIC: Foreign exchange Theory

ANSWER: C: The number of ounces of silver that can be bought with one ounce of gold

The Gold/Silver ratio is the number of ounces of silver that can be bought with one ounce of gold.

QUESTION 23: TOPIC: Foreign exchange Theory

ANSWER: A: the interest rates in the two currencies.

Forward Foreign exchange swap points are calculated from the interest rates in the two currencies for the period quoted.

QUESTION 24: TOPIC: Foreign exchange Theory

ANSWER: D: GBP interest rates will fall

If the 1 month GBP/USD forward swap points are quoted at a GBP discount they must be quoted High-low. If you set up a position at 30 points your favour that must be on the market maker's offered side (assume a quote of 35-30). You have taken the points your favour and therefore sold and bought Sterling meaning your view on GBP interest rates is that they will fall (assuming Spot GBP/USD and USD interest rates remain the same).

QUESTION 25: TOPIC: Foreign exchange Theory

ANSWER: D: you have bought GBP spot against SEK and sold GBP 3 months forward against SEK

If on a quote of 370/350 the customer deals on your forward Offer of GBP of at 350 you have bought GBP spot against SEK and sold GBP 3 months forward against SEK.

QUESTION 26: TOPIC: Foreign exchange Theory

ANSWER: C: Austria, Spain, Germany and Ireland

Of these lists only Austria, Spain, Germany and Ireland are currently all members of the euro zone.

QUESTION 27: TOPIC: Foreign exchange Theory

ANSWER: C: EUR premium would reduce

Here the EUR is at a forward premium (USD discount) so USD interest rates are higher than EUR. IF USD rates fall the swap differential will reduce, i.e. discount swap points will move numerically lower.

QUESTION 28: TOPIC: Foreign exchange Theory

ANSWER: A: AUD interest rates are higher than EUR interest rates in the 6 months

If 6-month EUR/AUD is quoted at 29-32, the EUR is at a forward premium and therefore AUD interest rates are higher than EUR interest rates in the 6 months.

QUESTION 29: TOPIC: Foreign exchange Theory

ANSWER: B: the Canadian "Maple Leaf"

The Canadian "Maple Leaf" bullion coin has a 999.9/1000 gold purity (.9999 fineness).

QUESTION 30: TOPIC: Foreign exchange Theory

ANSWER: B: they widen

If the differential between 3-month USD interest rates and 3-month GBP interest rates widens, the 3-month GBP/USD forward points will also widen.

QUESTION 31: TOPIC: Foreign exchange Calculations

ANSWER: D: 21/19

Subtract the forward outright from the spot rate (left from left and right from right) to calculate the swap points to be 21-19.

QUESTION 32: TOPIC: Foreign exchange Calculations

ANSWER: D: 111/106

Divide the difference between the prices by 90 and multiply by 60 to achieve the correct 5 months forward price (assuming straight line interpolation).

QUESTION 33: TOPIC: Foreign exchange Calculations

ANSWER: B: 1.6270

ACI formula page 7 Data: Spot GBP/USD (mid-point): 1.6347, Ccy1 Bid (91 days): 0.0593, Ccy2 Offer (91 days): 0.0394, annual basis: GBP: Act/365, USD: Act/360 = 1.6270.

QUESTION 34: TOPIC: Foreign exchange Calculations

ANSWER: A: JPY 1,250,000

One point on USD 1 million in USD/JPY is worth JPY 10,000 (calculated from the number of decimal places) therefore 25 points X USD 5 million X JPY 10,000 = he has LOST JPY 1,250,000

QUESTION 35: TOPIC: Foreign exchange Calculations

ANSWER: A: Profit USD 32,000.00

Short EUR/USD and market closes lower. One point on EUR 1 million in EUR/USD is worth USD 100.00 (calculated from the number of decimal places) therefore here the books show a PROFIT of (1.3787 minus 1.3755) 32 points on EUR 10 million 10 X 32 X 100 = USD 32,000.00.

QUESTION 36: TOPIC: Foreign exchange Calculations

ANSWER: C: 47 pts GBP Discount

1 month outright USD/CHFY 1.0000 minus 0.0007 = 0.9993 X 1 months outright GBP/USD 1.6500 minus 0.0035 = 1.6465. 0.9993 X 1.6465 = 1.6453 (outright GBP/CHF). Spot GBP/CHF: 1.6500 X 1.0000 = 1.6500, therefore mid GBP/CHF swap points: 1.6500-1.6453 = 47 pts lower than spot therefore GBP Discount (swap would be quoted high-low in dealer terms).

QUESTION 37: TOPIC: Fwd/fwds, FRAs, Money market Futures and Swaps

ANSWER: D: Revaluation against the closing price on the exchange

The variation margin on a futures contract is calculated daily against the closing price on the exchange and is payable to your clearing member or the Exchange by 10 a.m. the day following valuation date.

QUESTION 38: TOPIC: Fwd/fwds, FRAs, Money market Futures and Swaps

ANSWER: A: an OTC instrument to swap interest rate payments or receipts

An interest rate swap is an OTC instrument enabling counterparties to swap interest rate payments or receipts over an agreed period.

QUESTION 39: TOPIC: Fwd/fwds, FRAs, Money market Futures and Swaps

ANSWER: D: You will pay GBP 123,287.67

You are the fixed rate payer in a 5 year GBP interest rate swap nominal principal GBP 100 million fixed v. 6 months LIBOR. The fixed rate is 2.25 p.c. and back in March 201X the floating rate until this month's re-rating date (March to September 201X) was set at 2.00 p.c. meaning that the net payment to be made is 0.25 p.c. (100,000,000 X 0.25 X 180 / 365 X 100) = GBP 123,287.67. You, the fixed rate payer will pay a net figure of GBP 123,287.67 to the floating rate payer.

QUESTION 40: TOPIC: Fwd/fwds, FRAs, Money market Futures and Swaps

ANSWER: D: buy a 1X4 USD FRA at 2.10 p.c.

To hedge this risk against rates rising the corporate treasurer should buy a 1-4 USD FRA at 2.10 p.c.

QUESTION 41: TOPIC: Fwd/fwds, FRAs, Money market Futures and Swaps

ANSWER: A: 23rd March 201X

USD are always settled on Spot date therefore the USD LIBOR rate two days before the start of the forward/forward FRA period (23rd March 201X) will be used as the settlement rate for the derivative.

QUESTION 42: TOPIC: Fwd/fwds, FRAs, Money market Futures and Swaps

ANSWER: B: daily

Variation margin (marking to market outstanding futures position to determine profits and losses) is settled on a daily basis.

QUESTION 43: TOPIC: Fwd/fwds, FRAs, Money market Futures and Swaps

ANSWER: D: 100 minus the implied forward-forward interest rate

Short Sterling STIR futures contracts are quoted on NYSE Euronext.liffe on an index basis i.e. 100 minus the implied forward-forward interest rate.

QUESTION 44: TOPIC: Fwd/fwds, FRAs, Money market Futures and Swaps

ANSWER: A: Short June ED futures, short 3s v. 6s USD FRA

The only valid arbitrage position of those listed is: Short June ED futures, short 3s v. 6s USD FRA.

QUESTION 45: TOPIC: Fwd/fwds, FRAs, Money market Futures and Swaps

ANSWER: C: an exchange of fixed for floating interest flows over a 2 year period

Of these definitions the only one which describes a plain vanilla interest rate swap is 'an exchange of fixed for floating interest flows over a 2 year period'.

QUESTION 46: TOPIC: Fwd/fwds, FRAs, Money market Futures and Swaps

ANSWER: C: EUR FRA

An FRA is a contract for difference (here denominated in EUR) whereas all the other instruments noted can be described as being negotiable or tradable.

QUESTION 47: TOPIC: Fwd/fwds, FRAs, Money market Futures and Swaps

ANSWER: A: March ED futures 98.00 ask, 1X4 USD FRAs Offered at 1.95 p.c.

Of these possible cross product positions only the purchase of March ED futures at the 98.00 ask price and the purchase of 1X4 USD FRAs at the Offered rate of 1.95 p.c. would produce a profitable arbitrage.

QUESTION 48: TOPIC: Fwd/fwds, FRAs, Money market Futures and Swaps

ANSWER: B: receive LIBOR floating, pay 3 year fixed

Of the choices available the only structure to suit your requirements would be to receive LIBOR floating and pay 3 year fixed.

QUESTION 49: TOPIC: Options

ANSWER: A: Buy a USD Put/CHF Call

If a corporate treasurer wants to hedge against the CHF appreciating against the USD, he should Buy a USD Put/CHF Call - giving him the right to sell USD BUY CHF at the chosen level.

QUESTION 50: TOPIC: Options

ANSWER: C: the options have moved ITM and you should hold 60% of the position in cash as a delta hedge

If you are short GBP Puts/USD Calls strike 1.7500 and the delta of the position is 0.45 and then moves to 0.60 this means that the options have moved ITM (in the money) and there is a greater probability of the options being exercised and you should hold 60% of the position in cash as an anticipatory hedge.

QUESTION 51: TOPIC: Options

ANSWER: D: 1.3700

EUR Call/USD Put strike price 1.3600 plus 0.100 premium = break-even of 1.3700.

QUESTION 52: TOPIC: Options

ANSWER: C: Long cap and short floor at zero premium

A collar is a simultaneous purchase of a Cap and Sale of a Floor at differing strike prices. Where the premium payable on the Cap purchase equals the premium receivable on the Floor sale this is described as a zero cost collar.

QUESTION 53: TOPIC: Options

ANSWER: C: 1.3715

The Break-even of a purchased Call option is strike plus premium paid. EUR 10,000,000 at 1.3700 is USD 13,700,000 plus premium paid 15,000.00 = USD 13,715,000 divided by 10,000,000 = break-even of 1.3715.

QUESTION 54: TOPIC: Options

ANSWER: A: buy a USD Put / JPY Call and sell a USD Call / JPY Put at the same strike price with the same expiry

To construct a Synthetic Short position in USD against JPY you should buy a USD Put / JPY Call and sell a USD Call / JPY Put at the same strike price with the same expiry. Market up counterparty exercises against you and you sell USD. Market down you exercise your Put option and you sell USD.

QUESTION 55: TOPIC: Principles of ALM

ANSWER: B: as a given deposit with a term of one month and a taken deposit with a term of four months

A sold JUN 3-month STIR-future should be reported in the gap report as of 22 May under its quasi cash movements: a given deposit (loan or asset) with a term of one month and a taken deposit (liability) with a term of four months.

QUESTION 56: TOPIC: Principles of ALM

ANSWER: C: lengthen the maturity of its asset portfolio

If the bank expects interest rates to fall with a parallel downward shift in the yield curve, if it wants to benefit from this view it should lengthen the maturity of its asset portfolio.

QUESTION 57: TOPIC: Principles of ALM

ANSWER: C: Planning the maturity structure and net funding requirements arising from banking book and trading book transactions.

Planning the maturity structure and net funding requirements arising from banking book and trading book transactions is part of the typical scope of Asset Liability Management.

QUESTION 58: TOPIC: Principles of ALM

ANSWER: B: the specification and management of the bank's market risk

ALCO is responsible for the specification and management of the bank's market risk.

QUESTION 59: TOPIC: Principles of ALM

ANSWER: C: A negative gap of GBP 200 million

With maturing liabilities greater than assets in the 3-6 month time bucket the gap for this period can be described as being 'a negative gap of GBP 200 million'.

QUESTION 60: TOPIC: Principles of ALM

ANSWER: C: a minimum 3.0 % leverage ratio

In addition to the Liquidity Coverage Ratio and the Net Stable funding ratio, Basel III introduces a minimum 3.0 % leverage ratio.

QUESTION 61: TOPIC: Principles of ALM

ANSWER: D: if an anticipated underlying risk is no longer certain to occur

Of these, the only valid reason to discontinue hedge accounting is if an anticipated underlying risk is now no longer certain to occur.

QUESTION 62: TOPIC: Principles of ALM

ANSWER: A: lending long, borrowing short

As the yield curve steepens a strategy of lending long, borrowing short would give rise to a negative mark to market as the yield curve steepens.

QUESTION 63: TOPIC: Principles of Risk

ANSWER: A: the time the portfolio or position is not altered or sold

The holding period used in any VaR calculation is defined as being the time the portfolio or position is not altered or sold.

QUESTION 64: TOPIC: Principles of Risk

ANSWER: B: problems with processing, product pricing, and valuation

For Basel capital purposes Operational risk in foreign exchange involves problems with processing, product pricing, and valuation.

QUESTION 65: TOPIC: Principles of Risk

ANSWER: D: a purchase of a USD CD from Mega Bank originally issued by Major Bank

The credit risk on a secondary market CD (here purchased from Mega Bank) is on the original issuer - Major Bank.

QUESTION 66: TOPIC: Principles of Risk

ANSWER: D: Credit Conversion Factor

Under Basel rules the meaning of CCF is Credit Conversion Factor.

QUESTION 67: TOPIC: Principles of Risk

ANSWER: D: a minimum common equity capital ratio of 4.5 % and a capital conservation buffer of 2.5 %

Under Basel III a minimum common equity capital ratio of 4.5 % and a capital conservation buffer of 2.5 % are required.

QUESTION 68: TOPIC: Principles of Risk

ANSWER: D: all of these

Operational risk, legal risk and liquidity risk are all increased by taking collateral which is merely for the reduction, mitigation of credit risk on the counterparty to any transaction – therefore 'all of these'.

QUESTION 69: TOPIC: Principles of Risk

ANSWER: B: Operational

Fraud is generally considered to be an Operational risk.

QUESTION 70: TOPIC: Principles of Risk

ANSWER: D: 99% confidence level and 10-day holding period.

BIS guidelines for calculations in bank VaR models require a 99% confidence level and a 10-day holding period.

End of Mock examination No. 3

QUESTION 1: TOPIC: Basic Interest Rate Calculations

ANSWER: B: 0.7029

Formula (not included in ACI formulae sheet) Data: EUR/GBP: 0.7000, EUR int rate (180 days): 0.029, EUR annual basis: Act/360, GBP int rate (180 days): 0.038, GBP annual basis: Act/365 = 0.7029.

QUESTION 2: TOPIC: Basic Interest Rate Calculations

ANSWER: D: 2 and 3 months standard period interest rates

To calculate a 2 1/2 months interest rate from spot you need the standard period interest rates for the periods either side i.e. 2 months and 3 months.

QUESTION 3: TOPIC: Basic Interest Rate Calculations

ANSWER: A: i) 03/04 inverted, ii) 03/05 positive

Interest rates quoted here indicate a negative yield curve on the first date (3rd April) which reverses and becomes positive on the second date (3rd May), therefore the correct answer is i) inverted and ii) positive.

QUESTION 4: TOPIC: Basic Interest Rate Calculations

ANSWER: D: 1 to 12 months standard period interest rates

To plot a spot yield curve you need the 1 to 12 months standard period interest rates from spot value.

QUESTION 5: TOPIC: Basic Interest Rate Calculations

ANSWER: B: Daily fixing for EUR interbank money market rates in the European market

EURIBOR is the official daily fixing for EUR interbank deposit rates in the European market as calculated by the ECB.

QUESTION 6: TOPIC: Basic Interest Rate Calculations

ANSWER: B: market sentiment is that over time interest rates will fall

The shape of a yield curve is one of many pointers as to current market sentiment in respect of the anticipated level of interest rates. A negative yield curve identifies the market's sentiment that over time interest rates are going to fall. Demand for short term money exceed supply and the professional market is looking to lend now at higher rates than anticipated in the future (supply exceeding demand). The maxim being "If you believe rates are going lower then borrow only on short term rather than lock into longer term rates which may indeed be cheaper tomorrow".

QUESTION 7: TOPIC: Cash Money markets Theory

ANSWER: A: 1.85 p.c.

Buying a primary Certificate of Deposit is like lending the issuer money. Selling on a CD in the secondary market is like bidding for a deposit. Therefore to make a profit on trading CDs during the same dealing day you must sell them at a lower rate of interest than you originally bought them, here 1.85 p.c.

QUESTION 8: TOPIC: Cash Money markets Theory

ANSWER: B: the break-even rate at which it is possible to buy a bond, repo it out and sell a futures contract

The implied repo rate is the break-even rate at which it is possible to buy a bond, repo it out and sell a futures contract (cash and carry arbitrage).

QUESTION 9: TOPIC: Cash Money markets Theory

ANSWER: B: A 3-month deposit of USD 10,000,000.00 offered by a US bank in London

A 3-month USD deposit offered by a US bank in London can be referred to as a Eurocurrency transaction as it is traded away from the currency's domestic centre (New York) i.e. a deposit placed in a currency (USD) not the local currency of the dealing centre (London = GBP).

QUESTION 10: TOPIC: Cash Money markets Theory

ANSWER: A: US BA, US T-bill, US CP

US Bankers Acceptances, US T-Bills and US Domestic Commercial Paper are all Discount instruments redeemed at face value at maturity.

QUESTION 11: TOPIC: Cash Money markets Theory

ANSWER: A: It is a negotiable instrument

A CD is a negotiable instrument. A buyer of a CD can sell the security in the secondary market if funds are required earlier than maturity date of the certificate.

QUESTION 12: TOPIC: Cash Money markets Theory

ANSWER: D: provides Sell/buy backs with a legal framework

The latest version of the Global Master Repurchase Agreement provides Sell/buy backs with a legal framework.

QUESTION 13: TOPIC: Cash Money markets Calculations

ANSWER: B: USD 9,948,888.89

ACI formulae page 3 Data: face value: USD 10,000,000.00, discount rate (92 days): 0.02, annual basis: Act/360. ANSWER: USD 9,948,888.89.

QUESTION 14: TOPIC: Cash Money markets Calculations

ANSWER: D: a gain of USD 373,599.00

ACI formulae page 3 Data: principal: 50,000,000.00, issue rate (90 days): 0.045, Sec CD yield (30 days): 0.045, annual basis: Act/360. ANSWER: USD 50,373,599.00 a gain of USD 373,599.00.

QUESTION 15: TOPIC: Cash Money markets Calculations

ANSWER: C: GBP 51,250,000.00

If as repoer the dealer is able to charge 2.50% margin (haircut) on a cash advance of GBP 50,000,000 the value of collateral will be 50,000,000 X 1.025 = USD 51,250,000.00.

QUESTION 16: TOPIC: Cash Money markets Calculations

ANSWER: C: USD 19,897,197.81

ACI formulae page 3 Data: face value: USD 20,000,000.00, yield (30 days): 0.062 (LIBOR 6.00 + 0.20), annual basis: Act/360. ANSWER: USD 19,897,197.81.

QUESTION 17: TOPIC: Cash Money markets Calculations

ANSWER: D: Blair Bank Paris, EUR 4,989,583.33

ACI formulae page 3 Data: face value: EUR 5,000,000.00, discount rate (30 days): 0.025 (the best offer of BAs/bid for cash), annual basis: Act/360. ANSWER: Blair Bank Paris at 2.50 p.c. and will pay EUR 4,989,583.33 for your purchase of BAs.

QUESTION 18: TOPIC: Cash Money markets Calculations

ANSWER: A: GBP 20,176,988.75

ACI formulae page 3. Data: principal: 20,000,000.00, issue rate (181 days): 0.0375, Sec CD yield (91 days): 0.03875 (market maker's Bid), annual basis: Act/365. ANSWER: A: GBP 20,176,988.75

QUESTION 19: TOPIC: Foreign exchange Theory

ANSWER: B: it will move towards par

Here the USD is at a forward premium (GBP discount) so USD interest rates are currently lower than GBP. IF USD rates rise the swap differential will narrow, i.e. move towards par.

QUESTION 20: TOPIC: Foreign exchange Theory

ANSWER: D: 6 months EUR rates are lower than 6 months GBP rates

The only thing you can positively identify from this quote is that the EUR is at a Premium (GBP is at a Discount) therefore EUR interest rates are lower than GBP in the 6 months period.

QUESTION 21: TOPIC: Foreign exchange Theory

ANSWER: B: if not dealt on immediately, the price is subject to change and should be rechecked before dealing

In basic spot FX dealing terminology "Your risk" indicates to the receiver of the quote that, if not dealt on immediately, the price may have to be re-quoted at the receiver's risk.

QUESTION 22: TOPIC: Foreign exchange Theory

ANSWER: A: A time/delivery forward contract

A time/delivery option forward contract involves physical settlement of the currency amounts on one or more value dates (i.e. a contractual obligation during the option period).

QUESTION 23: TOPIC: Foreign exchange Theory

ANSWER: B: a screen-based anonymous dealing system for professional spot traders

An example of an automatic trading system (ATS) or electronic broker in the spot FX market is EBS which is described as "a screen-based anonymous dealing system for professional spot traders, operating 24 hours a day, and seven days a week.

QUESTION 24: TOPIC: Foreign exchange Theory

ANSWER: B: commission paid by both parties at rates agreed beforehand

Voice-brokers in spot FX are remunerated with commission paid by both parties at rates agreed beforehand.

QUESTION 25: TOPIC: Foreign exchange Theory

ANSWER: C: the original n-d-f exchange rate is compared with the current spot and the difference is settled on value date

On fixing date the original n-d-f exchange rate is compared with the current spot and the difference is settled by a difference payment on value date (fixing date + 2).

QUESTION 26: TOPIC: Foreign exchange Theory

ANSWER: B: Big figure = 107, points adjustment -1.00

If the mid-point Spot EUR/JPY is quoted: 108.00 and 6 months forward swap is quoted: 100 points EUR Discount, the outright rate (108.00 minus 1.84 points = 107.00) can be described as Big figure = 107 and points adjustment minus 100 (-100).

QUESTION 27: TOPIC: Foreign exchange Theory

ANSWER: D: A market situation where prices for future delivery are lower than the spot price

In precious metals trading 'Backwardation' is a market situation where prices for future delivery are lower than the spot price caused by shortage or tightness of supply.

QUESTION 28: TOPIC: Foreign exchange Theory

ANSWER: D: 31st March

Because of "End/end" convention the forward dealing value date for 1 month deals dealt for Spot value 27th February will be Tuesday (Wednesday in a leap year) 31st March.

QUESTION 29: TOPIC: Foreign exchange Theory

ANSWER: B: it eliminates credit risk with the counterparty

There will always be credit risk in FX swaps. The counterparty could cease trading any time between deal date and the value date of the forward leg of any FX swap. This is deemed to be a market replacement risk. The other three alternatives can all be used to describe the linked set of transactions making up an FX swap.

QUESTION 30: TOPIC: Foreign exchange Theory

ANSWER: A: 23 – 25

You have given 'Voice-brokers Limited' a better Offer than he was quoting therefore your Offer of 25 replaces the previous offer of 27 making his new price to the market 23 – 25.

QUESTION 31: TOPIC: Foreign exchange Calculations

ANSWER: B: 1.6605

The outright is 1.6500. The forward points are quoted 110-105 therefore the points are subtracted from the spot to achieve the outright quote. The bank is selling GBP so the dealer uses the Spot offer (of GBP) and the Offered points -105, meaning that the Spot rate must be 1.6500 + 0.0105 = 1.6605.

QUESTION 32: TOPIC: Foreign exchange Calculations

ANSWER: D: KRW 10,000,000 payable to Seoul International Industries

The n-d-f is marked to market using the comparator rate of 1091.00. Seoul International Industries bought the n-d-f to protect against the USD rising. The USD has risen and the payment KRW 10,000,000 (USD 10 million at 1091.00 less USD 10 million at 1090.00) is in favour of the client Seoul International Industries and will be paid on value date (fixing plus 2).

QUESTION 33: TOPIC: Foreign exchange Calculations

ANSWER: D: 1.00005

You can buy CHF value spot at 1.0000 and you can buy and sell CHF (Sell and Buy USD) at 1/2 (0.00005) point your favour therefore ADD 0.00005 to 1.0000 = 1.00005.

QUESTION 34: TOPIC: Foreign exchange Calculations

ANSWER: B: Profit JPY 720,000

Having sold EUR at JPY 146.60 per CHF you revalue and can now buy them back lower at 146.00 therefore by marking to market at this rate you can record a profit of JPY 720,000.

QUESTION 35: TOPIC: Foreign exchange Calculations

ANSWER: A: 198 pts GBP discount

ACI formula page 7 Data: Spot GBP/USD: 1.6600, USD int rate (180 days): 0.0175, annual basis: Act/360, GBP int rate (180 days): 0.0425, annual basis: Act/365. ANSWER: 198 pts GBP Discount.

QUESTION 36: TOPIC: Foreign exchange Calculations

ANSWER: B: 1.62098/1.62153

Either use the reverse logic approach for ante spot calculations (add GBP discount and subtract GBP premium) or think about the adjustment to the near date rate i.e. the rate for tomorrow against spot.

QUESTION 37: TOPIC: Fwd/fwds, FRAs, Money market Futures and Swaps

ANSWER: D: 14th June

The fixing date for a eurocurrency FRA (here USD) settled against LIBOR is always two days before the start (Settlement) date of the FRA here 14th June for the settlement date 16th June 201X.

QUESTION 38: TOPIC: Fwd/fwds, FRAs, Money market Futures and Swaps

ANSWER: D: 2.15 p.c.

Data: equiv int rate1 (90 days): 0.0198, equiv int rate2 (90 days): 0.023. ANSWER: 2.14(9569) p.c. rounded to 2.15 p.c.

QUESTION 39: TOPIC: Fwd/fwds, FRAs, Money market Futures and Swaps

ANSWER: D: should make clear their intention to do so when initially negotiating the deal

Principals who enter into an interest rate swap with the intention of shortly afterwards assigning or transferring the swap to a third party should make clear their intention to do so when initially negotiating the deal.

QUESTION 40: TOPIC: Fwd/fwds, FRAs, Money market Futures and Swaps

ANSWER: A: sell 40 Short Sterling June at 97.90 and sell 40 Short Sterling September contracts at 97.87

ACI Formula sheet (not provided). Data: equiv int rate1 (90 days): 0.021 p.c., equiv int rate2 (90 days): 0.0213 ANSWER: June/Set strip in 40 contracts at 2.12(059) p.c. which is better than buying the 2s v. 10s FRA at 2.15 p.c.

QUESTION 41: TOPIC: Fwd/fwds, FRAs, Money market Futures and Swaps

ANSWER: B: the futures price closed below 96.20

If you are being asked to pay a margin call this means your current open interest position is showing a loss. If you are Long of Short Sterling contracts this means the closing price must have been LOWER than 96.20.

QUESTION 42: TOPIC: Fwd/fwds, FRAs, Money market Futures and Swaps

ANSWER: A: two days after maturity by net payment

A USD Overnight Indexed Swap (OIS) is settled two days after maturity by net payment

QUESTION 43: TOPIC: Fwd/fwds, FRAs, Money market Futures and Swaps

ANSWER: D: You will pay the counterparty on settlement date

Under FRABBA terms if the LIBOR rate is higher than the FRA contractual rate then the Seller pays the buyer the discounted difference on settlement date. Here 6.00 is higher than 5.50 therefore you (the seller) will pay the customer (the buyer) the settlement amount on settlement date.

QUESTION 44: TOPIC: Fwd/fwds, FRAs, Money market Futures and Swaps

ANSWER: B: Buy the FRA at 1.36 p.c.

If you are worried about interest rates rising you would buy the FRA. At 1.36 p.c. - better than selling futures at 98.62 (equivalent to an interest rate of 1.38 p.c.).

QUESTION 45: TOPIC: Fwd/fwds, FRAs, Money market Futures and Swaps

ANSWER: A: 25th January 201X

Sterling is a value same day currency therefore the LIBOR rate on the start date of the forward/forward FRA period (25th January 201X) will be used as settlement rate for the derivative.

QUESTION 46: TOPIC: Fwd/fwds, FRAs, Money market Futures and Swaps

ANSWER: B: 3.50 p.c.

If the net payment at maturity is calculated as EUR 4,861.11 in the dealer's favour the average compounded EURONIA for the period was 3.50 p.c.

QUESTION 47: TOPIC: Fwd/fwds, FRAs, Money market Futures and Swaps

ANSWER: D: 1.55 p.c.

ACI formula sheet (page 4): long int rate (90 days): 0.0215, short int rate (30 days): 0.0175, annual basis: Act/360. ANSWER: fwd/fwd interest rate = 1.547228 rounded to 1.55 p.c.

QUESTION 48: TOPIC: Fwd/fwds, FRAs, Money market Futures and Swaps

ANSWER: D: SONIA

SONIA is the Overnight Index for GBP and is used as the floating side of Overnight index swaps.

QUESTION 49: TOPIC: Options

ANSWER: D: Limited profit, unlimited loss

The seller of an option has limited profit potential (maximum premium received) and unlimited loss potential (he has to complete the contract if exercised regardless of where the exchange rate is at that time.

QUESTION 50: TOPIC: Options

ANSWER: C: zero intrinsic value + small time value

An OTM option has zero intrinsic value. Provided the option still has some time to expiry (here one month) its premium will be made up solely of time value.

QUESTION 51: TOPIC: Options

ANSWER: B: an interest rate guarantee involves an up-front premium payable, an FRA does not

Of those available the principal difference between an interest rate guarantee and an FRA is that an interest rate guarantee involves an up-front premium payable, an FRA does not.

QUESTION 52: TOPIC: Options

ANSWER: C: sell a Put and sell a Call at the same ATM strike price with the same expiry

To construct a Short Straddle you must sell a Put and sell a Call at the same ATM strike price with the same expiry.

QUESTION 53: TOPIC: Options

ANSWER: D: USD 3,000.00

Eurodollar 0.01 movement value = USD 25.00. 10 options will cost 10 X 12 X 25.00 = USD 3,000.00.

QUESTION 54: TOPIC: Options

ANSWER: C: A short strangle

By selling a put and selling a call at different strike prices for the same expiry, the dealer has created a Short Strangle position.

QUESTION 55: TOPIC: Principles of ALM

ANSWER: B: as a given deposit with a term of one month and a taken deposit with a term of four months

A sold JUN 3-month STIR-future should be reported in the gap report as of 22 May under its quasi cash movements: a given deposit (loan or asset) with a term of one month and a taken deposit (liability) with a term of four months.

QUESTION 56: TOPIC: Principles of ALM

ANSWER: A: Assets and Liabilities are assessed currency by currency.

Under Basel III, Assets and Liabilities are assessed currency by currency. E.g. Sterling liabilities need to be supported by Sterling assets.

QUESTION 57: TOPIC: Principles of ALM

ANSWER: B: a strategic management tool to manage interest rate risk and liquidity risk

An accurate description of Asset and Liability Management in the dealing room is a strategic management tool to manage interest rate risk and liquidity risk.

QUESTION 58: TOPIC: Principles of ALM

ANSWER: D: Rising interest rates can result in mark-to-market losses on fixed-rate assets.

Rising interest rates can result in mark-to-market losses on fixed-rate assets where these assets carry interest rates below the marked to marked level.

QUESTION 59: TOPIC: Principles of ALM

ANSWER: D: as an asset maturing in 3 months time and a liability maturing in 6 months time

A 3s v. 6s purchased FRA appears in the bank's gap reportage as an asset maturing in 3 months time and a liability maturing in 6 months time.

QUESTION 60: TOPIC: Principles of ALM

ANSWER: C: 6 months

The maximum possible Macaulay Duration of an FRN resetting at 6 months LIBOR is 6 months.

QUESTION 61: TOPIC: Principles of ALM

ANSWER: A: all time horizons which are relevant to banks' maturity profiles

Basel III recommends that stress tests should cover all time horizons which are relevant to banks' maturity profiles.

QUESTION 62: TOPIC: Principles of ALM

ANSWER: D: a means to allocate inter-divisional profits in an equitable fashion

Funds Transfer Pricing, with the rate set by agreement between ALCO and a bank's business unit directors, is a means to allocate inter-divisional profits in an equitable fashion.

QUESTION 63: TOPIC: Principles of Risk

ANSWER: B: The revaluation using appropriate current market rates of dealing risk positions

The term "mark to market" is a method used to revalue dealing risk positions i.e. spot foreign exchange positions can be marked to market using current market rates for Profit and loss and risk evaluation purposes.

QUESTION 64: TOPIC: Principles of Risk

ANSWER: C: Basis risk

Basis risk applies to Futures trading NOT forward foreign exchange transactions.

QUESTION 65: TOPIC: Principles of Risk

ANSWER: D: 1250%

Under Basel Securitisation rules the highest potential risk weight is 1250%.

QUESTION 66: TOPIC: Principles of Risk

ANSWER: D: Risk Weighted Assets

Under Basel rules RWA stands for Risk Weighted Assets

QUESTION 67: TOPIC: Principles of Risk

ANSWER: A: Forward price simulation

Monte Carlo simulation, Variance-covariance approach and Historical simulation are all recognised methods to calculate VaR whereas Forward price simulation is not.

QUESTION 68: TOPIC: Principles of Risk

ANSWER: B: Economic exposure

This sub-heading of Exchange Exposure is referred to as Economic risk.

QUESTION 69: TOPIC: Principles of Risk

ANSWER: C: an exporter invoicing goods and services in USD with its cost base in GBP

Transaction risk is suffered by an exporter invoicing goods and services in USD with its cost base in GBP.

QUESTION 70: TOPIC: Principles of Risk

ANSWER: D: zero

Where you have sold an FRA and interest rates rise by 1% the credit risk is zero. FRAs credit risk is assessed on market replacement risk and where (as in this instance) you would owe the counterparty on settlement there is no risk.

End of Mock examination No. 4

QUESTION 1: TOPIC: Basic Interest Rate Calculations

ANSWER: B: investors lending funds for longer periods expect to earn a higher interest rate

According to the Liquidity Preference Theory investors lending funds for longer periods expect to earn a higher interest rate and are prepared to give up liquidity or access to their money in exchange for the higher interest rate.

QUESTION 2: TOPIC: Basic Interest Rate Calculations

ANSWER: B: 1.28 p.c.

Simple int formula Data: Principal CHF 15.500,000.00, interest (182 days): 100,000.00, annual basis: Act/360. ANSWER: 1.28 p.c.

QUESTION 3: TOPIC: Basic Interest Rate Calculations

ANSWER: A: 4.055 p.c.

ACI formulae page 2 Data: Mmkt int rate: 0.04, ANSWER: 4.055 p.c.

QUESTION 4: TOPIC: Basic Interest Rate Calculations

ANSWER: B: Actual/360

Yen interest in the Euromarkets is calculated on a day count/annual basis convention of Actual/360.

QUESTION 5: TOPIC: Basic Interest Rate Calculations

ANSWER: D: 2.30 p.c.

ACI formulae (not included) Data: Principal: EUR 25,000,000.00, int rate1 (90 days): 0.0225, int rate2 (91 days): 0.0215, int rate3 (92 days): 0.0215, int rate4 (92 days): 0.0219, annual basis: Act/360. ANSWER: 2.30 p.c.

QUESTION 6: TOPIC: Basic Interest Rate Calculations

ANSWER: A: 31st January to 1st February 201X

If today is Thursday 27th January 201X the correct dates for a Spot/Next USD deposit taken in London is Monday 31st January to Tuesday 1st February 201X.

QUESTION 7: TOPIC: Cash Money markets Theory

ANSWER: A: you can raise the currency more cheaply via the FX swap than in the money market

Covered interest arbitrage is possible when the values of the forward points and the interest rate differential between the two currencies diverge and you can raise the currency more cheaply via the FX swap than in the money market.

QUESTION 8: TOPIC: Cash Money markets Theory

ANSWER: A: buy and sell the base currency on the market maker's 6 mos BID FX swap and borrow the variable currency

In an interest arbitrage operation to raise the base currency for 6 months as a market user you must buy and sell the base currency (sell and buy the variable currency) on the left hand side of the swap (the forward BID for base currency) and borrow the variable currency.

QUESTION 9: TOPIC: Cash Money markets Theory

ANSWER: B: discount paying instruments using the Actual/360 annual basis

US Treasury Bills are discount paying instruments quoted as a rate of discount using the Actual/360 annual basis.

QUESTION 10: TOPIC: Cash Money markets Theory

ANSWER: D: CHF Money Market Deposit

A Swiss Franc money market deposit is not negotiable.

QUESTION 11: TOPIC: Cash Money markets Theory

ANSWER: B: secondary market price OUT on value date, face value IN on maturity date

The purchase of a T-Bill in the secondary market gives rise to the following cash flows: secondary market price OUT on value date, face value IN on maturity date.

QUESTION 12: TOPIC: Cash Money markets Theory

ANSWER: B: 8 p.c. semiannual money market yield

The more frequently interest is payable the more attractive the investment. Semi-annual yield rates are therefore better than annual and the annual basis then decides which on money market and bond bases produces the best result. The money market basis pays on an Actual No. of days / 360 whereas the Bond basis only pays 360 / 360. An 8 p.c. payable semiannually on a money market basis is therefore the most attractive return of those quoted.

QUESTION 13: TOPIC: Cash Money markets Calculations

ANSWER: D: USD 20,005,000.00

You have lent USD 20,000,000 cash against a lower amount of collateral (due to the initial margin of 1.75% being charged by the repoer). The maturity consideration will be USD 20,005,000.00 (3 percent for 3 days on USD 20 million).

QUESTION 14: TOPIC: Cash Money markets Calculations

ANSWER: B: USD 19,933,333.33

ACI formulae page 3 Data: face value: USD 20,000,000.00, discount rate (30 days): 0.04, annual basis: Act/360. ANSWER: USD 19,933,333.33.

QUESTION 15: TOPIC: Cash Money markets Calculations

ANSWER: C: 4.04 p.c.

ACI formulae page 3 Data: discount rate (90 days): 0.04, annual basis: Act/365. ANSWER: 4.04 p.c.

QUESTION 16: TOPIC: Cash Money markets Calculations

ANSWER: B: 2.76 p.c.

ACI formulae page 3 Data: discount rate (60 days): 0.0275, annual basis: Act/360. ANSWER: 2.7627 (rounded to 2.76 p.c.).

QUESTION 17: TOPIC: Cash Money markets Calculations

ANSWER: C: EUR 10,102,135.56

ACI formulae page 3 Data: principal: EUR 10,000,000.00, issue rate (90 days): 0.04, yield (180 days): 0.03875, annual basis: Act/360. ANSWER: EUR 10,102,135.56.

QUESTION 18: TOPIC: Cash Money markets Calculations

ANSWER: C: USD 68,996.51

The maturity consideration is the initial consideration USD 9,581,000 plus repo interest calculated at 4.25 for 61 days = 68,996.51 - the answer required here.

QUESTION 19: TOPIC: Foreign exchange Theory

ANSWER: D: 1.3734

The rate quote is so many USD (cents) per EUR therefore you want to buy as many USD per EUR as possible (the highest bid for EUR - the highest rate on the left hand side of the market makers' quotations) hence 1.3734.

QUESTION 20: TOPIC: Foreign exchange Theory

ANSWER: C: Overbought GBP 3 million against USD

Cable is dealers' jargon for the GBP/USD exchange rate quotation. GBP is an indirectly quoted currency to a GBP base and dealers tend to describe their positions in terms of the base currency therefore in this case the dealer is confirming his open position as overbought 3 million Pounds Sterling against USD.

QUESTION 21: TOPIC: Foreign exchange Theory

ANSWER: B: You can buy GBP against EUR

As market user you can buy GBP against EUR at 0.9338 (1.4100 / 1.5100).

QUESTION 22: TOPIC: Foreign exchange Theory

ANSWER: B: multiply the GBP/USD Bid by the USD/CHF Bid

To calculate the rate at which you would buy GBP against CHF as market maker you would multiply the GBP/USD Bid (left hand side) by the USD/CHF Bid (left hand side).

QUESTION 23: TOPIC: Foreign exchange Theory

WHAT IS THE RELATIONSHIP OF THE STERLING EXCHANGE RATE TO THE EURO?

ANSWER: D: it is freely floating

The Sterling exchange rate remains freely floating against the Euro.

QUESTION 24: TOPIC: Foreign exchange Theory

ANSWER: C: Longer term OFFER minus Shorter term BID

To calculate the fwd/fwd right hand side (Offer of USD) adjust the right hand side (OFFER) of the furthest forward swap by the left hand side (BID) of the nearer period. i.e. Longer term OFFER minus Shorter term BID.

QUESTION 25: TOPIC: Foreign exchange Theory

ANSWER: B: The dealer must sell USD/JPY for value tomorrow and buy USD/JPY for value spot

If the dealer is long USD/JPY (Long USD - the base currency) then to roll this position forward Tom/Next the dealer must sell and buy USD (buy and sell JPY) in a Tom/Next swap, value tomorrow against the next day (Spot date).

QUESTION 26: TOPIC: Foreign exchange Theory

ANSWER: D: the interlinking mechanism that connects national RTGS payments systems in EU member states

TARGET2 is the interlinking mechanism that connects national RTGS payments systems in EU member states.

QUESTION 27: TOPIC: Foreign exchange Theory

ANSWER: D: GBP discount would increase

Here the GBP is at a forward discount (USD premium) so GBP interest rates are higher than USD. IF USD interest rates fall the swap differential will increase, i.e. discount swap points will move numerically higher.

QUESTION 28: TOPIC: Foreign exchange Theory

ANSWER: A: GBP interest rates are now higher than USD

If the 3 months forward GBP/USD swap moves from a 5 point GBP Discount to a 3 point GBP Premium and USD interest rates remain the same, GBP interest rates are now higher than USD.

QUESTION 29: TOPIC: Foreign exchange Theory

ANSWER: C: for physical delivery an institution must hold a LOCO account

The principal difference between precious metals trading for physical delivery and book entry is that for physical delivery an institution must hold a LOCO account.

QUESTION 30: TOPIC: Foreign exchange Theory

ANSWER: A: 0.90 98-03

On a spot quote of 0.90 98-03 you can buy USD (sell CHF) at 0.91 03 the best spot offer of USD (bid for CHF) available. The price is quoted 'around the figure' 0.91.

QUESTION 31: TOPIC: Foreign exchange Calculations

ANSWER: C: -125

3 months outright USD/JPY 76.00 less 0.33 = 75.67 X 3 months outright GBP/USD 1.5500 less 0.0097 = 1.5403 making the outright cross rate 116.55. Spot GBP/JPY: 1.5500 X 76.00 = 117.80, therefore mid GBP/JPY swap points: 116.55 minus 117.80 = -1.25 or -125 (Sterling discount) GBP/JPY points (swap would be quoted high-low in dealer terms).

QUESTION 32: EXAMINATION SECTION: TOPIC: Foreign exchange Calculations

ANSWER: D: Buy spot EUR from Bank A at 1.4052 and sell and buy EUR/USD with Bank B spot ag 6 mths at 55 pts

If You buy spot EUR from Bank A at 1.4052 and sell and buy EUR ag USD on Bank B's forward offer (spot against 6 months) at 55 points (against you) your all-in 6 months rate is (1.4052 plus 0.0055) 1.4107.

QUESTION 33: EXAMINATION SECTION: TOPIC: Foreign exchange Calculations

ANSWER: D: 1.3681

1 month swap 12-10 and 2 months swap 26-22. 14 points higher Offer for the extra 1 month (1-2 months) = 7 extra points for the half month (15 days), therefore the price is 17 points to be subtracted from the Spot making the Offer for forward EUR against USD 1.3700 minus 19 = 1.3681.

QUESTION 34: EXAMINATION SECTION: TOPIC: Foreign exchange Calculations

ANSWER: D: 0.8928-33

Data: 1 divided by 1.1200 = EUR Bid/GBP Offer, 1 divided by 1.1195 = EUR Offer/GBP Bid. ANSWER: 0.89928-33.

QUESTION 35: EXAMINATION SECTION: TOPIC: Foreign exchange Calculations

ANSWER: C: USD 1,032,700.00

On a spot AUD/USD quote of 1.03 27-32 you sell AUD 1,000,000 to the market maker's bid of 1.03 27 and you will receive value spot (1,000,000 multiplied by the rate of 1.03 27) = USD 1,032,700.00.

QUESTION 36: EXAMINATION SECTION: TOPIC: Foreign exchange Calculations

ANSWER: D: LOSS USD 45,000

You are short GBP 3 million at a rate of 1.6500 receiving USD 4,950,000.00 and you BUY back GBP at 1.6650 paying USD 4,995,000.00 you would make a loss of USD 45,000.00.

QUESTION 37: TOPIC: Fwd/fwds, FRAs Money market Futures and Swaps

ANSWER: C: You pay GBP 1,225.98

ACI formula sheet (page 4): principal: 10,000,000.00, FRA rate (90 days): 0.023, LIBOR (90 days): 0.028, annual basis: Act/365. ANSWER: you will pay GBP 1,225.98 on settlement date.

QUESTION 38: TOPIC: Fwd/fwds, FRAs Money market Futures and Swaps

ANSWER: B: 4.27 p.c.

ACI formula sheet (not provided): spot ag 3 months (90 days): 0.04, 3s/6s (90 days): 0.045, annual basis: Act/360. ANSWER: 4.27(25) p.c.

QUESTION 39: TOPIC: Fwd/fwds, FRAs Money market Futures and Swaps

ANSWER: A: sell March ED contracts on NYSE Euronext.liffe

If you are short EUR for a three month period commencing in one month's time (spot against 1 v. spot against 4 months) and you are worried about interest rates rising you should sell futures contracts with a delivery date matching the start of the mismatch period – here March 201X.

QUESTION 40: TOPIC: Fwd/fwds, FRAs Money market Futures and Swaps

ANSWER: B: the Euroyen futures contract traded on NYSE Euronext.liffe has a nominal value of JPY 100,000,000

Of these, only the statement 'The Euroyen futures contract trade on NYSE Euronext.liffe has a nominal value of JPY 100,000,000.' is correct.

QUESTION 41: TOPIC: Fwd/fwds, FRAs Money market Futures and Swaps

ANSWER: D: GLOBEX

The electronic trading platform on CME Group Chicago is called GLOBEX.

QUESTION 42: TOPIC: Fwd/fwds, FRAs Money market Futures and Swaps

ANSWER: D: LIBOR

The majority of interest rate swaps and currency swaps under ISDA terms use LIBOR 3 or 6 months as reference rate for the floating side of the agreement.

QUESTION 43: TOPIC: Fwd/fwds, FRAs Money market Futures and Swaps

ANSWER: D: Pay fixed and receive floating through swaps for the term of the portfolio

If you funded your fixed-income investment portfolio with short-term deposits, you could hedge your interest rate exposure by paying fixed and receive floating through an interest rate swap for the term of the portfolio.

QUESTION 44: TOPIC: Fwd/fwds, FRAs Money market Futures and Swaps

ANSWER: C: a 3s v. 6s 90 day FRA 'bid-offer' price coinciding with the Sept 1X futures nominal dates

The IMM September price the broker is looking for a 3s v. 6s 90 day FRA 'bid-offer' price coinciding with the September futures nominal dates

QUESTION 45: TOPIC: Fwd/fwds, FRAs Money market Futures and Swaps

ANSWER: B: pay fixed and receive floating on an interest rate swap

A corporate treasurer concerned about interest rates rising and wanting to hedge his longer term funding could pay fixed and receive floating on an interest rate swap.

QUESTION 46: TOPIC: Fwd/fwds, FRAs Money market Futures and Swaps

ANSWER: B: 2.00 p.c.

You are the fixed rate payer in a 5 year GBP interest rate swap nominal principal GBP 100 million fixed v. 6 months LIBOR. The fixed rate is 2.25 p.c. and if you are paying the net amount the floating rate must has been fixed lower at 2.00 p.c. on the last rate fixing date.

QUESTION 47: TOPIC: Fwd/fwds, FRAs Money market Futures and Swaps

ANSWER: C: 6.88 p.c.

Data: equiv int rate1 (90 days): 0.0678, equiv int rate2 (90 days): 0.0687 p.c., ANSWER: 6.88(3223) p.c.

QUESTION 48: TOPIC: Fwd/fwds, FRAs Money market Futures and Swaps

ANSWER: C: you have sold a 2s v. 3s EUR FRA

The calling counterparty has to deal on your 'Bid - Offer' price (you are market maker). If he wants to buy he must buy on your offer at 3.74 (right hand side) in the 2s v. 3s FRA.

QUESTION 49: TOPIC: Options

ANSWER: A: A synthetic short position

The purchase of a Put and sale of a Call at the same strike price and same expiry is a synthetic forward, meaning that whichever way the exchange rate moves the trader will be short the underlying currency (If lower the trader exercises the Put, if higher the Call is exercised against him). Either way he will be short the underlying currency.

QUESTION 50: TOPIC: Options

ANSWER: D: an option to enter into an FRA

An interest rate guarantee is an option product permitting the buyer to fix the interest rate payable/receivable for a single period in the future, e.g. an option to enter into an FRA.

QUESTION 51: TOPIC: Options

ANSWER: A: increasing his long USD delta hedge position

In respect of this outstanding short position the options trader will be increasing his long USD delta hedge position against CHF as an "in of the money" USD Call/CHF Put option has a higher probability of being exercised by the buyer, hence the Delta tends towards 1.

QUESTION 52: TOPIC: Options

ANSWER: B: USD 975.00

A British Pound option price quoted as 1.5600 is equivalent to 1.5600 X 0.01 = 0.0156 when the price is quoted in full. The cash price (premium) of the option is 0.0156 X 62,500 (contract size) = USD 975.00.

QUESTION 53: TOPIC: Options

ANSWER: B: Swaption

A Swaption is an option to enter into an interest rate swap and involves the payment of an up-front premium by the buyer.

QUESTION 54: TOPIC: Options

ANSWER: A: intrinsic value + time value

An ITM option has intrinsic value – it is immediately exercisable for profit. Provided the option still has some time to expiry (here one month) its premium will be made up additionally of time value.

QUESTION 55: TOPIC: Principles of ALM

ANSWER: B: more assets than liabilities will be repriced in the near term

A bank's balance sheet is considered asset-sensitive to market interest rate changes if more assets than liabilities will be repriced in the near term.

QUESTION 56: TOPIC: Principles of ALM

ANSWER: A: off-setting risk in one market with protection in a closely correlated market

Hedging involves off-setting risk in one market with temporary protection in another, using a market or financial instrument with close correlation to the underlying risk. To comply with the accurate definition of a hedge the market or product used as a hedge must have the ability to be unwound (lifted). Any hedge cost/benefit must be identified and treated differently from trading activities, the cost/benefit usually spread over the life of the risk originally hedged.

QUESTION 57: TOPIC: Principles of ALM

ANSWER: C: Net interest income would hardly change at all.

In an environment of decreasing interest rates if a bank ran a zero gap, net interest income would hardly change at all.

QUESTION 58: TOPIC: Principles of ALM

ANSWER: D: providing a guarantee

When considering credit derivatives Basel rules regard the sale of credit protection as providing a guarantee.

QUESTION 59: TOPIC: Principles of ALM

ANSWER: C: A means by which to reduce a risk

A hedge is a temporary substitute for a known future requirement. It is a means to reduce risk. Dealers can use various off-balance sheet treasury derivatives to hedge interest rate risks in their cash market activities.

QUESTION 60: TOPIC: Principles of ALM

ANSWER: A: buy a 2s v. 5s GBP 10 million FRA

In these circumstances your best hedge is to buy a 2s v. 5s GBP FRA in GBP 10 million.

QUESTION 61: TOPIC: Principles of ALM

ANSWER: B: running a matched trading book

Of these statements only running a matched book is a function of asset and liability management.

QUESTION 62: TOPIC: Principles of ALM

ANSWER: D: a form of CDO that invests in credit default swaps or other non-cash assets to gain exposure to a portfolio of fixed income assets

A Synthetic CDO is a form of CDO that invests in credit default swaps (CDSs) or other non-cash assets to gain exposure to a portfolio of fixed income assets

QUESTION 63: TOPIC: Principles of Risk

ANSWER: C: Delivery risk and Market replacement risk

You have dealt today for an outright FX transaction value 3 months forward with your corporate client Madoff Investments. Without any other information the risks that you are running are Delivery risk and market replacement risk.

QUESTION 64: TOPIC: Principles of Risk

ANSWER: D: multiple offsetting FX contracts which can be agreed to be netted in event of default

Close-out netting is when counterparties have multiple offsetting foreign exchange forward contracts and have agreed to net these obligations in the event that one of the counterparties defaults (as permitted under IFEMA master agreements).

QUESTION 65: TOPIC: Principles of Risk

ANSWER: D: to assess interest rate risk

Gap (also called mismatch) analysis is a means to assess interest rate risk.

QUESTION 66: TOPIC: Principles of Risk

ANSWER: D: Stress testing only

Stress testing is used to assess market risk under abnormal market conditions.

QUESTION 67: TOPIC: Principles of Risk

ANSWER: B: Bilateral netting

This is an example of Bilateral netting.

QUESTION 68: TOPIC: Principles of Risk

ANSWER: D: USD 22.5 million

Delivery risk (also known as Settlement risk) is recorded from the moment any exchange transaction is entered into and remains the same up to and including the value date of the deal when the funds are exchanged. This is because payment has to be made in one currency before confirmed receipt of the countervalue. With currency payments being made in different centres the risk is deemed to be equivalent to the total value (gross NOT net) of purchases and sales of currencies outstanding with a counterparty for each value date. Maturing forward contracts will impact this figure alongside Spot deals effected for that value date.

QUESTION 69: TOPIC: Principles of Risk

ANSWER: C: Market risk

The risk described here is exchange or interest rate risk, both of which are described as "market risk".

QUESTION 70: TOPIC: Principles of Risk

ANSWER: A: hedging offsets an existing risk in one market, arbitrage is simultaneous trading for profit

Of these statements the accurate one is 'hedging offsets an existing risk in one market (with protection in another closely correlated market), arbitrage is simultaneous trading for profit (to take advantage of price discrepancies between markets)'.

End of Mock examination No. 5

ACI Dealing Certificate MOCK EXAMINATION No. 6 - ANSWERS

QUESTION 1: TOPIC: Basic Interest Rate Calculations

ANSWER: D: +66.5 pts

ACI formulae page 7 Data: EUR/USD: 1.3500, USD int rate (180 days): 0.04, EUR int rate (180 days): 0.03, annual basis (both ccies): Act/360. ANSWER: Outright: 1.35665 = 66.5 points EUR Premium.

QUESTION 2: TOPIC: Basic Interest Rate Calculations

ANSWER: A: numerically lower than its equivalent yield

The rate of discount on a discount-paying money market instrument is always numerically lower than its equivalent yield.

QUESTION 3: TOPIC: Basic Interest Rate Calculations

ANSWER: C: 3.325 p.c.

ACI formulae (not included) Data: 3 months (91 days): 0.029, 3s v. 6s fwd/fwd (92 days): 0.037187, annual basis: Act/360. ANSWER: 3.325 p.c.

QUESTION 4: TOPIC: Basic Interest Rate Calculations

ANSWER: A: Volume-weighted average overnight EUR deposit rate

EONIA is the Volume-weighted average overnight EUR deposit rate published daily by the ECB.

QUESTION 5: TOPIC: Basic Interest Rate Calculations

ANSWER: A: 4.17 p.c.

Through straight line interpolation (no formula provided by ACI) the additional 30 days of the three months are worth 1.16666 r per day so for 1/2 month (15 days) the adjustment is 1.6666 X 15 = 17.49 added to the 2 months interest rate quote = 4.17 p.c. for a 2 1/2 months quote to a customer.

QUESTION 6: TOPIC: Basic Interest Rate Calculations

ANSWER: D: annually, then balance at maturity

Regardless of where you are based, interest on fixed deposits is payable at maturity and if the deposit is accepted for a period in excess of one year (in this case 19 months), annually on the anniversary and at maturity.

QUESTION 7: TOPIC: Cash Money markets Theory

ANSWER: C: GBP 3 months Bankers Acceptance purchased at 2.97 p.c.

Of these financial instruments all except the GBP Bankers Acceptances pay a return as a yield. The GBP BAs are "Discount paying instrument quoted as a rate of discount" and the discount rate of 2.97 is equivalent to a higher yield of 2.99 p.c.

QUESTION 8: TOPIC: Cash Money markets Theory

ANSWER: B: Actual/365

All GBP short term money market transactions (including the interest on repos) have interest calculated on an Actual / 365 annual basis.

QUESTION 9: TOPIC: Cash Money markets Theory

ANSWER: C: Delivery repo

A |Delivery repo is the least risky for the buyer as it will be delivered to and held by him (as reverse repoer).

QUESTION 10: TOPIC: Cash Money markets Theory

ANSWER: A: US T-Bills

US T-BIlls are quoted at a discount rate in the interbank market.

QUESTION 11: TOPIC: Cash Money markets Theory

ANSWER: A: Repo

Of those listed the Repo is the only transaction type which is "collateralized". All the others are short term security transaction types.

QUESTION 12: TOPIC: Cash Money markets Theory

ANSWER: A: USD Money Market deposit

Of these instruments only USD Money market deposits are quoted as a yield, the rest are all quoted and traded on a discount basis.

QUESTION 13: TOPIC: Cash Money markets Calculations

ANSWER: D: 3.1669 p.c.

ACI formulae page 3 Data: discount rate: 0.0315, annual basis: Act/360. ANSWER: 3.1669 p.c.

QUESTION 14: TOPIC: Cash Money markets Calculations

ANSWER: A: GBP 9,622,342.67

The Repo amount is GBP 9,581,000 (the rounded dirty price of the Gilt and interest at 5.25 p.c. is payable in addition at maturity of the Repo therefore the maturity consideration is GBP 9,622,342.67.

QUESTION 15: TOPIC: Cash Money markets Calculations

ANSWER: B: EUR 10,565,503.42, EUR 10,571,153.03

EUR 10,565,503.42 is the dirty price of the bond and this is the initial consideration of the repo. Interest of 5,649.61 is payable on the cash advance for the 7 days making the maturity consideration EUR 10,571,153.03.

QUESTION 16: TOPIC: Cash Money markets Calculations

ANSWER: D: EUR 97,869,000.00

EUR 100 million with a dirty price of 96.90 = EUR 96,900,000.00 on which the dealer (the repoer) charges a 1% margin: 96,900,000.00 X 1.01 means he will receive EUR 97,869,000.00 initial consideration

QUESTION 17: TOPIC: Cash Money markets Calculations

ANSWER: A: 4.6654 p.c.

ACI formulae (not included) Data: Principal: USD 10,000,000.00, int rate1 (92 days): 0.045, int rate2 (91 days): 0.0457, int rate3 (90 days): 0.0462, int rate4 (92 days): 0.0465, annual basis: Act/360. ANSWER: 4.6654.

QUESTION 18: TOPIC: Cash Money markets Calculations

ANSWER: C: GBP 201,994,520.55

Simple int formula Data: principal: GBP 200 million, issue rate (91 day 'coupon'): 0.04, annual basis: Act/365. ANSWER: GBP 1,994,520.55 making the maturity value GBP 201,994,520.55.

QUESTION 19: TOPIC: Foreign exchange Theory

ANSWER: D: 1.38 52-55

You want to buy EUR at 1.38 52, you put the broker on (you advise him of your BID for the base currency EUR at 52). He is currently BID 1.38 50. Your bid is an improvement on his current bid of 1.38 50, making his new price to the market 1.38 52-55.

QUESTION 20: TOPIC: Foreign exchange Theory

ANSWER: A: you would take as bid rate the bid side of the 2-month forward and as offered rate the offered side of the 1-month forward

When quoting a 1- to 2-month forward FX time option price in a currency pair trading at a discount to a customer you would take as bid rate the bid side of the 2-month forward and as offered rate the offered side of the 1-month forward.

QUESTION 21: TOPIC: Foreign exchange Theory

ANSWER: D: He buys USD 5,000,000.00 at 0.9426

You are market maker here and on your quote the calling bank (He) buys USD 5,000,000.00 at 0.9426.

QUESTION 22: TOPIC: Foreign exchange Theory

ANSWER: D: JPY 100,000

EUR/JPY is quoted to two decimal places. One big figure therefore equals 100 points - the difference between 79.50 and 80.50 and is worth JPY 1,000,000.

QUESTION 23: TOPIC: Foreign exchange Theory

ANSWER: C: Tuesday 30th April 201X

If today is Tuesday 27th February then Spot date will be Thursday 29th February 201X (a leap year). The standard period forward value date will normally be the same date in the appropriate forward month. But if today's spot date is the last business day in the current month for forward date calculation purposes this is deemed to be the month-end date, and all other standard period forward dates are then the last business dates in the appropriate forward months. The two months maturity date from Spot date Thursday 29th February 201X (a leap year) will therefore be Tuesday 30th April 201X. This rule is termed the "End/end" rule.

QUESTION 24: TOPIC: Foreign exchange Theory

ANSWER: B: the specification of a gold bar to meet the requirements of the LBMA

The term 'London Good delivery' in Precious metals trading refers to the specification of a gold bar to meet the requirements of the LBMA (London Bullion Market Association).

QUESTION 25: TOPIC: Foreign exchange Theory

ANSWER: C: sold GBP 5 million at 1.5575

'Yours' is a way of advising the broker that you are selling the base currency (here GBP). It is important that you always quantify this expression as noted above '5 yours!' meaning you are selling GBP 5 million to the broker's bid of 1.5575

QUESTION 26: TOPIC: Foreign exchange Theory

ANSWER: D: Australian Dollars (AUD)

For ease of position keeping, rate tracking and profit and loss calculations dealers in the interbank spot AUD/USD market (an indirectly quoted currency against the USD) would tend to deal in round amounts of the base currency AUD.

QUESTION 27: TOPIC: Foreign exchange Theory

ANSWER: A: at a forward Discount

In forward exchange terminology, the currency with the higher interest rate can be described as being at a forward Discount and if this currency is the base currency (here the EUR) in an indirect currency pair (EUR/GBP), then the numbers in the forward swap points will be quoted "High-Low".

QUESTION 28: TOPIC: Foreign exchange Theory

ANSWER: D: They reflect the interest rate differential between two currencies

The forward swap points reflect the interest differential between the two currencies in the FX quotation for the period quoted.

QUESTION 29: TOPIC: Foreign exchange Theory

ANSWER: B: USD interest rates are higher than CAD

With the 1 month forward USD/CAD points quoted High - Low the USD is at a forward discount and the USD interest rates are higher than CAD in this period.

QUESTION 30: TOPIC: Foreign exchange Theory

ANSWER: B: 4-Par

If the interest rate for the base currency in a foreign exchange swap quotation (here the GBP) is marginally higher than the countercurrency (here USD) the base currency is described as being at a forward Discount and the numbers in the swap bid-offer spread will be quoted and displayed "High-Low" (international terminology). Where the 3 months GBP interest rate is marginally higher than USD then the only possible price of those quoted is 4-Par.

QUESTION 31: TOPIC: Foreign exchange Calculations

ANSWER: B: 1.625125

The method to calculate an ante spot outright is to add/subtract the benefit or cost of bringing the cashflows back from the spot date to the desired ante spot date. Here add the 1.25 pts benefit of selling and buying Tom/next GBP against USD to the spot rate of 1.6250 = 1.625125.

QUESTION 32: TOPIC: Foreign exchange Calculations

ANSWER: D: 110/100

30 day swap = 100-90, 60 day swap 160-150. There is a difference of 60 points for the 30 days meaning 2 points a day. For the 35 day swap therefore 10 points are added (2 X 5 days) making the swap 110-100.

QUESTION 33: TOPIC: Foreign exchange Calculations

ANSWER: D: 0.8479

ACI formula page 7 Data: Spot EUR/GBP = 0.8500, EUR int rate (90 days): 0.02, annual basis: Act/360, GBP int rate (90 days): 0.01, annual basis: Act/365. ANSWER: 0.8479.

QUESTION 34: TOPIC: Foreign exchange Calculations

ANSWER: A: 0.90 40-45

3 months outright fwd EUR/USD is 0.9020-30 and the swap = -20 to -15 making the spot 0.90 40-45 (0.9040 minus 0.0020 - 0.9045 minus 15).

QUESTION 35: TOPIC: Foreign exchange Calculations

ANSWER: D: Spot: - GBP 10,000,000, + USD 16,005,000, 7 days: + GBP 10,000,000, - USD 15,998,000

You are market maker, if you have been dealt at 7 points your favour on the swap you have just quoted you have sold and bought base currency (forward bid) and so you sell and buy GBP, buy and sell USD rates 1.6005 and 1.5998.Spot cash movements: - GBP 10,000,000, + USD 16,005,000, 7 days forward cash movements: + GBP 10,000,000, - USD 15,998,000.

QUESTION 36: TOPIC: Foreign exchange Calculations

ANSWER: A: 0.9050, USD 5,524,861.87

You must take 5 points therefore the customer rate will be lower (you give him less CHF per USD). Rate = 0.9055 minus 0.0005 = 0.9050 and the USD equivalent is USD 5,524,861.87.

QUESTION 37: TOPIC: Fwd/fwds, FRAs Money market Futures and Swaps

ANSWER: D: all of these

All of these statements relating to STIR futures contract specifications are correct.

QUESTION 38: TOPIC: Fwd/fwds, FRAs Money market Futures and Swaps

ANSWER: A: BBAIRS

BBAIRS = British Bankers Association Interest Rate Swaps agreement is frequently used for GBP interest rate swaps between London based banks. The International Swaps and Derivatives Association (ISDA) produce the most frequently encountered standard terms for interest rate swaps in the international markets.

QUESTION 39: TOPIC: Fwd/fwds, FRAs Money market Futures and Swaps

ANSWER: C: Sell 1-4 FRAs, Sell June Futures

To set up an arbitrage position in Futures and FRAs in May you would Sell 1-4 FRAs, Sell June Futures.

QUESTION 40: TOPIC: Fwd/fwds, FRAs Money market Futures and Swaps

ANSWER: B: has established the price sensitivities of a longer-term fixed-rate liability and a floating-rate asset

In a plain vanilla interest rate swap, the "fixed-rate payer" is said to have established the price sensitivities of a longer-term fixed-rate liability and a floating-rate asset.

QUESTION 41: TOPIC: Fwd/fwds, FRAs Money market Futures and Swaps

ANSWER: C: You receive USD 32,258.06

ACI formula sheet (page 4): FRA: 20,000,000.00, FRA rate (90 days): 0.0235 (market maker's offer), LIBOR 0.03, annual basis: Act/360. ANSWER: 32,258.06 in your favour.

QUESTION 42: TOPIC: Fwd/fwds, FRAs Money market Futures and Swaps

ANSWER: D: permits the risk and return on an asset to be achieved without actually owning it

A Total return swap permits the risk and return on an asset to be achieved without actually owning it.

QUESTION 43: TOPIC: Fwd/fwds, FRAs Money market Futures and Swaps

ANSWER: B: less than 98.70

If you are short Futures and today receive variation margin (a profit) then the end-of-day settlement price must have been lower than your open interest price of 98.70.

QUESTION 44: TOPIC: Fwd/fwds, FRAs Money market Futures and Swaps

ANSWER: D: Sterling interest rates are more volatile

Any suggestion of higher volatility in the markets could dramatically increase NYSE Euronext.liffe traders' potential for losses. To dissuade too many traders from holding large open interest positions at times of increased risk the Exchange raises the initial margins.

QUESTION 45: TOPIC: Fwd/fwds, FRAs Money market Futures and Swaps

ANSWER: A: Federal Funds Effective rate compounded

The floating rate in an OIS is always the daily overnight index (here Federal Funds Effective rate) compounded during the swap period, netted with the fixed rate (here 7 day USD fixed) and paid on maturity date plus 2 days (USD specific).

QUESTION 46: TOPIC: Fwd/fwds, FRAs Money market Futures and Swaps

ANSWER: C: 6 month USD LIBOR against 5 year US Treasuries

An index or basis swap is a swap between two floating rate indices or two markets quoted on different bases i.e. both LIBOR, CDs to Commercial Paper or LIBOR to Prime. Here therefore the odd one out is the 6 month USD LIBOR against 5 year US Treasuries which is a 'plain vanilla' interest rate swap.

QUESTION 47: TOPIC: Fwd/fwds, FRAs Money market Futures and Swaps

ANSWER: D: You will receive GBP 1,875.00

ACI Formula sheet (not provided). Data: 15 'points' profit (GBP 12.50) on 10 contracts. ANSWER: GBP 1,875.00.

QUESTION 48: TOPIC: Fwd/fwds, FRAs Money market Futures and Swaps

ANSWER: A: The risk of an adverse change in the spread between futures and cash prices

Basis risk is the risk of an adverse change in the spread between futures and cash prices.

QUESTION 49: TOPIC: Options

ANSWER: A: the price of the option - payable on deal date

The premium of a European style OTC currency option is the price of the option payable on deal date.

QUESTION 50: TOPIC: Options

ANSWER: D: USD 25,000.00

Here the OTC option premium is expressed as a flat percentage of the underlying currency, here 1,000,000 X 2.50 / 100 = USD 25,000.00.

QUESTION 51: TOPIC: Options

ANSWER: A: tends towards zero

An "out of the money" option has less probability of being exercised and the Delta tends towards zero, indicating to the Options trader that he needs less position in the underlying commodity to hedge his risk under these conditions.

QUESTION 52: TOPIC: Options

ANSWER: D: a volatility trade

The purchase of a Put at one strike price and the purchase of a Call at a higher strike price (both with the same expiry) is a volatility strategy – meaning that whichever way the exchange rate moves, provided it moves above the Call or below the Put break-even rates the trader will exercise his options and make money.

QUESTION 53: TOPIC: Options

ANSWER: D: GBP 69,000.00

If the option's premium is quoted as 0.023 then on an underlying amount of EUR 3 million the premium is GBP 69,000.00 (3,000,000 X 0.023).

QUESTION 54: TOPIC: Options

ANSWER: D: Zero cost Collar

Where the customer has bought an interest rate collar where the Premium on Cap purchased equals the premium on the floor sold this is described as a zero cost collar.

QUESTION 55: TOPIC: Principles of ALM

ANSWER: D: a 9-month liability and a 6-month asset, both for USD 10 million

A long hedge position in a 6X9 FRA for USD 10 million will be considered as a 9-month liability and a 6-month asset, both for USD 10 million when performing a gap analysis.

QUESTION 56: TOPIC: Principles of ALM

ANSWER: B: all of these

All these issues represent weaknesses of a traditional approach to gap analysis.

QUESTION 57: TOPIC: Principles of ALM

ANSWER: A: 100% of qualifying bank reserves and 100% of domestic sovereign or central bank debt in domestic currency

Under the LCR within Basel II regulations level 1 assets include 100% of qualifying bank reserves and 100% of domestic sovereign or central bank debt in domestic currency

QUESTION 58: TOPIC: Principles of ALM

ANSWER: C: assumes the credit risk on a reference bond from the issuer in exchange for a periodic protection fee similar to an insurance premium, and is obliged to pay only if a negative credit event occurs

The credit protection seller in a CDS assumes the credit risk on a reference bond from the issuer in exchange for a periodic protection fee similar to an insurance premium and is obliged to pay only if a negative credit event occurs.

QUESTION 59: TOPIC: Principles of ALM

ANSWER: D: total assets minus intangible assets

Under Basel III 'Adjusted assets' are total assets minus intangible assets.

QUESTION 60: TOPIC: Principles of ALM

ANSWER: D: sell Sept 1X STIR ED futures, receive/pay profit/loss daily, buy back futures, take cash

In June 1X to hedge a short 3s v. 6s forward-forward short USD interest rate risk position in the cash market the ALM dealer would sell the appropriate delivery month STIR ED futures (here Sept 1X), the bank would receive/pay profit/loss daily and then near to the start date of the hedge period the short futures position would be closed-out (bought back) and the dealer would take the cash to fund the shortage.

QUESTION 61: TOPIC: Principles of ALM

ANSWER: D: when its liabilities subject to re-pricing exceed its assets subject to re-pricing in that time bucket

A bank is deemed to be interest rate sensitive in a particular maturity bucket when its liabilities subject to re-pricing exceed its assets subject to re-pricing in that time bucket.

QUESTION 62: TOPIC: Principles of ALM

ANSWER: A: a parameter used in the calculation of Economic Capital or Regulatory Capital for a banking institution

Loss given default (LGD) is a parameter used in the calculation of Economic Capital or Regulatory Capital under Basel rules for a banking institution. Exposure is the amount of an investment that the bank may lose.

QUESTION 63: TOPIC: Principles of Risk

ANSWER: C: 100%

Under Basel rules the risk weight for claims on unrated sovereigns and their central banks in the standardized approach is 100%.

QUESTION 64: TOPIC: Principles of Risk

ANSWER: A: 1 minus recovery rate, probability of default and exposure at default

Under Basel rules, expected credit loss is a function of 1 minus recovery rate (Loss Given Default), probability of default and exposure at default.

QUESTION 65: TOPIC: Principles of Risk

ANSWER: B: Simple historic volatility

The Correlation or Variance / co-variance VAR methodology relies on Simple historic volatility.

QUESTION 66: TOPIC: Principles of Risk

ANSWER: B: in 1 out of 10 days it is expected that the portfolio value will decline by USD 10,000.00 or more.

If the daily 90% confidence level VaR of a portfolio is correctly estimated to be USD 10,000.00, in 1 out of 10 days it is expected that the portfolio value will decline by USD 10,000.00 or more.

QUESTION 67: TOPIC: Principles of Risk

ANSWER: C: Monitoring counterparty credit risk

Monitoring counterparty credit risk is not strictly a function of position keeping though this task may frequently be delegated to the position clerk within the dealing room.

QUESTION 68: TOPIC: Principles of Risk

ANSWER: D: an independent credit assessment department

Procedures may differ from bank to bank but no parties to any potential deals should have the ability to set up credit limits to facilitate transactions. Dealers, the other bank and brokers are therefore ruled out, leaving the independent credit assessment department as the only viable choice.

QUESTION 69: TOPIC: Principles of Risk

ANSWER: D: all subordinated claims on corporates, sovereigns and banks

Under the foundation approach all subordinated claims on corporates, sovereigns and banks attract a 75% LGD.

QUESTION 70: TOPIC: Principles of Risk

ANSWER: D: the expected loss in those cases where the loss exceeds the VaR at the 95% level

The expected shortfall is the expected loss in those cases where the loss exceeds the VaR at the 95% level.

End of Mock examination No. 6

ACI – THE FINANCIAL MARKETS ASSOCIATION EXAMINATION FORMULAE

(as at September 2017)

INTEREST RATE	250
MONEY MARKET	251
FORWARD-FORWARDS and	
FORWARD RATE AGREEMENTS	252
FIXED INCOME	*ACI Diploma only*
FOREIGN EXCHANGE	255
OPTIONS	*ACI Diploma only*

Useful formulae for the **ACI Dealing Certificate** are included in the text. Where these formulae are included in the **ACI Formula sheet** these are annotated ***<ACI preferred>***. Note that the actual ACI formulae sheet provided in the examination is slightly differently laid out. Formulae are also available on-screen during the examination. The official ACI formulae sheet can be downloaded from the ACI website: www.acifma.com.

In all the formulae…

- interest rates, yields, coupon rates and rates of discount are expressed as a decimal, e.g. 2.53% will be expressed as 0.0253

- 'annual basis' is the number of days in a year assumed under the appropriate rate convention

- 'term' is the number of days from settlement to maturity of the instrument in question

- 'day count' is the number of days from settlement to maturity of the instrument in question.

> **Note:** This formulae sheet should be available to candidates at the examination test centre. Just in case it is not it is recommended that candidates obtain a *clean* copy (download from ACI website www.acifma.com) beforehand to take with them.

INTEREST RATE CONVERSIONS *(page 1)*

Converting between bond basis and money market basis

From money market to bond (full year)

$$rate_{bond\,basis} = rate_{money\,market\,basis}\,\frac{365}{360}$$

From bond to money market (full year)

$$rate_{money\,market\,basis} = rate_{bond\,basis}\,\frac{360}{365}$$

Converting between annually and semi-annually compounding frequencies

From semi-annual to annual

$$rate_{annually\text{-}compounded} = \left(1 + \frac{rate_{semi\text{-}annually\,compounded}}{2}\right)^2 - 1$$

From annual to semi-annual

$$rate_{semi\text{-}annually\,compounded} = \left(\sqrt{1 + rate_{annually\,compounded}} - 1\right) \times 2$$

The formulae for converting between annually and semi-annually compounded rate apply only to rates quoted on a bond basis, not a money market basis.

MONEY MARKET *(page 2)*

Certificates of deposit

$$\text{proceeds at maturity} = \text{face value} \left(1 + \frac{\text{coupon} \times \text{term}}{\text{annual basis}} \right)$$

$$\text{secondary market proceeds} = \frac{\text{proceeds at maturity}}{1 + \dfrac{\text{yield} \times \text{day count}}{\text{annual basis}}}$$

Discount-paying instruments quoted as a true yield

$$\text{secondary market proceeds} = \frac{\text{face value}}{1 + \dfrac{\text{yield} \times \text{day count}}{\text{annual basis}}}$$

Discount-paying instruments quoted as a rate of discount

$$\text{discount amount} = \text{face value} \, \frac{\text{rate of discount} \times \text{day count}}{\text{annual basis}}$$

$$\text{secondary market proceeds} = \text{face value} \left(1 - \frac{\text{rate of discount} \times \text{day count}}{\text{annual basis}} \right)$$

True yield of a discount instrument

$$\text{true yield} = \frac{\text{rate of discount}}{1 - \dfrac{\text{rate of discount} \times \text{day count}}{\text{annual basis}}}$$

Forward price of sell/buy-back   (ACI Diploma ONLY)

$$\text{forward price} = \frac{\left(\text{repurchase price} - \text{accrued interest on collateral at termination} \right)}{\text{nominal price of collateral}} \, 100$$

FORWARD-FORWARDS / FORWARD RATE AGREEMENTS

Forward/forward interest rate

(for periods up to one year)

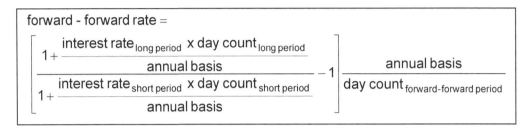

$$\text{forward - forward rate} = \left[\frac{1+\dfrac{\text{interest rate}_{\text{long period}} \times \text{day count}_{\text{long period}}}{\text{annual basis}}}{1+\dfrac{\text{interest rate}_{\text{short period}} \times \text{day count}_{\text{short period}}}{\text{annual basis}}} - 1\right] \frac{\text{annual basis}}{\text{day count}_{\text{forward-forward period}}}$$

FRA settlement

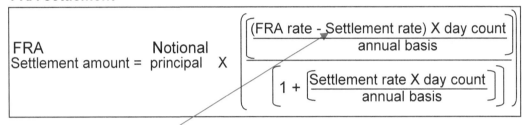

$$\text{FRA Settlement amount} = \text{Notional principal} \times \left(\frac{\dfrac{(\text{FRA rate} - \text{Settlement rate}) \times \text{day count}}{\text{annual basis}}}{1 + \left[\dfrac{\text{Settlement rate} \times \text{day count}}{\text{annual basis}}\right]}\right)$$

Note: *The ACI FRA Settlement formula above only gives guidance on the direction of any settlement payment if the top line is always input as "**FRA rate minus Settlement rate**".*

*If so then a '**positive**' result means **"Buyer pays Seller"***

*…and a '**negative**' result means "**Seller pays Buyer**".*

Clean and dirty price of bond with annual coupons on coupon date

clean price / dirty price (on coupon date) =

$$100\left|\left[\frac{coupon}{yield}\left(1-\frac{1}{\left(1+\frac{yield}{coupon\ frequency}\right)^{remaining\ coupons}}\right)\right]+\frac{1}{\left(1+\frac{yield}{coupon\ frequency}\right)^{remaining\ coupons}}\right]$$

Dirty price of bond with annual coupons

$$dirty\ price = \frac{first\ cashflow}{(1+yield)^{\frac{days\ to\ next\ coupon}{annual\ basis}}} + \frac{second\ cashflow}{(1+yield)^{1+\frac{days\ to\ next\ coupon}{annual\ basis}}} + L + \frac{n^{th}\ cashflow}{(1+yi} + ... + \frac{}{}^{\frac{rs\ to\ next\ coupon}{annual\ basis}}$$

Duration at issue or on a coupon date

Macaulay duration

Macaulay Duration =

$$\frac{\left[(first\ coupon\ amount\ \times\ time\ to\ first\ coupon)+(second\ coupon\ amount\ \times\ time\ to\ second\ coupon)+...\right.}{\left.+\ ((last\ coupon\ amount + nominal\ amount)\times\ time\ to\ last\ coupon)\right]}{net\ present\ value\ of\ bond}$$

Modified duration

$$Modified\ Duration = \frac{Macaulay\ Duration}{\left(1+\frac{yield}{compounding\ frequency}\right)}$$

Calculating zero-coupon yield from yield-to-maturity (bootstrapping)

$$\text{zero - coupon yield for n - year term}$$

$$= \left(\sqrt[n]{\frac{\text{final coupon amount} + \text{nominal amount}}{\text{implied present value of final coupon and nominal amount}}} - 1 \right) 100$$

The implied present value of the final coupon and nominal amount is calculated by subtracting from the net present value of the bond the sum of the present values of all coupons except the final one, where each present value is calculated using the appropriate zero-coupon yield.

FOREIGN EXCHANGE *(page 6)*

Forward FX rate

$$\text{forward rate} = \text{spot rate} \frac{1 + \dfrac{\text{interest rate}_{\text{quoted currency}} \times \text{day count}}{\text{annual basis}_{\text{quoted currency}}}}{1 + \dfrac{\text{interest rate}_{\text{base currency}} \times \text{day count}}{\text{annual basis}_{\text{base currency}}}}$$

Note: If the swap points are required these can be ascertained by comparing the result of this calculation with the spot rate.

Result: Forward outright rate HIGHER than spot = **Base currency PREMIUM**
(LOW-HIGH - Positive points)

Result: Forward outright rate LOWER than spot = **Base currency DISCOUNT**
(HIGH-LOW - Negative points)

Covered interest arbitrage

Variable (quoted) currency interest rate calculation
(for periods up to one year)

synthetic quoted currency interest rate =

$$\left[\left(\left(1 + \frac{\text{interest rate}_{\text{base currency}} \times \text{day count}}{\text{annual basis}_{\text{base currency}}}\right)\frac{\text{forward rate}}{\text{spot rate}}\right) - 1\right]\frac{\text{annual basis}_{\text{quoted currency}}}{\text{day count}}$$

Base currency interest rate calculation
(for periods up to one year)

synthetic base currency interest rate =

$$\left[\left(\left(1 + \frac{\text{interest rate}_{\text{quoted currency}} \times \text{day count}}{\text{annual basis}_{\text{quoted currency}}}\right)\frac{\text{spot rate}}{\text{forward rate}}\right) - 1\right]\frac{\text{annual basis}_{\text{base currency}}}{\text{day count}}$$

Standard deviation

$$\text{standard deviation} = \sqrt{\frac{\sum_{t=1}^{n}(\text{return at time t} - \text{mean return})^2}{\text{number of observations} - 1}}$$

Calculating the volatility over a period from annualised volatility

$$\text{volatility over period t} = \text{annualised volatility}\sqrt{t}$$

Where **t** is in years or fractions thereof.

In standard deviation calculations the ACI exams assume a year of **252** working days.

Principal ISO / SWIFT currency codes

Americas

Argentina	ARS
Bahamas	BSD
Bermuda	BMD
Brazil	BRL
Canada	CAD*
Mexico	MXN*
Panama	PAB
USA	USD*

Asia Pacific

Australia	AUD*
China	CNY
Hong Kong	HKD*
India	INR
Indonesia	IDR
Japan	JPY*
Korea (Republic of)	KRW*
Macau	MOP
Malaysia	MYR
New Zealand	NZD*
Pakistan	PKR
Philippines	PHP
Singapore	SGD*
Sri Lanka	LKR
Thailand	THB

Europe

Austria	*EUR**
Belgium	*EUR**
Channel Islands	GBP*
Croatia	HRN
Cyprus	*EUR**
Czech Republic	CZK
Denmark	DKK*
Estonia	*EUR**
Finland	*EUR**
France	*EUR**
Georgia	GEL
Germany	*EUR**
Greece	*EUR**

Europe *(cont.)*

Hungary	HUF
Iceland	ISN
Ireland	*EUR**
Italy	*EUR**
Latvia	*EUR**
Lithuania	*EUR**
Luxembourg	*EUR**
Macedonia	MKD
Malta	*EUR**
Monaco	*EUR**
Netherlands	*EUR**
Norway	NOK*
Poland	PLN
Portugal	*EUR**
Romania	ROL/RON
Slovakia	*EUR**
Slovenia	*EUR**
Spain	*EUR**
Sweden	SEK*
Switzerland	CHF*
United Kingdom	GBP*

Middle East and Africa

Bahrain	BHD
Egypt	EGP
Israel	ILS*
Jordan	JOD
Kenya	KES
Kuwait	KWD
Lebanon	LBP
Mauritius	MUR
Saudi Arabia	SAR
South Africa	ZAR*
Tanzania	TZS
Tunisia	TND
United Arab Emirates	AED

19 EU Eurozone countries (plus Monaco) in *italics*

CLS currencies as indicated *

***WinFOREX* test selection screen**

WinFOREX test selection screen

The selection of the **FROM SELECTED TOPICS** button invokes the list of available **WinFOREX Module DC** question libraries (1,855 as at September 2017). Please refer to the System users' guide <sysguide_20*nn*.pdf> included on the installation USB flashdrive for full details of the product and its operation.

Whilst there are nine (9) questions baskets in the examination to assist the candidate in his/her studies/revision **WinFOREX** contains fourteen separate question categories (as shown above) of interactive theory and calculation multiple choice questions relating to the **ACI Dealing Certificate** (**September 2017)** syllabus / examination format.

For ease of training/revision, there are separate individual theory and calculation question baskets for Repos (**DC topic 2**) and Precious metals (**DC topic 3**) and **DC topic 4** is split into three sub-topic question baskets... Forward/forwards and FRAs, Money market Futures *and* Money market swaps.

After selecting the desired topic the system displays each interactive question in turn. On the user selecting/confirming an answer the outcome is evidenced by a yellow Smiley face (correct answer) or a red sad face (incorrect answer) and the correct answer plus a brief descriptive text is then displayed in the lower (blue) section.

TOPIC: CASH MONEY MARKETS CALCULATIONS

Today you buy a EUR CD yielding 3.875 p.c. for 90 days. The CD has a face value of EUR 10 million and was originally issued at a rate of 4 p.c. for 180 days. What is the maturity value?

⊙	A	EUR 10,059,069.40
☺	B	EUR 10,200,000.00
	C	EUR 10,102,135.56
	D	EUR 10,100,749.69

CONFIRM	Click for Correct Answer	NEXT QUESTION

Not the right one. You should have selected answer B.....
EUR 10,200,000.00

Simple int formula (not included) Data: principal EUR 10,000,000.00, yield (90 days): 0.03875, annual basis: Act/360. ANSWER: EUR 10,000,000 plus 200,000.00 interest (simple interest formula).

Progress - 40%   Question 2 of 5   Pause

WinFOREX test question and answer screen

At the bottom of the screen there are icons to access the interactive Excel spreadsheet-based ACI formulae sheet <aciformulae1.xls> and the screen viewable accompanying text <winforextextModDCnn.pdf> (both available in the full SUL version).

On selection of the centre button <**ACI EXAM**> on the test selection screen the system creates a unique timed random-generated full 70 question 'mock' (trial) examination – correctly weighted and marked (See page 15) enabling candidates to test themselves on theory, calculations *and* time management techniques. All such mock examinations can be debriefed by the candidate question by question after the event.

If you haven't yet purchased the **WinFOREX** product this is available on-line at the company website www.lywood-david.co.uk or www.multimediatradewind.co.uk

There are also textbooks and software products available on the website for the other *level 1* examination **ACI Operations Certificate 2019** and the *level 2* **ACI Diploma 2019** (also re-released in September 2017).

Multimedia TradeWind Limited
Warren Cottage,
Melfort Road,
Crowborough,
East Sussex, TN6 1QT
United Kingdom

Phone: +44 1892 652806

e-mail: mmtw@lywood-david.co.uk